Total British Football

Publisher and Creative Director: Nick Wells
Project Editor: Sara Robson
Co-ordination and Design: Chris Herbert
Picture Research: Melinda Révèsz

Special thanks to: Christine Delaborde,
Jeff Fletcher, Scott Morgan, Sonya Newland,
Colin Rudderham, Claire Walker, Polly Willis

FLAME TREE PUBLISHING

Crabtree Hall, Crabtree Lane
Fulham, London, SW6 6TY
United Kingdom
info@flametreepublishing.com
www.flametreepublishing.com

First published 2006

06 07 08 09

2 3 4 5 6 7 8 9

Flame Tree is part of The Foundry
Creative Media Company Limited

The CIP record for this book is available from
the British Library.

ISBN 1 84451 403 X

Every effort has been made to contact the copyright
holders. We apologize in advance for any omissions
and would be pleased to insert the appropriate
acknowledgement in subsequent editions
of this publication.

While every endeavour has been made to ensure the
accuracy of the reproduction of the images in this book,
we would be grateful to receive any comments or
suggestions for inclusion in future reprints.

Printed in China

Authors and contributors

NICK HOLT was born and raised in Bolton. Unlike its
favourite son Nat Lofthouse, he spent much of his
footballing career on the wing. An early penchant for
alcohol and good living produced a wide player in the
John Robertson mould, only without the talent. A natural
abrasiveness made him ill-suited for retail; he is now a
successful buying magnate. He lives in a small village
with wife Emma, rendered less peaceful than it should be
by his four large dogs.

GUY LLOYD was raised and schooled in Slough, and to
his credit managed to survive the experience. He
attended university, but declined their kind offer of a
fifth term. His working career has taken in the wacky
world of record retailing and a number of years in
various roles in publishing. Guy's awesome knowledge
of obscure footballing trivia is of concern to friends and
family alike. At 6 ft 3 in he has the natural physique of
a goalkeeper. If only he'd had the talent.

MARK GONNELLA (Contributor) is a freelance sports
writer with a number of football books to his credit. A
journalist since leaving school, his career has spanned
local and national newspapers and broadcasting. He
also works as a media consultant to a number of
bluechip companies and sporting organisations.
Married with two children, Mark holds an FA coaching
badge, continues to play local league football and is a
lifelong fan of his hometown club Reading.

Picture Credits

All photographs courtesy of Allsport, except: Action Images:
21; Empics: 89, 189, 231, 237, 300, 342, 411, 470;
Foundry Arts: 51, 85, 101, 365, 479; Offside Sports
Photography Ltd: 9, 157, 177, 197, 287, 353, 505; (Mark
Leech): 147; Orion Books: 161, 225; Popperfoto: 69, 172,
315, 419; Topham: 108, 116, 137, 169, 199, 215, 221,
225 (l), 243, 254, 273, 283, 293, 355, 403 (all), 405,
427, 433, 447, 485, 493, 495; VinMag Archive: 395.

Publisher's Note

Some entries in this book have previously appeared in
Total Football.

Total British Football

Nick Holt & Guy Lloyd

Foreword: Sir Bobby Robson

FLAME TREE
PUBLISHING

Contents

How To Use This Book

You are encouraged to use this book in a variety of ways, each of which caters for a range of interests, knowledge and uses.

- The book is organized alphabetically by entry.
- The entries relate to all aspects of the game: players, managers, matches, dream teams, national and club sides.
- Also included are entries which focus on everything else about football, from tactics and cheating to fanzines and chanting, stadia and the World Cup to bizarre hairstyles and penalty shoot-outs.
- The A–Z format enables the reader to find well-known names quickly and easily, and to discover less well-known players, teams and topics alongside the familiar ones.
- There is a comprehensive index that allows specific entries to be located.

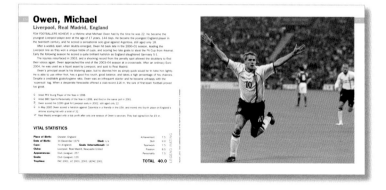

2. Subtitle gives extra information about the subject of the entry

1. Entry title

3. Information and authors' opinion on the person, team or topic the entry is about

7. Bullet-points give additional information to the main text

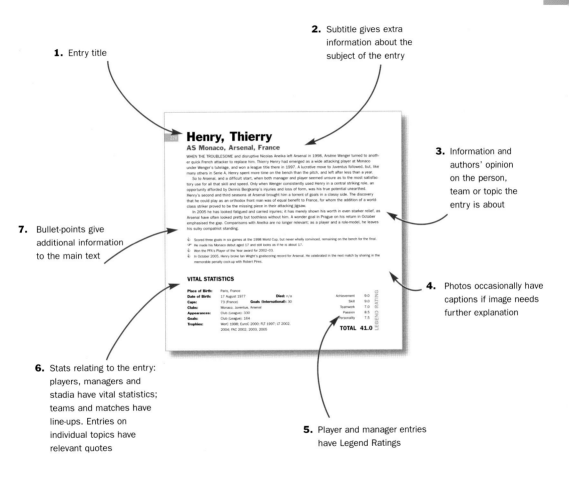

4. Photos occasionally have captions if image needs further explanation

6. Stats relating to the entry: players, managers and stadia have vital statistics; teams and matches have line-ups. Entries on individual topics have relevant quotes

5. Player and manager entries have Legend Ratings

Foreword

With the 2006 World Cup in Germany and the outstanding success of Euro 2004 in Portugal following on from the 2002 World Cup Finals in Japan and South Korea, the global popularity of our wonderful game of football continues to grow.

The remarkable skills of the players – especially the dazzling Brazilians in the World Cup, of course; the amazingly high levels of fitness and stamina, plus the hard-nosed tactical battles fought out by the coaches, made fascinating viewing for all those watching those matches.

Football continues to evolve, and the balance of power may be shifting. It is predicted that an African country will win the World Cup in the near future – and we had better not rule out the possibility of an Asian team from becoming World Champions.

Football in the early years of the twenty-first century remains the highest-profile sport on the planet and its future looks very bright indeed. British football in particular is hugely popular around the globe and the Premiership remains the most followed league in the world.

All those lucky enough to earn a living from football – including players, managers and those involved in the media – owe a huge debt to the past giants of the sport. The players and managers make today's headlines, but it is the supporters of the game that form the bedrock of the sport. It is their passion, their enthusiasm and, ultimately, their money that helps keep the game alive.

Thousands of books on football have been published over the years. Some have been notorious and self-seeking, others well-crafted works of literature. And many excellent reference books, containing all kinds of information and statistics, have been produced.

Total British Football is a worthy addition to the list. It has been written and compiled *by* genuine football fans *for* genuine football fans. The book is not a just a list of statistics, nor an in-depth history of the game, but one that tries to identify key people, events and themes that have changed or enlivened the game for better or worse.

It pays tribute to the past and present heroes of the game. *Total British Football* takes an honest, thoughtful and affectionate view of our marvellous sport and will be a good read for all football fans, young and old.

Sir Bobby Robson

Introduction

Football is unique amongst sports in the degree of passion it arouses in non-combatants. Not for the football fan the pure voyeurism of watching two people belt the living daylights out of each other in a ring, nor the tortuous but cerebral intrigue of a fluctuating test match. Football is about intensity, the thrill of a moment, the excitement of a game revolving around a single piece of action. The fans live every moment, feel every moment, kick every ball.

We've done our share of suffering watching Chelsea under-perform and Bolton get relegated (but not this time, at least for another year!). We've also done our fair share of running around screaming as Chelsea win the FA Cup or Bolton win at Highbury. We've tried to write this book from a fan's perspective, and capture some of the agony and the ecstasy, the hysteria and the humour.

This is not a list of stats; Rothmans and others cover that. Nor is it an in-depth history of the game; that involves too much stuff that no one really cares about – and too much work! This book tries to identify key people, events and themes that have changed or enlivened the game for better or worse. From Henry to Hairstyles, New Theories to Nicknames, we've given a page – no more – to the best and worst of the Beautiful Game. If we think a player was talented but a bit of a lightweight, we've said so; if we think a side was dirty or arrogant, we've said so. We've said so not just because we think we're right, but because football fans want an opinion and an argument.

legend rating

Throughout the book you will note that each player or manager has a legend rating. These are based on the following criteria:

PLAYERS

Achievement: how much the player achieved in football – very little sympathy is accorded players who eschew 'the big move' in this mark.
Skill: pure talent.
Teamwork: ability to turn a game with a moment of skill or leadership.
Passion: overall contribution to a side, heart.
Personality: charisma, personal style.

MANAGERS

Achievement: as above.
Tactical Awareness: ability to read the way a game is going or will go and to act accordingly.
Motivation: gung-ho up-and-at 'em style or man-management – whatever it takes to get the best out of your best.
Transfer Dealing and Team Selection: the ability to distinguish a Cantona from a Marco Boogers.
Personality: as above.

Like the Dream Teams, these are based on opinion, rather than any tangible measurement, and are meant to invite discussion and disagreement. If you think we've rippled Row F rather than the back of the net with our selections, please e-mail us with your abuse (not too ripe!), or your own selections. You could even e-mail us if you agree – but where's the fun in that?

Nick Holt and *Guy Lloyd*
football@flametreepublishing.com

Adams, Tony

Arsenal, England

IN HIS EARLY YEARS Adams was frequently subjected to cries of 'donkey' from the terraces, as he appeared to be a traditional English centre half – physically dominant but maladroit with the ball at his feet. The fact that he is now treated with universal respect wherever he plays is testimony to the commitment and hard work he has shown in eliminating many of those early deficiencies in his game. The back line of David Seaman, Lee Dixon, Nigel Winterburn and Adams, with first Steve Bould and later Martin Keown, could reasonably lay claim to be the best-ever British club defence.

An outstanding reader of the game, he became a natural leader and an inspirational talisman for both England and Arsenal, both of whom were notably weaker in his absence. Adams' fight against alcohol addiction became a symbol of his strength of character, and his readiness to address personal flaws earned him respect well beyond the football world. His brief stretch in prison gave him a glimpse of life that few of today's pampered professionals would comprehend.

- Arsenal's miserly defence conceded only 18 goals as they waltzed away with the Championship in 1991.
- Adams took over two years to score his first league goal, finally bagging against Liverpool in 1986.
- In Adams's 11 matches as England captain they were only beaten once.
- Adams's honesty and self-awareness has mistakenly led some journalists to use him as a sage and philosopher, when he is clearly neither. He is a decent man who has learned to grow up.
- Adams' long-awaited introduction to management in 2003–04 proved a baptism of fire as he failed to rescue beleaguered Wycombe from relegation, and he resigned in November 2004.

VITAL STATISTICS

Place of Birth:	Romford, England
Date of Birth:	10 October 1966 **Died:** n/a
Caps:	66 (England) **Goals (International):** 5
Clubs:	As Player: Arsenal; As Manager: Wycombe Wanderers
Appearances:	Club (League): 504
Goals:	Club (League): 32
Trophies:	LT 1989, 1991, 1998, 2002; FAC 1993, 1998, 2002; LC 1987, 1993; CWC 1994

LEGEND RATING

Achievement	8.0
Skill	6.5
Teamwork	8.5
Passion	9.5
Personality	8.0
TOTAL	**40.5**

Allison, Malcolm
Manchester City, Crystal Palace

THE TACKY 1970s image should not disguise the ability of Malcolm Allison, one of England's finest post-war coaches. Like Ron Atkinson and Graham Taylor, Allison only truly established himself in football after hanging up his boots. A contributor to the West Ham 'academy' of the late 1950s, he was a senior professional at Upton Park when an awestruck Bobby Moore came under his tutelage. But it was at Manchester, first working as a coach during Joe Mercer's reign at Maine Road, that he honed his managerial abilities. Mercer and Allison presided over the most successful spell in the club's history, winning promotion in 1966, and the First Division title two years later.

In 1972 the marriage went sour and Allison was handed control of the team. He was a disastrous manager, and his graceless comments about Mercer earned him no plaudits. City lost seven of their first 10 league games and Allison jumped ship to Palace before the axe fell. The Eagles were relegated the same season. After Third Division Palace's Cup run brought them to within one game of Wembley in 1976, City forgave him and he returned to Maine Road. This time he was worse, squandering millions on mediocre players. He was sacked in 1980 and has since remained in the footballing wilderness, a sad demise for a man who shaped England's most famous captain.

👍 1968. Allison gave a famous half-time team-talk in City's final league game at Newcastle. With the score at 2-2 and a win needed, he remained completely silent, believing that the players knew the task ahead. They duly obliged.

☞ 'I've served more time than Ronnie Biggs did for the Great Train Robbery.' Allison reflecting ruefully on his lifetime touchline ban.

👍 1978–79. Broke British transfer record, paying £1.4 m for Steve Daley. Other signings include £750,000 for Preston's Michael Robinson, a player with a handful of league games, plus £250,000 for untried Palace teenager Steve MacKenzie.

☞ After City and Palace, Allison went to Farense in Portugal before returning to England to take over non-league Fisher Athletic.

VITAL STATISTICS

Place of Birth:	Dartford, England	
Date of Birth:	5 September 1927	**Died:** n/a
Caps:	0	**Goals (International):** 0
Clubs:	As Player: West Ham; As Manager: Plymouth,	
	Manchester City, Crystal Palace, Middlesbrough,	
	Bristol Rovers	
Trophies:	LT 1968; FAC 1969; LC 1970 (all as assistant	
	manager at Manchester City)	

LEGEND RATING	
Achievement	5.0
Skill	9.0
Teamwork	7.0
Passion	5.0
Personality	9.0
TOTAL	**35.0**

All-Rounders

Sporting Polymaths

LIFE ISN'T FAIR. MOST of us would settle for a modicum of talent in any activity; some blessed souls were not only talented enough to play professional football, they excelled at other sports as well.

The doyen was C.B. Fry. The hero of the late-Victorian and Edwardian eras, Fry played football and cricket for England, held the world long-jump record and was offered the throne of Albania for good measure.

Sportsmen who played both football and cricket were relatively commonplace in the days of lower wages and football seasons that didn't extend endlessly into the summer. By the early 1980s, a dwindling breed that included Ted Hemsley, Phil Neale, Jim Cumbes, Arnie Sidebottom and Alan Ramage had disappeared completely.

Pride of place in this era goes to Chris Balderstone, most notably for his efforts on 15 September 1975. After scoring an undefeated 50 for Leicestershire against Derbyshire, a waiting taxi took him to Doncaster, where he turned out in a Fourth Division game for Rovers against Brentford. He returned to Chesterfield the following morning to complete his century.

Follow that Ronaldo!

☞ Sporting brothers Denis & Leslie Compton both played football for Arsenal and England in the pre-and post-war era. They were also county cricketers for Middlesex; Denis is regarded by many as England's finest post-war batsman.

✑ England's World Cup hat-trick hero Geoff Hurst played for the Essex first XI; Gary Lineker also excelled at cricket.

☞ Other athletes have shown good footballing skills in their early years. England cricketer Graham Thorpe was a talented player, as was athlete Duane Ladejo. Viv Richards occasionally turned out for the Leeward Islands.

☞ Alan Hansen, Kenny Dalglish and Michael Owen are all excellent golf players, using their ample leisure time to hone their skills.

'Had he been playing today, there would not have been one unsponsored inch of him.'

Broadcaster and journalist Michael Parkinson pays tribute to Arsenal, Middlesex and England legend Denis Compton

Anderson, Viv
Nottingham Forest, England

VIV ANDERSON DID NOT SINGLE-HANDEDLY banish racism from the game of football, but he did advance the cause of enlightenment by becoming the first black player to win a full England cap. No tokenism here: Anderson was a cultured, overlapping fullback with genuine pace and an ease on the ball not normally associated with English defenders. His best club football came early in his career at Nottingham Forest where, under Brian Clough's tutelage, he became an integral member of their First Division and European Cup-winning teams. His reputation was enhanced further at Arsenal, but faded after a later move to Manchester United where injuries hampered his spell in the mid-1980s. Thus far, his coaching career has been a disappointment. Promoted from player to the backroom staff at Middlesbrough, he was Bryan Robson's assistant during their topsy-turvy Riverside reign that ended with them both being shown the door in 2001. Yet, while he still has much to prove in the management game, Anderson's legacy as a pioneer of black footballers is not something that can ever be taken away from him. Through his skill, courage and dignity he helped turn the volume down on the bigots. And for that alone, he deserves considerable respect.

- Played his first cap against Czechoslovakia in 1979. Anderson was sent a bullet in the post before the game; the accompanying note claimed the next one was for him if he played.
- Anderson was Alex Ferguson's first signing at Man United.
- He should have won far more than 30 caps (right-back plodder Phil Neal reached 50).
- Anderson remained a professional for 23 years, almost unheard of for a modern outfield player.
- Anderson was awarded an MBE in 2000.

VITAL STATISTICS

		LEGEND RATING
Place of Birth: Nottingham, England		
Date of Birth: 29 August 1956 **Died:** n/a	Achievement	8.0
Caps: 30 (England) **Goals (International):** 2	Skill	6.0
Clubs: Nottingham Forest, Arsenal, Manchester United,	Teamwork	8.0
Sheffield Wednesday, Barnsley	Passion	7.0
Appearances: Club (All Matches): 574	Personality	7.0
Goals: Club (All Matches): 31		
Trophies: LT 1978; LC 1978, 1979, 1987; EC 1980	**TOTAL**	**36.0**

Archie's Passion
Holland 2 Scotland 3, 1978

GOING INTO THIS MATCH, Scotland's hopes of glory at the 1978 World Cup Finals were already in tatters. With only one point from their first two games they were virtually out of the competition – a fate they could only avoid by beating the mighty Holland by three clear goals. Unbelievably, they came close to pulling it off.

The Scots gave everything. They hit the bar, had a goal disallowed and found themselves a goal down for their troubles, when Rensenbrink converted a penalty. Dalglish volleyed a deserved equaliser just before half-time, and Gemmill scored from the spot after Souness was brought down. Then came the goal that set Scottish hearts beating like the clappers. Gemmill, picking the ball up wide on the right, swerved past two defenders, nutmegged a third and coolly chipped the advancing Jongbloed. As he turned away Gemmill's face was a glorious and unforgettable fusion of elation, determination and passion. A midget player with a giant's heart had scored one of the greatest goals in the history of the game. Sadly for Gemmill, Dalglish and the rest, Scotland could not force a fourth, and had their hopes finally, and emphatically extinguished by Johnny Rep's 30-yard howitzer three minutes later.

☞ No less a judge than the great Dutch coach Rinus Michels had tipped Scotland as dark horses to win the tournament.

☜ Scottish winger Willie Johnston was sent home after the first match for taking a banned substance.

☞ Martin Buchan was chosen as fullback against Peru, where he struggled against Munante, one of the world's fastest wingers.

☜ Ally MacLeod stayed on as manager for one more game before resigning, blaming everyone else for a disastrous tournament.

☜ Complacent and off-key in the first two games, Scotland had been beaten by Peru and drawn with Iran, Ally MacLeod having omitted Graeme Souness for both these games.

SCORERS	**Holland:** Rensenbrink (pen), Rep
	Scotland: Dalglish, Gemmill 2 (1 pen)
EVENT	World Cup group match, Mendoza, 11 June 1978
HOLLAND	(Man: Ernst Happel)
	1. Jongbloed 2. Suurbier 3. Krol 4. Jansen 5. Rijsbergen
	6. Poortvliet 7. van der Kerkhof, R 8. Rep 9. Rensenbrink
	10. Neeskens 11. van der Kerkhof, W
SCOTLAND	(Man: Ally MacLeod)
	1. Rough 2. Kennedy 3. Donachie 4. Rioch 5. Forsyth 6. Buchan
	7. Gemmill 8. Hartford 9. Jordan 10. Souness 11. Dalglish

Ardiles, Osvaldo ('Ossie')
Argentina, Tottenham Hotspur

ARDILES WAS UNKNOWN IN EUROPE before the 1978 World Cup, where he was the fulcrum of the Argentina side that won the tournament, so when he and Ricky Villa were persuaded to come to England immediately after, it was, rightly, regarded as a stunning coup for Spurs. Ardiles returned to the World Cup stage in 1982, but Argentina found it harder work playing in Europe and lost their crown.

With the exception of his 1981 Cup final performance Villa was only a partial success at Spurs. Ardiles, on the other hand, was a revelation. His push-and-go style was easy to adapt to English football, and he formed a hugely effective partnership with the more flamboyant Glenn Hoddle. A better defence would surely have seen Spurs win more than an FA Cup and UEFA Cup in the early 1980s.

As a manager, Ardiles proved surprisingly inept for such an intelligent player. After a reasonably successful spell at Swindon Town, he suffered disastrous tenures at Newcastle and back at Spurs where, despite bringing in expensive signings such as Jurgen Klinsmann, Gica Popescu and Ilie Dumitrescu, he could not mould the team into an effective unit. In 2003 he settled in Japan as manager of Tokyo Verdy 1969.

☞ His only success as a manager, promotion with Swindon, was annulled due to financial irregularities under the previous incumbent, Lou Macari.

☞ Ardiles and Maradona only briefly overlapped for Argentina, when Ossie was past his energetic best. They would have been some combination in their mutual pomp.

☞ Ardiles' most embarrassing moment was a brief cameo in Spurs' 1981 FA Cup song. The memory of that squeaky little voice trilling out 'Tottingham' still sends shivers down the spine of music lovers everywhere.

☞ Ardiles owned a Yorkshire Terrier called Gazza.

VITAL STATISTICS

Place of Birth:	Cordoba, Argentina	
Date of Birth:	3 August 1952	**Died:** n/a
Caps:	53 (Argentina)	**Goals (International):** 8
Clubs:	Instituto de Cordoba, Huracan, Tottenham Hotspur, Paris Saint Germain, Blackburn Rovers, Queen's Park Rangers	
Appearances:	Club (for Tottenham): 315	
Goals:	Club (for Tottenham): 25	
Trophies:	WorC 1978; FAC 1981; UEFAC 1984	

Achievement	8.0
Skill	8.0
Teamwork	9.0
Passion	8.0
Personality	7.0
TOTAL	**40.0**

LEGEND RATING

Armfield, Jimmy

Blackpool, England

AS HONEST, ONE-CLUB MEN GO, there was none finer than the pipe-smoking Jimmy Armfield. Arguably England's best-ever fullback, Armfield approached fixtures at Bloomfield Road or the Maracana with the same dedicated, professional attitude. The England international spent 20 seasons with Blackpool, starting as a fresh-faced team-mate of Stanley Matthews and ending it alongside the long-haired mavericks of the 1970s. Signed originally as an amateur, his sporting attitude brought him a reputation as a fine tackler but never a dirty one, while his speed and enthusiasm to link with the attack made him the English pioneer of the modern wing-back position. His peak was the 1962 World Cup, where journalists voted him the tournament's best right back. But, amazingly, he was dropped to accommodate George Cohen before the next Finals tournament and never regained his place. Thus, with Jimmy Greaves, he became one of the best England players of his generation not to collect a 1966 World Cup winner's medal (to add to his woes that year, he was also beaten to the PFA Player of the Year award by Bobby Charlton). Loyal even now, Armfield still lives in Blackpool where, like his original mentor Matthews, he continues to be held in high esteem by the locals.

☞ A natural sportsman, Armfield excelled as a schoolboy at cricket, swimming and athletics.

✍ Armfield holds the Blackpool record for league appearances (568) and is the club's most capped player (43).

☞ In 1959 he made his England debut at the Maracana in front of 120,000 fanatical Brazilians.

✍ In 1963 Armfield shocked Blackpool by requesting a transfer, although he played at Bloomfield Road for a further eight years.

☞ Now a summariser for BBC radio, Armfield was awarded the OBE in 2000.

VITAL STATISTICS

Place of Birth:	Manchester, England	
Date of Birth:	21 September 1935	**Died:** n/a
Caps:	43 (England)	**Goals (International):** 0
Clubs:	Blackpool	
Appearances:	Club (League): 568	
Goals:	Club (League): 0	
Trophies:	None	

Achievement	5.0	
Skill	8.0	
Teamwork	8.0	
Passion	7.0	
Personality	7.0	
TOTAL	**35.0**	

LEGEND RATING

Atkinson, Ron

West Bromwich Albion, Manchester United

QUITE HOW RON ATKINSON EMERGED as a flamboyant, big-time manager and media pundit is something of a surprise, given his nondescript playing career kicking round the lower divisions at places like Barrow and Oxford United. It speaks volumes for his self-confidence that he was able to manage players whose ability far exceeded his own and, despite never having won a league title, convince those around him that he was a success.

His best team, the late-1970s West Bromwich Albion of Bryan Robson, Cyrille Regis and Laurie Cunningham, gave him the opportunity to fry bigger fish at Old Trafford. A record of two third places, three fourths and two FA Cups would have been more than good enough for most, but at United it cost him his job and heralded the arrival of Alex Ferguson. Perhaps it was signing Remi Moses for a ridiculous sum that the United board found unacceptable.

For four seasons United fans considered the Atkinson era a relatively golden one but, following their recent run of success, his tenure is now regarded as a failure. An Indian summer at Villa threatened an elusive title, but by this time his tanned presence was better known on television, where his unique jargon still entertains and irritates audiences in equal measure.

☞ Atkinson took Cambridge United from Fourth to Second Division in successive seasons.

☟ 1988. Sacked from his only foreign job at Atlético Madrid after just 88 days by notorious president, Jesus Gil.

☞ 1991. Vilified by Sheffield Wednesday fans after leaving for Villa, Atkinson was to return to Hillsborough six years later.

☞ 1986. 'The sacking of Ron Atkinson is the best thing that could happen to Manchester United,' said former United boss, Tommy Docherty on hearing the news. Despite comparisons, there was no love lost.

VITAL STATISTICS

Place of Birth:	Liverpool, England	
Date of Birth:	19 March 1939	**Died:** n/a
Caps:	0	**Goals (International):** 0
Clubs:	As Player: Aston Villa, Oxford United;	
	As Manager: Kettering Town, Cambridge United,	
	West Bromwich Albion, Manchester United,	
	Atlético Madrid, Sheffield Wednesday, Aston	
	Villa, Coventry City	
Trophies:	FAC 1983, 1985; FLT 1991, 1994	

LEGEND RATING	
Achievement	6
Tactical Awareness	6
Motivation	8
Team Selection/Transfers	8
Personality	9
TOTAL	**37**

Back From The Dead

Comebacks

TEN MINUTES FROM TIME, the ball rolls into touch. The camera catches pitted gaps in the crowd, upturned seats vacated by sections of the crowd who have decided that this one-sided contest is a foregone conclusion. Usually, they're right. Usually...

The greatest comeback? The Valley, 21 December 1957. With an hour played, 10-man Charlton trailed Huddersfield 5-1. Their outside left Johnny Summers suddenly realised a game was taking place and blasted a six-minute hat-trick. With two minutes left Charlton led 6-5 but appeared to have blown it when the Yorkshireman stole an equaliser. Enter Summers, providing John Ryan with a last-gasp winner. Huddersfield's manager was one Bill Shankly. He was still learning his trade.

In recent years, Spurs' soft centre has cost them dear. Their capitulation, when 3-0 up, to Manchester United, is worthy of (and gets) its own entry. Whether Mancunian opposition holds a particular terror, we shall never know, but in January 2004 lightning struck again. Spurs hosted City in the FA Cup fourth round. Half-time oranges were sucked secure in the knowledge of a three-goal cushion, whilst City's contribution consisted of a red card for Joey Barton. When Jonathan Macken headed the Sky Blues' winner (and City's fourth goal) in injury time, most Tottenham fans must have begun to wonder whether God was a Gooner. We've all been there.

✎ Liverpool's recovery from 3-0 down to Milan in the 2005 Champions League final must rank as the biggest fightback on a major occassion, even though technically they didn't win the game in open play.

☞ February 2001. In their fifth-round FA Cup tie Tranmere were 3-0 down at half-time to Premiership Southampton, a Paul Rideout hat-trick and Stuart Barlow's winner earned them a quarter-final dream encounter with Liverpool.

☞ Season 2003–04. Wolves' 4-3 defeat of Leicester was achieved the hard way after the Foxes had led 3-0. Black Country neighbours West Brom provided a carbon copy at Upton Park, this after the Hammers scored three in the first 18 minutes.

☞ November 2002: Mansfield lead Bristol City 4-2 with 88 minutes on the watch. It must have stuck, as six minutes of injury time gave City enough wriggle room for three goals, and three unforgettable points.

☞ Most famous international comeback – the 1966 World Cup Finals. Small-fry North Korea, having already despatched Italy, led 3-0 against fancied Portugal. They reckoned against Eusebio, who roused the Potuguese to a famous 5-3 win.

'Dear Dad, I hope you don't mind but I don't want to be a Spurs fan any more. Love Sam.'

Letter from nine-year-old Sam Curtis to journalist father Adrian, after Tottenham blow a three-goal lead to Manchester City

Man City battle with Spurs before their injury time winner, January 2004.

Baggies' Best
The West Bromwich Albion Dream Team

THE MODERN BAGGIES' FAN will not remember their team's greatest years. Nor, come to that, would their fathers. One of the founder members of the league, two of West Brom's five FA Cup victories came in the nineteenth century, and their only league title was in 1920. Jesse Pennington, the upstanding and gentlemanly Victorian centre half represents that era.

Another competent side was built in the 1950s. They won the FA Cup in 1954, with much-capped Welsh right back Stuart Williams, a young Bobby Robson, midfield worker Ray Barlow and the exciting centre forward Ronnie Allen in the side.

The rest of this Dream Team is made up of stars from the 1960s and 1970s; Albion maintained a respectable berth in the top flight for most of those years, including a third and a fourth place under Ron Atkinson. Their star turn was Bryan Robson, but left winger Willie Johnston was an outstanding maverick and a real crowd favourite too. Latterly West Brom have struggled to hold on to their better players, and despite regular appearances in the top six in Division One, look ill-equipped to compete in the modern Premier League.

☞ Ron Atkinson's departure spelt the end of the competitive years for Albion. Bryan Robson decamped to join him at Old Trafford, and Remi Moses and Laurie Cunningham went the same way.

☜ Derek Statham was desperately unlucky. Three caps for England, compared with 86 for Kenny Sansom should have been raised at Prime Minister's Question Time, as it clearly constitutes a national disgrace.

☞ Alongside Cyrille is the late Jeff Astle. Astle was a good centre forward who fell on hard times – why else would he have agreed to sing karaoke on Baddiel and Skinner's *Fantasy Football* show?

☟ Tony Brown remains the club's top scorer in the league and overall. He relegates the popular Cyrille Regis to the bench.

Manager: Ron Atkinson
4-4-2

John Osborne (60s/70s)

Don Howe (50s/60s) John Wile (C) (60s/70s) Jesse Pennington (1890s/00s) Derek Statham (70s)

Ray Barlow (40s/50s) Bobby Robson (60s) Bryan Robson (80s) Willie Johnston (70s)

Tony Brown (60s) Ronnie Allen (50s/60s)

Subs: Jim Cumbes (G) (60s/70s) Brendan Batson (D) (70s) Asa Hartford (M) (70s) Cyrille Regis (F) (80s) Jeff Astle (F) (60s)

Baggies' legend Jeff Astle celebrates after scoring the winner in the 1968 Cup Final versus Everton.

Ball, Alan

Everton, Southampton, England

THERE ARE FEW PLAYERS who reach their peak at 21, but as the youngest member of England's World Cup winning side, Alan Ball had the world at his feet. A teenage talent at Blackpool, his six-figure transfer to Everton the same year, the first of that size between English clubs, correctly identified Ball as one of English football's major talents. His Everton years saw Ball in his domestic pomp. With Howard Kendall and Colin Harvey he formed the 'Holy Trinity' that was the Everton midfield and saw them continue the north-west's dominance of the league title. Ball's adherence to the fiery redhead stereotype provided any team with its engine room, but often brought him to the attention of referees and earned him the rare distinction of becoming one of only a handful of players to be sent off while playing for England.

After a lean period at Arsenal, during which his fall-out with Don Revie put paid to his international career, his renaissance at Southampton was typical of other ageing ex-England stars. However, he could not repeat his on-field success in management, where his record thus far reads promotions two, relegations five.

- ☞ Despite being a World Cup winner, his 1970 league title is Ball's only domestic trophy.
- ☝ He was the first player to make 100 league appearances for four different clubs (Blackpool, Everton, Arsenal and Southampton).
- ☞ He scored one of the quickest-ever First Division goals, in 12 seconds for Arsenal v Man Utd.
- ☞ His £220 k move to Arsenal made Ball England's most expensive player for a second time.
- ☞ Ball on Revie's England selections: 'Some of the players are donkeys. Give them a lump of sugar and they run all day and play bingo all night.'

VITAL STATISTICS

Place of Birth:	Farnworth, Lancashire, England
Date of Birth:	12 May 1945 **Died:** n/a
Caps:	72 (England) **Goals (International):** 8
Clubs:	Blackpool, Everton, Arsenal, Southampton, Bristol Rovers
Appearances:	Club (League): 743
Goals:	Club (League): 170
Trophies:	WorC 1966; LT 1970

LEGEND RATING	
Achievement	9.0
Skill	7.0
Teamwork	8.0
Passion	9.0
Personality	7.0
TOTAL	**40.0**

Banged Up
Car-Crashers, Counterfeiters And Other Crooks

SADLY, FOOTBALL'S RECORD is as long as your arm. It is not simply that the game is prey to match-fixing, betting scandals and brown envelopes. Some of its participants are just plain criminal.

Top of the crime league is Arsenal. Five players in as many years were banned from driving in the early 1980s, while Tony Adams went one better in 1990, earning a four-month sentence after wrapping his car around a telegraph pole while driving under the influence. In 1988, Liverpool's Jan Molby joined the motoring school of infamy, when he was detained for three months at Her Majesty's pleasure on a reckless driving charge. These efforts were nothing compared to former Gunner Peter Storey. His rap sheet included headbutting a lollipop man, forgery and living off immoral earnings. Small wonder that one of his later trial judges sentenced him with the words: 'you already know what prisons are like, Mr Storey'.

The most tragic case is probably that of George Best. The flawed Belfast genius drank and drove once too often but failed to show in court. Eventually tracked to his Chelsea flat, he escaped and later resisted arrest, a small squad of officers being occupied in the process. The magistrate failed to see the funny side and gave him three months. The bigger they are….

🖑 Colombian keeper Rene Higuita is known to English audiences for his spectacular 'scorpion-kick' at Wembley in 1996. Less publicised was his absence from the 1994 World Cup Finals, when he was in jail as a result of kidnapping charges.

🖑 August 2005 – ex Paris Saint-Germain and Strasbourg defender Godwin Okpara is sentenced to four years by a Parisian court for imprisoning and raping a 13-year-old girl. Okpara claimed he had adopted her.

🖑 Duncan Ferguson's nickname of 'Duncan Disorderly' came after convictions for violence ended in a three-month jail term. Ferguson had assaulted Raith Rovers' fullback John McStay, a rare example of an on-field incident standing up in court.

🖑 Wrexham's Mickey Thomas was convicted of forgery in 1992. The incriminating evidence included his passing of dodgy banknotes to the club's YTS players.

🖑 In February 2005, Aresnal's Jermaine Pennant was sentenced to three months after a string of motoring offences. At the time he was on loan to Birmingham, for whom he played with an electronic tag after his release on parole.

🖑 October 2005 – former West Ham, Manchester City and Everton midfielder Mark Ward is dealt an eight-year gaol term after his conviction for possessing cocaine with intent to supply. Four kilos of the drug had been unearthed at a house Ward was renting in Merseyside.

'For a man who commanded the respect of thousands of people, to find yourself here, believe me, it is heartbreaking.'

Peter Storey's trial judge

1996: Colombian keeper Rene Higuita shows off his scorpion kick at Wembley.

Banks, Gordon
England

ENGLAND'S POST-WAR TRADITION is richer in goalkeepers than in any other position. The pick of a distinguished crop is a man once sacked from Romarsh Welfare in the Yorkshire League after conceding 15 goals in two games. Fortunately for England, Gordon Banks put this disappointment behind him to become his country's automatic choice for nine years, making his debut in Alf Ramsey's second game in charge. It was Ramsey who gave him all his 73 caps, but his worth to England's cause was perhaps most tellingly illustrated by a game he missed. Stricken by a stomach bug the night before the 1970 World Cup quarter-final against West Germany in Mexico, Banks was forced to watch helplessly as his replacement, Peter Bonetti, conceded three goals as England let slip a 2-0 lead. Despite his ability Banks's club career was largely unsuccessful (Leicester and Stoke provided top-division football but little else). Indeed, Leicester practically gave him away to Stoke (£50,000), although they did have an ace up their sleeve in the form of a teenager called Peter Shilton to take over his mantle. The end of his career made headline news for the wrong reasons, the loss of the sight in his right eye following a car crash making his fitness and athleticism irrelevant.

- He lost two FA Cup finals (1961 and 1963) with Leicester in three seasons.
- With Banks between the posts, England lost only nine of 73 games.
- He pulled off what is regarded as the world's greatest-ever save, diving to push a header from Pelé over the bar at the 1970 World Cup Finals in Mexico.
- During his spell with the Fort Lauderdale Strikers in the USA Banks was voted NASL's most valuable keeper. He could only see out of one eye at the time.
- In 1972 he became the first goalkeeper since Bert Trautmann (1956) to win the Footballer of the Year award.

VITAL STATISTICS

Place of Birth: Sheffield, England

Date of Birth: 20 December 1937 **Died:** n/a

Caps: 73 (England) **Goals (International):** 0

Clubs: Chesterfield, Leicester City, Stoke City, Fort Lauderdale Strikers

Appearances: Club (League): 510

Goals: Club (League): 0

Trophies: WorC 1966; LC 1964, 1972

Achievement	8.0
Skill	10.0
Teamwork	8.0
Passion	9.0
Personality	7.0
TOTAL	**42.0**

LEGEND RATING

Bastin, Cliff
Arsenal, England

WHILE STILL A TEENAGER Cliff Bastin won a league title, the FA Cup and his first England cap. He carried on achieving great things, and who knows what he might have accomplished had the war not arrived while he was still only 27.

Herbert Chapman went to watch a player called Tommy Barnett at Watford, but ended up buying the opposition winger. Thus Bastin arrived at Highbury where his left-sided partnership with Alex James proved the creative core in the most successful club side of the 1930s. Most wingers at that time simply tried to go round their marker, but Bastin gave Arsenal an extra option by frequently cutting in and shooting, hence his remarkable goal tally for a winger.

When centre-forward Ted Drake joined Arsenal Bastin scored fewer goals, but his constant 'assists' for the barnstorming Drake helped Arsenal maintain their march towards three consecutive titles. Bastin was still with Arsenal after the war, but his increasing deafness and the legacy of earlier cartilage trouble meant he was a spent force, and he retired at the end of that first season.

- Bastin was one of seven Arsenal players in the England team for the 1934 'Battle of Highbury' against Italy.
- His 33 goals in 1933 remains a record for a winger.
- Rome radio claimed Bastin was a POW during the war; actually he was an air-raid warden, unable to enter active service due to encroaching deafness.
- Bastin remained Arsenal's top scorer until Ian Wright eclipsed his record in 1997.
- Bastin joined other Arsenal stars as a pallbearer at Herbert Chapman's funeral.

VITAL STATISTICS

Place of Birth:	Exeter, England	
Date of Birth:	14 March 1912	**Died:** 4 December 1991
Caps:	21 (England)	**Goals (International):** 12
Clubs:	Exeter City, Arsenal	
Appearances:	Club (All Matches): 395	
Goals:	Club (All Matches): 178	
Trophies:	LT 1931, 1933, 1934, 1935, 1938;	
	FAC 1930, 1936	

LEGEND RATING	
Achievement	8.0
Skill	9.0
Teamwork	8.0
Passion	7.0
Personality	7.0
TOTAL	**39.0**

Baxter, Jim

Rangers, Scotland

A MIDFIELD, BALL-PLAYING GENERAL whose medal tally never matched those of a Billy McNeill or an Ally McCoist, but whose skill, personality and lifestyle filled endless column inches on the front and back pages of Scotland's press.

The architect of Rangers' dominance in the early 1960s, Baxter's talent elevated him to the status of team-mate to the likes of Alfredo Di Stefano, Ferenc Puskas and Eusebio in a Wembley appearance for the Rest of the World against England in 1963. Four years later it was the same venue and opponents who provided Baxter with a moment that epitomised his talent and sense of occasion when, during Scotland's famous defeat of the World Champions, he sat on the ball inviting the English players to dispossess him. While the tanner-ball Scottish stereotype suited Baxter, he also lived up to his nation's drinking traditions and a decline following a transfer to Sunderland in 1965 ensured he was never again to win a major trophy. His death at 61 in April 2001 jogged memories of a greater glory and prompted Rangers fans to line the streets in their thousands to mourn his passing.

- Baxter's best-ever Rangers performance was probably the 1963 Cup final replay against Celtic. He was imperious in a 3-0 victory.
- Scotland's failure to qualify for the 1966 World Cup Finals was put down largely to the absence of Baxter, who missed crucial qualifiers against Poland and Italy.
- Baxter never played in the Finals of a major international tournament, so remains largely unknown outside Britain.
- After four unsuccessful years away, Baxter returned to Rangers for a last hurrah in 1969, but was not the force of old.
- Scotland's 1967 victory at Wembley condemned England to their first defeat since winning the World Cup a year earlier.

VITAL STATISTICS

Place of Birth: Hill O'Beath, Fife, Scotland

Date of Birth: 29 September 1939 **Died:** 14 April 2001

Caps: 34 (Scotland) **Goals (International):** 3

Clubs: Rangers, Sunderland, Raith Rovers, Nottingham Forest

Appearances: Club (for Rangers): 254

Goals: Club (for Rangers): 24

Trophies: SLT 1961, 1963, 1964; SFAC 1962, 1963, 1964

LEGEND RATING	
Achievement	6.0
Skill	9.0
Teamwork	7.0
Passion	8.0
Personality	8.0
TOTAL	**38.0**

Beckenbauer, Franz

Bayern Munich, Germany

'THE KAISER', as Franz Beckenbauer became known (such were the imperious nature of his displays for club and country), was one of the finest players in the history of the game. An outstanding captain and tactician, it was no surprise that he went on to win everything, including the World Cup as player and manager.

Beginning his international career as a deep-lying midfielder, Beckenbauer revolutionised the notion of the attacking sweeper, bursting out of defence to set up attacks, often even finishing them himself. He had every attribute a footballer requires: control, passing, strength and uncanny vision. Only Ruud Gullit has since shown a comparable range of skills, but he lacked Beckenbauer's iron will. Retiring from international football in 1977, Beckenbauer teamed up with Pelé at New York Cosmos in the North American Soccer League, before returning to claim one last domestic honour with SV Hamburg.

Once retired he was appointed national coach almost immediately, and injected the same discipline and indomitable steel into the German side in the 1980s that it was famed for under his captaincy 10 years earlier. More success followed, and Beckenbauer, as President of Bayern Munich, remains at the forefront of German and European football to this day.

- Many commentators believe Beckenbauer's best performance came in the 3-2 win over England at the 1970 World Cup in Mexico. He inspired the Germans to a 3-2 win after they fell two goals behind.
- Only Mario Zagalo has equalled Beckenbauer's feat of World Cup medals as player and manager; Zagalo was not captain of Brazil.
- Beckenbauer was twice named European Footballer of the Year, in 1972 and 1976.
- He was picked for Germany after only 27 appearances for Bayern.
- Beckenbauer was detailed to man-mark Bobby Charlton in the 1966 World Cup Final, and later admitted he was not ready for the challenge.

VITAL STATISTICS

Place of Birth:	Munich, Germany	
Date of Birth:	11 September 1945	**Died:** n/a
Caps:	104 (W. Germany) **Goals (International):** 15	
Clubs:	Bayern Munich, Hamburg, New York Cosmos	
Appearances:	Club (All Matches): 720	
Goals:	Club (All Matches): 94	
Trophies:	WorC 1974 (1990); EuroC 1972; BLG 1969, 1973, 1974, 1975, (1994); EC 1974, 1975; CWC 1967	

LEGEND RATING	
Achievement	10.0
Skill	9.0
Teamwork	9.0
Passion	9.0
Personality	8.0
TOTAL	**45.0**

Beckenbauer covets the World Cup with the West German team in 1974.

Beckham, David
Manchester United, Real Madrid, England

WHEN DAVID BECKHAM curled a last-minute free kick over the Greek wall to win England a place at the 2002 World Cup Finals, it completed a comeback more remarkable than his national side. It also capped one of the most complete performances by any player in an England shirt.

Three years previously, he was the nation's hate figure, reviled after his petulant kick and red card against Argentina had cost England their place at France 98. If he had taken the easy option and moved abroad immeadiately, he may not have become what he is; the single most influential player for his country. His passing and crossing are of the highest order, and his shooting from set pieces is simply Brazilian in its power and accuracy.

That he has matured beyond adolescent cockiness is more surprising, his looks, style and pop-star wife have made 'Becks' the most hounded footballer since George Best. A much-publicised spat with Alex Ferguson led to Beckham's departure for Real Madrid, where he has sometimes struggled alongside the other *galacticos*. A similar recent dip in form for England has led to some short-term thinking over his international future. England's midfield, for all the industry of Lampard and Gerrard, still needs the vision of its most experienced member.

- Arrives in English football with an outrageous 50 m goal at Wimbledon.
- 1999. Marries Spice Girl Victoria Beckham. 'Posh and Becks' become Britain's most photographed couple.
- December 2001. Voted BBC Sports Personality of the Year, and runner-up as World Footballer of the Year for a second time.
- October 2004. Claims to have deliberately earned a booking (and subsequent suspension) with a silly tackle in the England v Wales game, as he was injured and would have missed the next game anyway. Apparently this proves he's not stupid. Yes, David. Follows this a year later by becoming the first England player to be sent off twice, albeit very harshly, against Austria.

VITAL STATISTICS

Place of Birth:	Leytonstone, England	
Date of Birth:	2 May 1975	**Died:** n/a
Caps:	84 (England)	**Goals (International):** 16
Clubs:	Manchester United, Real Madrid	
Appearances:	Club (All Matches): 443	
Goals:	Club (All Matches): 93	
Trophies:	LT 1996, 1997, 1999, 2000, 2001, 2003;	
	FAC 1996, 1999; EC 1999	

Achievement	9.0
Skill	8.0
Teamwork	8.0
Passion	9.0
Personality	7.0
TOTAL	**41.0**

LEGEND RATING

Bellamy, Craig
Newcastle United, Blackburn Rovers, Wales

IF YOU ASK MODERN PREMIERSHIP defenders who they find hardest to handle, the name of Craig Bellamy will undoubtedly crop up. If you ask Premiership managers who is the hardest player to handle, Bellamy will definitey crop up, but in a less flattering context.

As a player, Bellamy's astonishing pace, allied to a decent skill level and a nose for goal, make him a threat to any defence. His presence has improved every side he has played for, and his absence cost Wales and Newcastle dear on more than one occasion. Those absences are often due to suspensions, as Bellamy's immature attitude has often seen him fall foul of club discipline, especially at Newcastle. A history of injuries adds to the feeling that he is a risk, even a liability, for any employer.

There is time for this gifted player to make more permanent and positive mark on the game, but it must happen soon, or he will be consigned to the 'what if' file alongside Alan Hudson and Willie Johnston and all the other wayward souls.

- A major fall-out with Graeme Souness (he publicly accused his manager of lying) at Newcastle saw Bellamy shipped out to Celtic on loan and then sold to Blackburn, managed by former Wales manager, Mark Hughes.
- Bellamy's best season was his first for Newcastle, in 2001–02. His form and goals in partnership with Alan Shearer saw Newcastle pushing at the top of the Premiership. An injury to the winger in February saw Newcastle falter without his pace and drive.
- The 'gobbiest' player Bobby Robson said he had ever worked with, Bellamy once made the headlines for an off-the-field altercation in Cardiff town centre. Maybe he should study John Terry's career to see how bad boys can grow up.

VITAL STATISTICS

Place of Birth:	Cardiff, Wales				
Date of Birth:	13 July 1979	**Died:** n/a	Achievement	5.0	
Caps:	34 (Wales)	**Goals (International):** 9	Skill	9.0	
Clubs:	Norwich City, Coventry City, Newcastle United,		Teamwork	7.0	
	Celtic (loan), Blackburn Rovers		Passion	7.0	
Appearances:	Club (All Matches): 233		Personality	5.0	
Goals:	Club (All Matches): 79				
Trophies:	None		**TOTAL 33.0**		

LEGEND RATING

Bellamy (No. 10) is congratulated by mentor Shearer.

Bergkamp, Dennis

Arsenal, Holland

DENNIS BERGKAMP BROKE INTO the Ajax team towards the end of the Gullit, Rijkaard, Van Basten era. Bergkamp gradually made his presence felt, and earned a high-profile move to Inter to replace Jurgen Klinsmann. Not suited to playing as a lone striker, he preferred to drop off defences, creating space to play others in or try a trademark curling shot. Inter offloaded him to Arsenal and initially, it seemed as if his spell at Highbury would be equally unfruitful, but the arrival of Arsène Wenger changed all that. Almost immediately Bergkamp was rejuvenated and, in tandem with Nicolas Anelka, inspired the Gunners to a League and Cup double in 1998.

After scoring the two goals at Wembley that effectively eliminated England in the qualifiers, Bergkamp had an outstanding 1994 World Cup in a transitional side. In France in 1998 Bergkamp showed his divine poise and touch in scoring the goal of the tournament against Argentina, but he wasn't fully fit and couldn't turn the semi-finals as Brazil beat the Dutch in a penalty shoot-out.

As the years have caught up with him, Bergkamp has settled into the role of vital squad player at Arsenal. Two more titles in 2002 and 2004 bear testimony to his enduring intelligence and skill – the old master can still galvanise the gifted youngsters alongside him.

- In August 1997 Bergkamp occupied the top three positions in the *Match Of The Day* goal-of-the-month competition. The winning goal, a cheeky control-and-finish against Leicester, also won the goal-of-the-season award.
- Bergkamp was named the Football Writers' and PFA Player of the Year in 1998.
- Bergkamp's fear of flying, which he thought he had conquered, was rekindled by a bomb alert as the Dutch team travelled to the 1994 World Cup in the USA. He has not flown since.
- Bergkamp was named after Denis Law. His parents mistakenly spelt his first name with two 'n's instead of one.

VITAL STATISTICS

Place of Birth:	Amsterdam, Holland	
Date of Birth:	18 May 1969	**Died:** n/a
Caps:	79 (Holland)	**Goals (International):** 36
Clubs:	Ajax, Inter Milan, Arsenal	
Appearances:	Club (All Matches): 646	
Goals:	Club (All Matches): 233	
Trophies:	LT 1998, 2002, 2004; FAC 1998, 2002, 2003;	
	DLT 1993; UEFAC 1992, 1994	

Achievement	7.0
Skill	9.0
Teamwork	8.0
Passion	7.0
Personality	7.0
TOTAL	**38.0**

LEGEND RATING

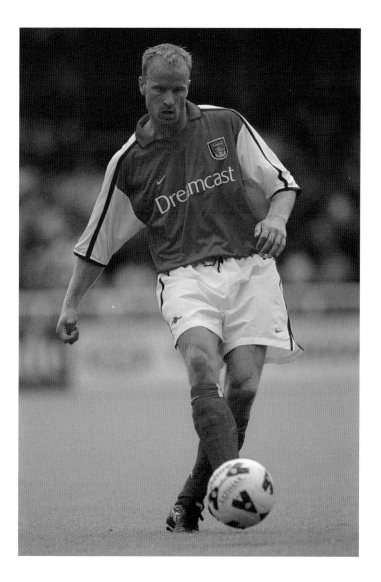

Best Football Team In The World

...Ever

THIS WAS REALLY EASY TO PICK. So few players elevate themselves to the level of these 16 players that the process of elimination is almost automatic. The criteria? Great technical ability, appetite for battle, sustained excellence over a number of years, and an ability to inspire others, either by example or leadership.

None of these players were perfect (although Pelé came close at times) and none are pre-war (football was a cruder game back then and the competition was less fierce), but all satisfy the criteria in abundance. Six of them played in the 1950s, four more started in the 1960s, two in the 1970s, and the last four in the 1980s.

There are nine Europeans and five South Americans (no country has more than two players), and there are no out-and-out fullbacks; the restrictive nature of the position makes it unattractive for the very best players. If 4-4-2 were required, Baresi would slot in alongside Moore, and Garrincha or Best would drop to the bench.

Only Paolo Maldini is still in active service, and he may play until he is 50 at the current rate! There are only a tiny handful of players still in the game capable of ascending to these heights; Thierry Henry, Kaka, Wayne Rooney and Robinho may yet ascend to the pantheon.

☞ No one got close to either of the goalkeeping slots; the next in line were Shilton, Schmeichel, Zoff and Jennings.

☞ Van Basten is another Dutchman unlucky to miss out, and Eusebio and Bobby Charlton wouldn't have looked out of place.

☞ Daniel Passarella had a case for inclusion, but was less sophisticated than the four defenders picked. Marcel Desailly falls just short of this status.

☞ Gullit is perhaps the most obvious omission from the midfield.

☞ Lothar Matthaus was a great player, but his biggest fan was Lothar Matthaus.

✍ Managing this collection of inflated egos would be impossible, so we thought we might as well appoint ourselves!

Managers: Guy Lloyd and Nick Holt

3-4-1-2

Lev Yashin (USSR)

Franz Beckenbauer (C) (W. Ger) Bobby Moore (Eng) Paolo Maldini (Ita)

Garrincha (Bra) Pelé (Bra)
Michel Platini (Fra) George Best (N. Ire)

Alfredo Di Stefano (Arg)

Johan Cruyff (Hol) Ferenc Puskas (Hun)

Subs: Gordon Banks (G) (Eng) Franco Baresi (D) (Ita) Diego Maradona (M) (Arg) Juan Schiaffino (F) (Uru) Gerd Muller (F) (W. Ger)

Lev Yashin (USSR)

Franz Beckenbauer (W. Ger) (c)

Bobby Moore (Eng)

Paolo Maldini (Ita)

Garrincha (Bra)

Pelé (Bra)

Michel Platini (Fra)

George Best (N. Ire)

Johan Cruyff (Hol)

Alfredo Di Stefano (Arg)

Ferenc Puskas (Hun)

Best, George

Manchester United, Northern Ireland

'I THINK I'VE FOUND YOU A GENIUS,' claimed the Belfast scout in an excited telephone call to Matt Busby. He wasn't wrong. Signed as a professional on his 17th birthday, George Best thrilled the Old Trafford faithful like no player before or since. Had Best played for a stronger country than Northern Ireland he may now be spoken of with the same reverence as Pelé.

The cocktail of outrageous ball skills and smouldering good looks proved to be an explosive one; Best's transformation from Belfast innocent to international playboy seemed to capture the spirit of the 1960s. He was even dubbed 'El Beatle' by the Portuguese press after a mesmerising display in Benfica's Stadium of Light. The free spirit that was Europe's most feared striker became society's hottest property, an advertiser's dream whose fame and fortune rocketed in a whirl of boutique openings and product endorsement. The inevitable falls from grace were frequent and glaring, and at 28 he was washed-up.

Despite an Indian summer at Fulham with fellow funster Rodney Marsh, and occasional spells in the NASL and elsewhere, the career of George Best has now been restricted to bar-room reminiscences for nearly 30 years.

- Best was originally recommended to Leeds. Unimpressed, the scout left his trial match during the first half.
- 1968. Best's *annus mirabilis*: Joint First Division top-scorer, European Cup winner, English and European Footballer of the Year.
- 1970. Suspended for four weeks for bringing the game into disrepute. On his return, scored six in an 8-2 win at Northampton.
- 1976. Scored after 71 seconds in his debut for Fulham. Also became their first recipient of a red card.
- A liver transplant in 2002 failed to curb Best's drinking bouts and he was convicted of drink driving in January 2004. Drink finally got the better of George in November 2005 when he died from a kidney infection brought on by excessive drinking.

VITAL STATISTICS

Place of Birth:	Belfast, Northern Ireland	
Date of Birth:	22 May 1946	**Died:** 25 November 2005
Caps:	37 (N. Ireland)	**Goals (International):** 9
Clubs:	Manchester United, Stockport County, Cork Celtic, Los Angeles Aztecs, Fulham, Hibernian, Fort Lauderdale Strikers, San Jose Earthquakes, Golden, Bournemouth	
Appearances:	Club (League for Man Utd): 361	
Goals:	Club (League for Man Utd): 137	
Trophies:	LT 1965, 1967; EC 1968 (all with Man Utd)	

Achievement	8.0
Skill	10.0
Teamwork	7.0
Passion	8.0
Personality	9.0
TOTAL	**42.0**

LEGEND RATING

Bingham, Billy

Northern Ireland

THERE WAS A TIME in the not-too-distant past when Northern Ireland was not simply cannon fodder for the rest of the world. Lest we forget, the nation now lumped in the same bracket as Cyprus reached the 1958 World Cup quarter-finals, distinguished themselves in Spain in 1982 and qualified again for the Mexico Finals four years later. The one connection? Mr Billy Bingham.

As a small, nippy, right winger, Bingham played in all five games during the 1958 campaign, but it was as manager that he made the greater impact. The blend was the key; from the vast experience of Pat Jennings to the 17-year-old exuberance of Norman Whiteside, Bingham built a well-balanced team. Unfancied before the 1982 World Cup Finals, Northern Ireland beat hosts Spain to win their group, and were later only undone by a Michel Platini-inspired France.

At the Mexico Finals four years later there was again no disgrace in losing to Spain and Brazil. Indeed, Bingham had earned international respect as a coach simply by qualifying again. Bingham's international record was in stark contrast to his record as a club manager; he achieved little as boss of a string of lowly club sides. But to the people of Ulster he will always be fondly remembered.

- He shared a record number of Northern Ireland caps with Danny Blanchflower (56).
- ☞ 1959. Won FA Cup runners-up medal with Luton Town.
- ☞ 1963. League Championship winner with Everton.
- ☞ 1983. Coached Northern Ireland to a shock 1-0 win over West Germany in Hamburg.
- ✎ 1981. Awarded an MBE for services to football.

VITAL STATISTICS

Place of Birth:	Belfast, Northern Ireland	
Date of Birth:	5 August 1931	**Died:** n/a
Caps:	56 (N. Ireland)	**Goals (International):** 10
Clubs:	As Player: Glentoran, Sunderland, Luton Town,	
	Everton, Port Vale; As Manager: Southport,	
	Plymouth Argyle, Linfield, Everton, Mansfield	
Trophies:	None	

Achievement	5
Tactical Awareness	7
Motivation	9
Team Selection/Transfers	7
Personality	8
TOTAL	**36**

LEGEND RATING

Blanchflower, Robert Dennis (Danny)

Tottenham Hotspur, Northern Ireland

DANNY BLANCHFLOWER is best remembered as the playmaker in the 1961 Spurs double-winning side. However, he was by then in the twilight of his career, having emerged in Irish football just after the war.

Not exceptionally quick or powerful, Blanchflower's game was all about passing. Blessed with exceptional vision, his ability to find team-mates with the ball was uncanny. His understanding of the game was deep and intuitive, and he used that knowledge to great effect on the pitch. 'Football is not really about winning … it's about doing things in style,' he once wrote. Any modern footballer uttering those words would be sold the next day!

After retiring, Blanchflower had a few forays into management. He managed the Northern Ireland national team in a tough spell prior to the golden years of Billy Bingham, and was in charge at Stamford Bridge as Chelsea suffered relegation in 1979. Thereafter he concentrated on his career as a journalist, where his erudite thinking about the game served him better.

☞ He famously refused to take part in the programme *This Is Your Life* when Eamonn Andrews surprised him.

✌ Danny's younger brother, Jackie, played for Manchester United and was injured in the Munich air crash, never to play again.

☝ Blanchflower was captain of the Northern Ireland team that reached the quarter-finals of the 1958 World Cup.

☝ He was also captain when Northern Ireland beat England at Wembley for the first time in 1957.

✌ He was Player of the Year in 1958 and 1961.

VITAL STATISTICS

Place of Birth:	Belfast, Northern Ireland
Date of Birth:	10 February 1926 **Died:** 9 December 1993
Caps:	56 (N. Ireland) **Goals (International):** 2
Clubs:	Glentoran, Swindon Town, Barnsley, Aston Villa, Tottenham Hotspur
Appearances:	Club (All Matches): 735
Goals:	Club (All Matches): 40
Trophies:	LT 1961; FAC 1961, 1962; CWC 1963

LEGEND RATING	
Achievement	8.0
Skill	9.0
Teamwork	7.0
Passion	8.0
Personality	8.0
TOTAL	**40.0**

Bloomer, Steve

Derby County, England

WITH HIS SLIGHT BUILD and sallow appearance, Steve Bloomer was an unlikely athlete. A dressing-room nickname of 'paleface' hardly suggested a man brimming with rude health but, during a remarkable career of 21 seasons, he became English football's first great goalscoring hero, and its undoubted star during the pre-First World War era.

His 352 league goals (a record that only Dixie Dean has beaten) were achieved courtesy of rare, two-footed skills that made him one of the game's most entertaining dribblers. His influence was exemplified by the 1903 FA Cup. Bloomer's goals had guided Derby to the final but, for the big day itself, he was absent with injury. Without him Derby succumbed 6-0 to Bury in what remains the heaviest final defeat of all time.

Two years later he made up one half of British football's then-biggest transfer, as Middlesbrough swooped for Bloomer and Sunderland's Alf Common in the first-ever four-figure deal. The gamble paid off. Boro, seemingly destined for relegation, hauled themselves clear in the final weeks of the season. For Bloomer, carrying inferior team-mates became the story of his career.

- He was England's seventh-highest scorer with 28 goals, despite winning only 23 caps.
- Bloomer never won a trophy, twice finishing on the losing side in the FA Cup final.
- 1914. Coaching in Berlin, Bloomer's career was only ended when he was interned at the onset of the First World War.
- Bloomer had a typically direct approach to the game: 'The purpose of play is the scoring of goals.'
- He was the leading league scorer five times in eight seasons.

VITAL STATISTICS

Place of Birth:	Cradley Heath, England		
Date of Birth:	20 January 1874	**Died:** 16 April 1938	
Caps:	23 (England)	**Goals (International):** 28	
Clubs:	Derby County, Middlesbrough		
Appearances:	Club (League): 598		
Goals:	Club (League): 352		
Trophies:	None		

LEGEND RATING	
Achievement	5.0
Skill	8.0
Teamwork	8.0
Passion	9.0
Personality	6.0
TOTAL	**36.0**

Bloomer (front row, seated second from left) poses with the England team.

Blue Heaven
The Chelsea Dream Team

THE 1955 TEAM may have won Chelsea's first title, but its sum was always greater than its individual parts. Hence captain and inspiration Roy Bentley is its only inclusion in this Dream Team, the remaining players being provided by teams of the 1970s and from the last decade.

The agile Bonetti was a better goalkeeper than England fans will ever credit. The rest of the defence is dominated by the recent sides, with the exception of the fullbacks, where Shellito and McCreadie shade the more reliable Ferrer and sometimes unpredictable Le Saux. With Terry and the fabulous Marcel Desailly at the back, there's no shortage of strength and ability on the ball. Dennis Wise adds a bit of attitude to the midfield alongside the gifted yet underachieving Hudson. Frank Lampard provides all-day running and a good goal quota. The puck-like skills of Gianfranco Zola are used in their best position, just behind the front two (the only downside to this being that ball artists Nevin and Cooke have to settle for a place on the bench).

In attack Osgood, a truly complete centre forward who should have played more internationals for England, creates a twin spearhead alongside the more industrious Bentley. Hughie Gallagher, perhaps better known as a Newcastle player, makes a potent substitute.

🖑 No place for Jimmy Greaves. Despite 124 goals in 157 games, his name is synonymous with Spurs.

☞ Bonetti is one of Chelsea's shorter keepers, dwarfed by 'Fatty' Foulke and Ed de Goey. Less of a complete keeper than either Cudicini or Cech, he wins his place due to loyalty over 20 seasons.

☞ Osgood and Le Saux both had two spells at the club. Osgood is included for his first, Le Saux his second.

Manager: Jose Mourinho (00s)

4-3-1-2

Peter Bonetti (60s/70s)

Ken Shellito (60s) Marcel Desailly (90s)
John Terry (00s) Eddie McCreadie (70s)

Dennis Wise (90s) Frank Lampard (00s) Alan Hudson (70s)

Gianfranco Zola (90s)

Roy Bentley (50s) Peter Osgood (60s/70s)

Subs: Carlo Cudicini (G) (00s) Graeme Le Saux (D) (90s) Pat Nevin (W) (80s) Charlie Cooke (W) (60s/70s) Hughie Gallagher (F) (30s)

Ron Harris (left) and Peter Osgood (right) brandish the FA Cup after Chelsea's victory in 1970.

Boot Room, The
Liverpool, 1972–90

IT SEEMS A LITTLE HARSH to lump this lot together and count them as one team, but to separate them would be to undervalue their core strength, namely the great continuity that ran through the club for nearly 30 years. Liverpool's legendary ability to hand over from one manager to the next, and to replace one great player with another was the platform on which their success was built.

Shankly stood down for Paisley and, briefly, Fagan. Lawrenson slotted in effortlessly for Thompson, Keegan became Dalglish – every few years the face of the team would morph like Dr Who and a new line-up would emerge, just as powerful as the last. The circuit seemed to have been broken with the installation of Dalglish as the team's first player-manager, but the mercurial Scot understood the Liverpool ethos, and brought more success, including the club's first League and Cup double in 1986. Liverpool won games on reputation alone – lesser teams quailed at the prospect of playing them, and Anfield became a fortress. They lost only nine home league games in the 1970s, compared with 33 in the less successful 1990s.

- Phil Neal, the right back, amassed eight championship medals, a record held jointly with Hansen. Add 50 caps and you have a remarkable tally for a player of modest abilities.
- Ray Kennedy, a double winner with Arsenal in 1971, missed the chance to become the first player to achieve that feat with a second club when Liverpool were beaten by Manchester United in the 1977 FA Cup final.
- Ronnie Whelan was an underrated player – athletic and strong, he could run all day and was a wonderful foil for the less mobile talents of Souness and Jan Molby.
- Liverpool never replaced the solidity of Ray Clemence in goal; current keeper Jerzy Dudek looked for a while to be a promising substitute, but has recently fallen from favour.

Managers: Bill Shankly, Bob Paisley, Joe Fagan, Kenny Dalglish

Key Players
Ray Clemence (G) Emlyn Hughes (D) Phil Thompson (D)
Phil Neal (D) Alan Hansen (D) Mark Lawrenson (D)
Graeme Souness (M) Jimmy Case (M) Ray Kennedy (M)
Ronnie Whelan (M) John Barnes (W) Kevin Keegan (F)
Kenny Dalglish (F) Peter Beardsley (F) Ian Rush (F)

Trophies
LT 1973, 1976, 1977, 1979, 1980, 1982, 1983, 1984, 1986, 1988, 1990;
FAC 1986; LC 1981–84; UEFAC 1973, 1976; EC 1977, 1978, 1981, 1984

Bosman, Jean-Marc
FC Liege

IN 1988, an unremarkable Belgian midfielder entered into a dispute with his club over what appeared to be nothing more than a contractual technicality. Seven years later, the outcome of this legal spat was to change football forever. Jean-Marc Bosman was signed by RFC Liege on a two-year contract in 1988. On its expiry, a prospective new deal would have reduced his wages by 60 per cent. A potential solution was offered in the form of French club Dunkerque, but their transfer valuation of Bosman was less than half the £250,000 that Liege were demanding. He remained stuck in Belgium. Undeterred, Bosman started a legal process that inched its way to the European Court of Justice. His argument was that by retaining his registration, and demanding a transfer fee even after his contract had expired, Liege were in breach of European Union law, which was supposed to safeguard the free movement of workers between member states. In December 1995, the court agreed and ruled in Bosman's favour. The ruling has made players more powerful than ever before, with many of them, like England stars Steve McManaman and Sol Campbell, choosing to see out their contracts in order to negotiate lucrative moves away from clubs where they had been nurtured, developed and idolised.

☞ The same ruling also quashed a UEFA regulation limiting the number of foreign players that could appear in European competition for a single club.

✍ The beneficiaries? Top players, as clubs began to offer improved wages to attract out-of-contract stars.

☝ The losers? Small clubs, who had relied on the transfer income from their rising talent. Bigger teams could now wait for their contracts to expire and pick them up for nothing.

VITAL STATISTICS

Place of Birth:	Belgium		Achievement	4.0
Date of Birth:	30 October 1964	**Died:** n/a	Skill	6.0
Caps:	0	**Goals (International):** 0	Teamwork	7.0
Clubs:	FC Liege		Passion	8.0
Appearances:	Club (League): 73		Personality	9.0
Goals:	Club (League): 3			
Trophies:	None		**TOTAL**	**34.0**

LEGEND RATING

Brady, Liam

Arsenal, Juventus, Republic Of Ireland

LIAM BRADY'S SKILL on the ball was a joy to behold – great touch, excellent dribbling skills and a sublime left foot. Little wonder then, that Arsenal fans quickly took him to their hearts. 'Chippy', as he became known, inspired the Gunners to their dramatic 3-2 FA Cup final win over Manchester United in 1979, creating the winning goal for Alan Sunderland in the dying moments.

A year later he was instrumental in Arsenal's run to the final of the European Cup Winners' Cup but, on the night, it was Brady's missed penalty in the shoot-out that handed the Cup to Valencia.

Possibly operating on the philosophy of 'if you can't beat 'em join 'em', Brady later moved to the continent where he became a huge success, winning two Serie A titles with Juventus, where he played alongside greats like Roberto Bettega in what many Juve fans still regard as their finest-ever team. Oddly though, Brady never played in a championship-winning side for Arsenal. In England Brady is perhaps best remembered for a goal he scored during a 5-0 thrashing of Spurs, an outrageous left-footed shot that curled into the top corner of the net.

- Brady was voted PFA Player Of The Year in 1979.
- He scored the penalty that sealed Juve's second successive title in 1982.
- Both Brady's brothers played professional football in Ireland.
- Brady had an unhappy two years as manager of Celtic, citing internal politics as his reason for leaving.
- He won surprisingly little in England, just his 1979 FA Cup medal.

VITAL STATISTICS

Place of Birth:	Dublin, Ireland	Achievement	6.0
Date of Birth:	13 February 1956 **Died:** n/a	Skill	9.0
Caps:	72 (R. Ireland) **Goals (International):** 9	Teamwork	7.0
Clubs:	Arsenal, Juventus, Inter Milan, Ascoli, West Ham	Passion	8.0
Appearances:	Club (for Arsenal): 306	Personality	7.0
Goals:	Club (for Arsenal): 59		
Trophies:	FAC 1979; SA 1981, 1982	**TOTAL 37.0**	

LEGEND RATING

Bremner, Billy

Leeds United, Scotland

THE FIRST GREAT LEEDS SIDE may have been created by Don Revie, but Billy Bremner was its midfield heartbeat. An assessment of him could just as easily describe the team itself – tough-tackling, measured in the pass and with a combative spirit that was by turns inspirational and illegal.

Bremner was indispensable even in a team packed with pedigree, a fact emphasised by a glance at the Elland Road record books. Incredibly, Bremner led Leeds to six of the seven major trophy successes in their entire history (the championship win of 1992 being the only triumph in which he did not participate).

Often in trouble with referees, the sight of Bremner throwing his shirt to the ground after becoming, with Kevin Keegan, the first British player to be dismissed at Wembley, led to parliamentary calls for him to be permanently suspended.

It was similar at an international level. In 1974 he captained a Scotland squad that emerged from the World Cup Finals as the only unbeaten team, but was shortly banned for life following incidents in a Danish nightclub after a game. His departure from Elland Road to Hull City in 1976 signalled the break-up of the great Leeds team, a schism which took the Yorkshire club 16 years to recover from.

☞ Bremner made his Leeds debut aged 17, as a winger.

👍 1965. Scored Leeds' first-ever goal at Wembley but they lose 2-1 to Liverpool in the FA Cup final.

👍 1970. Scored in British football's most epic club game, but Leeds went down to Celtic in a European Cup semi-final.

👎 1985. Became Leeds' manager by popular demand. Failed to revive an average Second Division team and was sacked in 1988.

👎 1997. His sudden death from a heart attack shocked and saddened the football world.

VITAL STATISTICS

Place of Birth:	Stirling, Scotland
Date of Birth:	9 December 1942 **Died:** 7 December 1997
Caps:	54 (Scotland) **Goals (International):** 3
Clubs:	Leeds United, Hull City, Doncaster Rovers
Appearances:	Club (League for Leeds Utd): 586
Goals:	Club (League for Leeds Utd): 90
Trophies:	LT 1969, 1974; FAC 1972; LC 1968;
	UEFAC 1968, 1971

LEGEND RATING	
Achievement	8.0
Skill	7.0
Teamwork	9.0
Passion	9.0
Personality	6.0
TOTAL	**39.0**

Wembley 1968: Bremner lifts Leeds' first major trophy, the League Cup.

Bring On Brazil
Italy 4 West Germany 3, 1970

LET'S GIVE DUE CREDIT to Karl-Heinz Schnellinger. This semi-final was drifting towards a sterile 1-0 Italian victory when he emerged in the last minute to smash a volleyed equaliser, thus setting up the greatest extra-time ever. Germany then appeared to have completed their smash-and-grab raid when Müller took advantage of an underhit back pass but, uncharacteristically, the German defence went to sleep, and two goals in six minutes saw the first period of extra-time finish with Italy 3-2 ahead.

The plot had yet more twists. An apparently harmless header from Müller was left by substitute Rivera – who had anticipated a goal kick – and the ball crept inside the post. But within a minute, the villain had turned hero, calmly placing the ball past a floundering Sepp Maier for the game's fifth goal in a breathless 22 minutes. In the light of what had gone before, a goalless last nine minutes was unexpected. By the final whistle, players and spectators were completely drained.

- England should have been playing in this match, but had blown a 2-0 lead against Germany in the quarter-finals.
- Goals may have flowed in this game, but Burgnich's effort was rare: in his 66 internationals, this was his second and last.
- The high altitude of Mexico produced enervating conditions. Extra-time was always likely to lead to a higher incidence of errors and goals.
- This is not a game Franz Beckenbauer will remember fondly. Germany's sweeper finished with four in the debit column and a heavily strapped arm.
- For Italy, victory proved bittersweet. Brazil were waiting to pick them off in the final.

SCORERS   **Italy:** Boninsegna, Burgnich, Riva, Rivera
W. Germany: Schnellinger, Müller (2)
EVENT   World Cup semi-final, Azteca stadium, Mexico City, 17 June 1970

ITALY   (Man: Feruccio Valcareggio)
1. Albertosi 2. Burgnich 3. Facchetti 4. Bertini 5. Rosato 6. Cera 7. Domenghini 8. Mazzola 9. Boninsegna 10. Di Sisti 11. Riva

W. GERMANY (Man: Helmut Schoen)
1. Maier 2. Vogts 3. Patzke 4. Beckenbauer 5. Schnellinger 6. Schulz 7. Grabowski 8. Seeler 9. Müller 10. Overath 11. Lohr

Rivera wraps himself around a post as Müller levels the scores at 3–3.

Brooking, Trevor
West Ham United, England

ONE FOOTED, could not tackle, could not head, really slow. How on earth did Trevor Brooking make it as a professional footballer, let alone win 47 caps? Largely because the one foot he mainly used was a cracker, and he had the brains to use it. He got someone else to do the tackling and heading, and didn't need to be quick because his passing and anticipation and timing were so good.

Like many other Hammers, he was intensely loyal to the club – he remains a director – and thus sacrificed the opportunity to win a cupboard full of medals. At international level he developed a fine understanding with Kevin Keegan, another intelligent footballer, and was unlucky to play in an ordinary team that struggled to qualify for major tournaments. When they did reach the World Cup Finals, in 1982, Brooking was injured and played only 20 minutes.

In his retirement he has become a popular TV and radio commentator, famously dubbed 'Mr Creosote' due to his habit of sitting on the fence.

☞ Brooking scored the only goal of the 1980 FA Cup final – with his head, to his and everybody else's amazement.

✍ He scored twice in a World Cup qualifier in Budapest as England beat Hungary 3-1, probably his finest game for his country.

☞ He was appointed Chairman of Sport England, a government advisory body, in 2000. In 2003, was appointed as Director of Football Development at the FA.

✍ England's fortunes in the 1982 World Cup might have been better if Brooking and Keegan had been fit.

☞ Like his BBC colleagues Hansen and Lineker, he does not appear to have aged, apart from a few grey hairs. Is it the White City tea or the make-up?

VITAL STATISTICS

Place of Birth:	Barking, London, England		
Date of Birth:	2 October 1948	**Died:** n/a	
Caps:	47 (England)	**Goals (International):** 5	
Clubs:	West Ham United		
Appearances:	Club (League): 528		
Goals:	Club (League): 88		
Trophies:	FAC 1975, 1980		

Achievement	5.5
Skill	8.5
Teamwork	7.5
Passion	7.0
Personality	7.0
TOTAL	**35.5**

LEGEND RATING

Busby Babes
Manchester United, 1955–58

ANY MENTION OF THE Manchester United team that dominated English football in the late 1950s inevitably evokes images of the terrible Munich air crash. The death of eight of football's brightest young talents was a tragedy that touched the lives of football fans all over the world. But just as tragic is that the players who perished are now largely remembered as passengers on an ill-fated aircraft rather than for what they were: extraordinary and remarkable footballers who might easily have gone on to dominate Europe for a decade.

At the heart of the team was Duncan Edwards. Looking at photographs now, it seems impossible to believe that such an imposing presence was only 21 years old when he died. Mark Jones was a similarly towering figure at centre half, while in goal Harry Gregg combined agility with rare courage (many press pictures of the time show him diving boldly at the feet of oncoming strikers).

Like all great United teams though, their strength lay in attack. Tommy Taylor was a fearless centre forward in the best English tradition, and Dennis Viollet and Bobby Charlton both chipped in with more than their fair share of goals. This team was together for less than two seasons. Yet even in this short time they established themselves as a formidable and widely feared European force.

☞ Under Busby, United had already won the league in 1952, but that ageing side was dismantled to make way for the Babes.

👍 United won the league in 1956 and 1957. They should have won the double in 1957, but lost to Aston Villa in the final.

👍 United were the first British entrants to the European Cup in 1956–57, defying the wishes of the myopic Football League. They reached the semi-finals in their first two competitions.

👍 The last league match played by the Busby Babes, five days before Munich, was one of their most memorable games. Arsenal 4 United 5 brought the curtain down in typical style.

👍 Of the Munich survivors, Bill Foulkes and Bobby Charlton were eventual European Cup winners in 1968.

Manager: Matt Busby

Key Players
Harry Gregg (G) Duncan Edwards (D)
Tommy Taylor (F) Bobby Charlton (M/F) Bill Foulkes (D)
Dennis Viollet (M) Roger Byrne (D)

Trophies
LT 1956, 1957

The last line-up of the Busby Babes, 5 February 1958, Belgrade. From left to right: Edwards, Colman, Jones, Morgans, Charlton, Viollet, Taylor, Foulkes, Gregg, Scanlon, Byrne.

Busby, Matt

Manchester United

IN 1945 MATT BUSBY became manager of Manchester United, a club whose 67 years had yielded just two league titles and a solitary FA Cup. The trophy cabinet had been bare for 34 years, Old Trafford was a bomb site and United were lodging at Maine Road. On his retirement in 1969, Matt Busby had added five Championships, two FA Cups and United had become England's first winners of the European Cup.

Although a remarkable haul, it would surely have been more but for the tragic Munich air crash in 1958 that robbed English football of one of its greatest-ever teams. It was indicative of his tenacity and strength of will that Busby not only cheated death himself in the disaster but that, within seven years, he had made United champions again, rebuilding his team around George Best, Denis Law and Bobby Charlton. The end of his tenure saw them relegated within five years.

A journey to Old Trafford today finishes with a walk down Sir Matt Busby Way to his statue. One senses a modest, hard-working Scotsman from humble, working-class origins would have been uneasy with such acclaim. However, for a club with legends to spare, it is fitting that the tribute is for him alone.

☞ No mean player himself, Busby played for United's deadliest rivals Manchester City and Liverpool!

☞ He was born within a few miles of two other managerial legends, Jock Stein and Alex Ferguson.

✎ He was awarded a CBE in 1958 and knighted 10 years later.

☞ On winning the European Cup: 'When Bobby took the cup it cleansed me. It eased the pain of going into Europe. It was my justification.'

☞ He defied the Football League to enter United as England's first European Cup contestants in 1956. The rift took 26 years to heal, before Busby was elected Football League vice-president in 1982.

VITAL STATISTICS

Place of Birth:	Bellshill, Glasgow, Scotland	
Date of Birth:	26 May 1909	**Died:** 20 January 1994
Caps:	1 (Scotland)	**Goals (International):** 0
Clubs:	As Player: Manchester City, Liverpool;	
	As Manager: Manchester United	
Trophies:	FAC 1948, 1963; LT 1952, 1956, 1957, 1965, 1967; EC 1968	

LEGEND RATING	
Achievement	10
Tactical Awareness	9
Motivation	10
Team Selection/Transfers	9
Personality	8
TOTAL	**46**

Butcher, Terry
Ipswich Town, Rangers, England

IT IS RARE for an English player to make a move north of the border at the height of his career and make an even greater impact. Terry Butcher was a man of enough resolve and spirit to set himself apart from the norm.

A 6 ft 4 in giant, Butcher made his reputation as a central defensive totem during the latter days of Bobby Robson's reign at Ipswich. A natural leader, he was unfazed by international football at 21 and was a key player in an England spine of Peter Shilton, Bryan Robson and Gary Lineker. His iconic match came in 1989 during a World Cup qualifier in Sweden, a tedious 0-0 draw that was memorable only for Butcher who, after receiving an injury in an aerial challenge in the second-half, played the remainder of the match with blood oozing on to his white shirt from a head wound. His insistence on lasting the 90 minutes was typical of his courage and professionalism. At Rangers, his partnership with Richard Gough was the rock on which their nine consecutive title wins were built. A broken leg in 1987 was followed by three successive Scottish titles, before a brief, and largely unhappy, foray into management at Coventry. Although his knees finally gave out, his spirit never wavered.

- 1987. Scored at Aberdeen in a 1-1 draw to clinch Rangers' first SPL title for 10 years.
- 1987. One of three ordered off in an Old Firm clash, Butcher was later fined in a civil court for a breach of the peace.
- 1990. Untried in management, Butcher took charge as boss and player at Coventry.
- Butcher is one of the few England players to play in three World Cups. He would have captained England in the final itself but for the penalty shoot-out loss to Germany in the semi-final at Italia 90.
- Now manager of SPL side, Motherwell, Butcher is often to be heard as a decent summariser on BBC radio.

VITAL STATISTICS

Place of Birth:	Singapore	
Date of Birth:	28 December 1958	**Died:** n/a
Caps:	77 (England)	**Goals (International):** 3
Clubs:	As Player: Ipswich Town, Glasgow Rangers,	
	Coventry, Sunderland; As Manager: Motherwell	
Appearances:	Club (League): 445	
Goals:	Club (League): 24	
Trophies:	UEFAC 1981; SLT 1987, 1989, 1990	

Achievement	7.0
Skill	7.0
Teamwork	8.0
Passion	10.0
Personality	7.0
TOTAL	**39.0**

LEGEND RATING

Sweden, 1989. Butcher donates blood for the England cause.

Campbell, Sol
Tottenham, Arsenal, England

SOL CAMPBELL was destined for big things at an early age. A schoolboy prodigy, he was one of the early vindications of the FA School of Excellence before signing professional forms with Spurs in 1992.

He immediately started attracting the sort of praise normally reserved for continental central defenders. Not only could he take the knocks and command in the air, he possessed the first touch, distribution and prescience that brought comparisons with Bobby Moore.

Despite becoming a permanent fixture for England, it became clear that major domestic honours would elude Campbell at White Hart Lane. In the summer of 2001, as a free agent, he became the most talked-about transfer in years when he thought the unthinkable, broke Spurs' hearts and became a Gunner.

The inevitable yet depressing hate campaign followed, Campbell's dignified response was typical of a player who has always let his feet do the talking. The answer was the Double in his first season.

Despite the fierce competition for England's centre-back places, it took Campbell only five games for Arsenal to regain his international spot after a lengthy injury lay-off; an early departure with a hamstring strain promptly re-opened the door for Rio Ferdinand.

- 👍 December 1992 – scores on his first-team debut against Chelsea.
- 👍 Only 23 yellow cards in over 400 games are testament to Campbell's pace and clean tackling.
- ☞ At the 1998 World Cup Finals, Campbell has an 81st-minute 'winner' against Argentina disallowed for Shearer's earlier foul. Sadly the rest is history.
- 👍 Campbell's first international goal is England's opener at the 2002 World Cup Finals, as he powers home a header against Sweden.
- 👍 2002 – Campbell is named in FIFA's Team of the World Cup Finals, surprisingly edging out the superior Ferdinand.

VITAL STATISTICS

Place of Birth:	London, England		
Date of Birth:	18 September 1974	**Died:** n/a	
Caps:	65 (England)	**Goals (International):** 1	
Clubs:	Tottenham Hotspur, Arsenal		
Appearances:	Club (League): 376		
Goals:	Club (League): 25		
Trophies:	LT 2002, 2004; FAC 2002; LC 1999		

Achievement	7.0
Skill	9.0
Teamwork	7.0
Passion	8.0
Personality	7.0
TOTAL	**38.0**

LEGEND RATING

'What's up with you?': Sol Campbell asks of Brazil's Rivaldo during England's clash with Brazil on 21 June 2002.

Cantona, Eric
Manchester United, France

WHETHER FOR HIS FOOTBALLING exploits or temperamental outbursts, few players have provoked headlines or incited debate like Eric Cantona. Not one to suffer fools gladly, he was too hot to handle for five French clubs.

An instant hit at Leeds, his arrival provided the Yorkshire club with the impetus to clinch the League title in 1992 but, while the fans idolised him, rumours of his clashes with manager Howard Wilkinson were rife. His shock £1.2 m transfer to Manchester United indicated Leeds' desire to be rid of him, but it turned out to be the most injudicious transfer sale of all time, as Cantona went on to inspire United to a period of domination unrivalled since Liverpool's run of success in the 1970s and 1980s.

It is a sad fact that Cantona will be remembered for one moment of madness when, at Crystal Palace in 1995, making his way off the pitch following yet another red card, Cantona launched a two-footed kung fu kick at a spectator who had racially abused him. A less gifted player may have been sacked, but Cantona survived and returned to lead United to more championship success. He retired at 31, and his recent incarnations as an actor and sports promoter have enhanced his reputation as the modern renaissance footballer.

- 1988. Banned from the French national side after describing manager Henri Michel as a 'sack of sh*t'.
- PFA Player of the Year, 1994 and 1996. Footballer of the Year 1996.
- 1994. Arrested and handcuffed by security guards after a row with officials at USA 94. Cantona was just there to watch.
- He had five league titles in six English seasons 1992–97, missing out only in 1995.
- He was voted Manchester United's most valuable player ever in 1999.

VITAL STATISTICS

Place of Birth: Paris, France

Date of Birth: 24 May 1966   **Died:** n/a

Caps: 45 (France)   **Goals (International):** 19

Clubs: Martigues, Auxerre, Marseille, Bordeaux, Montpellier, Leeds United, Manchester United

Appearances: Club (for Man Utd): 142

Goals: Club (for Man Utd): 64

Trophies: LT 1992, 1993, 1994, 1996, 1997; FAC 1994, 1996

Achievement	8.0
Skill	9.0
Teamwork	7.0
Passion	9.0
Personality	9.0
TOTAL	**42.0**

LEGEND RATING

Capped And Clueless
The All-Time Worst England Team

EVEN AT THEIR PEAK this lot would have struggled to win a pub league. Anyone with at least one functioning eye could see this, except, it seems, the England managers who selected them. You want detail? Okay, here we go.

Beasant was error-prone and nervy.... Bardsley was nondescript.... Foster and Blockley were cumbersome and slow.... Ruddock was overweight and over-rated.... Phelan looked a decent player at Norwich but became a laughing stock at Old Trafford ... while Geoff Thomas was a plodding journeyman elevated to the role of international playmaker (he and his Palace team-mate Andy Gray were selected on the basis of getting to the Cup final). And who on earth was Nick Pickering?

Peter Ward? Hands up if you were there on the day he played the stormer that earned him selection for the national side. Michael Ricketts was picked on the back of a scoring streak at Bolton that ended when he earned his cap and decided he was an international.

This XI are by no means the only players who should never have been picked for England, but they remain the most startling examples.

☞ We've restricted ourselves to players from our own era. It's unfair to deride a player you've never seen.

☞ Both Ward and Pickering made their appearances in tour friendlies against Australia. Only Thomas of this team was a contender for a place in a first-choice England team.

✌ Foster compounded his lack of ability by wearing that absurd headband. It added nothing to his game and looked ridiculous.

✌ Ruddock had a nice left foot, but was too slow to cope with top-class forwards, and lacked the wit to make up for it with anticipation and experience.

☟ Kevin Keegan, for all his tactical shortcomings, seemed to know the best players when he saw them.

Manager: Don Revie

4-4-2

Dave Beasant (2) (90)

David Bardsley (2) (93) Steve Foster (3) (82)
Jeff Blockley (1) (73) Neil Ruddock (1) (95)

Michael Phelan (1) (90) Geoff Thomas (9) (91, 92)
Andy Gray (1) (92) Nick Pickering (1) (83)

Peter Ward (1) (80) Michael Ricketts (1) (2002)

Carter, Raich

Sunderland, Derby County, England

IF YOU ASKED YOUR GRANDDAD (who obviously thinks all modern players are cissies) whom he admired the most, he would probably say something like: 'Raich Carter, laddie, there was a player. He had everything: skill, vision, and he was a bit tasty in the tackle as well.' Granddad of course would be right. Horatio 'Raich' Carter was indeed a terrific player, and it remains a mystery how he was picked a measly 13 times for England (plus a few more unofficial wartime caps).

Carter's halcyon days were with his local team, Sunderland, whom he led with great distinction in the 1930s. Carter was hurt when Sunderland let him go after the war, and proved there was plenty left in the tank by leading Derby County to an FA Cup victory.

He was still playing as he approached 40, as player-manager of Hull City, and led the Tigers out of the Third Division. His managerial career continued at Leeds, where after taking a John Charles-inspired side out of Division Two, he failed to make an impact in the top flight.

👌 He was the only player to win FA Cup winners' medals either side of the Second World War.

👌 He scored the winning goal in the 1937 Cup final victory over Preston.

👌 Carter's first season at Hull saw the team begin the season with nine straight wins, end it with promotion, and fill in with a cup run ended by eventual winners Manchester United. Unsurprisingly, attendances at Boothferry Park doubled that year.

☞ He made his England debut against Scotland in 1934.

☞ He captained Sunderland to their last Championship in 1936, scoring 31 goals.

VITAL STATISTICS

Place of Birth:	Sunderland, England
Date of Birth:	21 December 1913 **Died:** 9 October 1994
Caps:	13 (England) **Goals (International):** 7
Clubs:	Sunderland, Derby County, Hull City
Appearances:	Club (for Sunderland): 276
Goals:	Club (for Sunderland): 127
Trophies:	LT 1936; FAC 1937, 1946

LEGEND RATING	
Achievement	6.0
Skill	8.0
Teamwork	8.0
Passion	7.0
Personality	7.0
TOTAL	**36.0**

Chanting
Ee-Aye-Addio And All That

IN THE 1870s it would have appeared rather vulgar. One can't imagine the Old Carthusians goalkeeper standing resolute with flat cap and Victorian moustache to a backdrop of 'Who ate all the pies?' from the massed top hats of the Royal Engineers.

Some contemporary chanting can claim a distinguished pedigree. 'The Pompey Chimes' were ringing out at Fratton Park for the title winning teams of over 50 years ago, while 'I'm Forever Blowing Bubbles' has been handed down through the generations at Upton Park (although opposition fans now tend to shout their own alternative over the cockney chorus).

Over the past 30 years, club choirs have broadened their repertoires considerably from the quaint 'Ee-aye-addio'. The greater televising of matches means that copyrights can be quickly violated – a player can be vocally ridiculed at Old Trafford one week and hear the identical chant at Stamford Bridge the next. One fact remains a certainty, though. Any player guilty of the merest physical deformity, tabloid headline or on-field mishap can be sure it will be pointed out. For anyone playing in front of more than two men and a dog, 'you can run but you can't hide' is the biggest truism of all.

☞ To opposition fans scarce in number: 'Is that all you take away?', 'You must have come in a taxi,' or 'We'll see you both outside'.

☞ 'He's fat, he's round' also prefaced a memorable chant about Jan Molby, namely: 'He's fat, he's round, his car is in the pound.' Opposition fans were quick to remind him of his driving misdemeanours.

☞ To expensive opposition striker, preferably one who's just missed an open goal: 'What a waste of money', 'Hallo, hallo [insert previous club here] reject' to a melody originally recorded by Gary Glitter.

✎ Silliest chant: 'Boing! Boing! Baggies! Baggies!', accompanied by a vigorous pogo from West Bromwich Albion fans.

✎ References in this section to Elton John, Leslie Ash or Trevor Morley would be libelous. But you know what we're getting at, right?

☞ 'There's only two Andy Gorams' chorused Celtic fans to the unfortunate Rangers keeper, after tabloids alleged treatment for schizophrenia.

'He's fat, he's round, he's never in the ground, Captain Bob.'

Oxford fans to absent chairman Robert Maxwell

Gallic chic noticeably absent as French fans raise the roof.

Chapman, Herbert
Arsenal, Huddersfield

MANY GREAT MANAGERS have built one great team at one club, but Herbert Chapman is among the élite who have done it twice. An unconventional manager, he surrounded himself with intelligent players who fed him ideas and tactics. He responded to a change in the offside law by introducing a 3-4-3 formation with a defensive centre half, and he was the first manager to encourage his wingers, notably Cliff Bastin, to cut inside the fullback and go for goal.

His first great side was the Huddersfield Town team of the 1920s, built around the intelligent playmaker Clem Stephenson. He left Huddersfield for the challenge of managing Arsenal and turned them into the dominant side of the next decade. The Arsenal side featured many of the great players of that generation, often providing five, six or even seven players to the England team of that era. Under his stewardship Arsenal went on to win the title four times in five years, but tragically Chapman died of pneumonia in 1934, aged 55, and didn't enjoy the full fruits of his work. He was the game's first managerial genius.

☞ Chapman was a great innovator, and was an early advocate of floodlights, artificial pitches and numbered shirts.

☞ He was instrumental in the renaming of Gillespie Road tube station as 'Arsenal'.

☞ He was one of the first managers to offer a fee to lure big-name players away from other clubs. His purchase of David Jack from Bolton was the first £10,000 transfer.

☞ Most of the Arsenal team only heard of Chapman's death as they turned up to play a match. The pallbearers at the funeral were Cliff Bastin, Eddie Hapgood, Joe Hume, David Jack, Alex James and Jack Lambert.

VITAL STATISTICS

Place of Birth:	Kiverton Park, England	
Date of Birth:	19 January 1878	**Died:** 6 January 1934
Caps:	0	**Goals (International):** 0
Clubs:	As Player: Kiverton Park, Ashton North End,	Achievement 10
	Stalybridge Rovers, Rochdale, Grimsby Town,	Tactical Awareness 9
	Sheppey United, Worksop, Northampton Town,	Motivation 9
	Sheffield United, Notts County, Tottenham Hotspur;	Team Selection/Transfers 9
	As Manager: Northampton Town, Leeds City,	Personality 9
	Huddersfield Town, Arsenal	
Trophies:	LT 1924, 1925, 1926, 1931, 1933; FAC 1922, 1930	**TOTAL 46**

LEGEND RATING

Chapman (left) was always ready to oblige the media.

Charles, John

Leeds United, Juventus, Wales

WHETHER OPERATING AT centre half or centre forward John Charles was the most complete footballer Wales has ever produced. Although a hero at Leeds and Cardiff, he became the first British player to settle successfully on the Continent, succeeding for five years in Italy where Jimmy Greaves and Denis Law were later to fail. So adored was he in Turin that Juventus fans dubbed him the 'Gentle Giant' due to his power and sportsmanship.

As an international, he was the key to Wales's most successful era, a period that culminated in their appearance in the 1958 World Cup quarter-final in Sweden. Sadly, Charles was absent through injury that day and the Welsh went down narrowly 1-0 to the eventual winners Brazil.

Lured back to Leeds by Don Revie, he failed to settle and returned to his adopted Italy with AS Roma before ending his career at Cardiff, adding thousands to the Ninian Park attendances. In a land where sporting heroes have traditionally played with an oval ball, Charles increased the stature of football in the Valleys like no player before or since. His death in February 2004 was mourned equally in Britain and Italy. It signalled the passing of a true sporting gentleman.

☞ 1957. Charles moves from Leeds to Juventus for £70,000, more than double the British transfer record.

👍 He never won a trophy in Britain, but has three Italian titles and two cups to his name.

☞ The first rich British footballer, Charles' wages in Italy were £60 per week, more than four times the maximum permitted in Britain. A signing-on fee of £10,000 added to his fortune.

☞ He played with brother, Mel, in the same Welsh team as the Allchurch brothers, Len and Ivor. Two sets of brothers have never appeared together in any other international team.

👍 1973. Years after retirement, Charles lined up for Europe, scoring a hat-trick against Great Britain in a friendly international.

VITAL STATISTICS

Place of Birth:	Swansea, Wales
Date of Birth:	27 December 1931 **Died:** 21 February 2004
Caps:	38 (Wales) **Goals (International):** 15
Clubs:	Leeds United, Juventus, Roma, Cardiff City, Hereford United
Appearances:	Club (League for Juventus): 150
Goals:	Club (League for Juventus): 93
Trophies:	SA 1958, 1960, 1961

LEGEND RATING	
Achievement	7.0
Skill	9.0
Teamwork	8.0
Passion	9.0
Personality	7.0
TOTAL	**40.0**

Charlton, Bobby
Manchester United, England

HAVING SURVIVED THE Munich air crash, Bobby Charlton seized his chance to become one of England's most successful and admired players. He never commanded the huge transfer fees paid for Denis Law, nor could he boast the natural flair and ability of George Best, but in terms of achievement Charlton was by far the most successful of United's most famous forward line. His application was total. As a young player he would often train wearing just a slipper on his right foot – a ploy designed to make him practice shooting with his left until it could generate the same venomous power as his right.

For England, he became a national hero after helping them win the 1966 World Cup, but it was his substitution in the 1970 quarter-final against Germany that fans remember almost as vividly; brought off by Alf Ramsey with the score at 2-1 to England, Charlton's absence upset the balance of the team and they eventually capitulated 3-2. Charlton bowed out in 1973 – on the same day as his brother, Jack – when over 60,000 fans packed Old Trafford for his testimonial. Knighted in 1994, he remains a director at Old Trafford and ambassador for both United and the Football Association. Even the Glasers realised some things were sacrosanct at United, guaranteeing Charlton's position after taking over the club in 2005.

- His league appearances (606) and goals (199) remain United club records.
- Best England goal? A 30-yard rasper versus Mexico in the 1966 World Cup Finals.
- 106 caps was an England record only Bobby Moore and Peter Shilton have overtaken, his 49 goals remain unequalled.
- 1966. English and European Footballer of the Year. He also received a special PFA merit award in 1974.
- He was one of only two Munich air crash survivors to play in the European Cup-winning side 10 years later. Bill Foulkes was the other.

VITAL STATISTICS

Place of Birth:	Ashington, Northumberland, England		
Date of Birth:	11 October 1937	**Died:** n/a	
Caps:	106 (England)	**Goals (International):** 49	
Clubs:	Manchester United, Preston North End		
Appearances:	Club (All Matches): 798		
Goals:	Club (All Matches): 257		
Trophies:	WorC 1966; EC 1968; LT 1957, 1965, 1967; FAC 1963		

LEGEND RATING	
Achievement	10.0
Skill	8.0
Teamwork	9.0
Passion	8.0
Personality	7.0
TOTAL	**42.0**

Charlton, Jack

Leeds, England, Republic Of Ireland

AN ENGLAND WORLD-CUP WINNER he may have been, and the defensive rock of Don Revie's Leeds he undoubtedly was, but Jack Charlton's most celebrated achievements came more recently across the Irish sea. Foreign managers taking control of other countries' national teams no longer raises eyebrows, but Charlton's appointment to the Republic of Ireland post was a revolutionary step. Using the no-frills approach that had served him well in English club management, Charlton rebuilt the Irish team. Eschewing continental niceties for a long-ball style that was effective rather than pretty, and recruiting players through long-lost Irish family connections, he affected a dramatic turnaround in their international fortunes. The Republic qualified for the European Championships and the World Cup in 1988 and 1990 respectively. The World Cup in Italy was his finest hour, especially the penalty shoot-out victory over Romania that set up a quarter-final with Italy, bringing the nation to a standstill. The Republic's 1-0 defeat to the Italians cemented his status as Ireland's second most popular icon after the Pope. USA 94 saw revenge against Italy, but Ireland's lack of imagination cost them. Imagination wasn't a word associated with him as a player either, but he stood tall against some of the best the game could throw at him.

👍 Success arrived late for Charlton the player; not picked for England until nearly 30, he was a World Cup winner and Footballer of the Year (1967) in the two seasons that followed.

👎 1965. Policeman intervened during a Fairs Cup tie to stop Charlton exacting revenge on a Valencia player. Charlton and two Spaniards were dismissed.

☞ 1973–74. His first season in management saw Middlesbrough win Division Two by 15 points.

👎 Charlton was criticised as Irish manager for seeking out players with distant Irish heritage, but the practice is now common.

👍 He is the only member of England's 1966 World Cup-winning side who made a success of management.

VITAL STATISTICS

Place of Birth:	Ashington, Northumberland, England
Date of Birth:	8 May 1935 **Died:** n/a
Caps:	35 (England)
Goals (International): 6	
Clubs:	As Player: Leeds United; As Manager:
	Middlesbrough, Sheffield Wednesday,
	Republic of Ireland national side
Trophies:	As Player: WorC 1966; LT 1969;
	FAC 1972; LC 1968; None as manager

MANAGER		PLAYER	
Achievement	6	Achievement	9
Tactical Awareness	8	Skill	6
Motivation	9	Teamwork	7
Team Selection/Transfers	7	Passion	8
Personality	8	Personality	7
TOTAL	**38**	**TOTAL**	**37**

LEGEND RATING

Cheating
The Unacceptable Face

THE ORIGINAL CHEAT was also the biggest. One can only imagine what was going through William Webb Ellis's mind as he picked up the ball and sprinted for the goal-line. The referee's action was even more inexplicable. Instead of an automatic red, Ellis was slapped on the back and credited with inventing a new game. If only he'd gone to Our Lady of the Sacred Heart, rugby might never have got off the ground. In football, modern discussion is centred on the dive. While some xenophobic opinion incorrectly identifies diving as an exclusively foreign pastime, it is true that Jurgen Klinsmann raised the art to a new level. Still, at least he had the self-deprecating charm to diffuse the criticism that came his way, famously making an ironic plunge turfwards after scoring on his Spurs debut at Hillsborough. The Daddy of all cheats, though, is Maradona, who saved the 1986 World Cup quarter-final against England for his party piece. Although Diego lied, the camera didn't, and the image of his hand palming the ball past Peter Shilton still raises the ire of all England fans.

In recent years, on-field cheating has reached pandemic proportions. FIFA has now made the act of 'simulation' a yellow-card offence, yet many players persist in diving. The use of video replays, as practised in rugby league and cricket, has its drawbacks, but until drastic action is taken some persistent offenders will often get away with it.

☞ Frank Skinner gag during Euro 92: 'I brushed past the television and Klinsmann fell over.'

☜ Drugs have played their part. Jaap Stam is one of the latest to fall foul of the authorities for use of banned substances.

☜ Referees are not untouchables. The Greek referee was widely believed to have cheated Leeds out of the 1973 European Cup Winners' Cup final. Even his countrymen in the Salonika crowd booed him at the final whistle.

☜ 1891. Lest we think the Victorians were wholly Corinthian, Aston Villa's keeper kicked the ball out of the ground to prevent Stoke taking a penalty before the final whistle blew. His actions brought the advent of the extra-time law.

☞ The complaint of players collapsing to the ground clutching non-existent head wounds provokes strong reactions. Leicester boss Dave Bassett accused Spurs' Mauricio Taricco of cheating after a league match in 2002; a bit rich from Robbie Savage's boss.

'It was scored partly by the hand of God and partly by the head of Maradona.'

Diego puts a personal spin on THAT goal, 1986

The 'Hand of God' strikes. Maradona's hand reaches the ball marginally before Peter Shilton.

Christmas Trees and Catenaccio

Tactics

IN THE EARLY PART of the last century, tactics did not invite the degree of discussion they do today. Teams played with two defenders, a centre half, two half backs – who were expected to do most of the running – two inside forwards to create and score, two wingers to supply, and a centre forward. But in the 1930s, innovative managers like Arsenal's Herbert Chapman and Italy's Vittorio Pozzo tweaked this system. In their teams the centre half became a defender, and the inside forwards started to drop a little deeper. Wingers, too, were encouraged to add to their repertoire and tuck slightly further infield.

Throughout the 1950s Austria and Hungary introduced new attacking ideas and styles, and their intricate passing and use of a deep-lying centre forward initially confused many of their more conventionally structured opponents. Brazil's World Cup success started when they adopted a back four, with attacking fullbacks and two forwards feeding off two wingers. The Italian club sides in the 1960s introduced the notion of the sweeper behind two centre halves, and Franz Beckenbauer advanced that role. The Dutch threw away the book entirely in the 1970s, laying the foundations for the fluid, modern football we see today.

☞ 'Contrary to what some people might think I do not want to see the ball booted aimlessly up-field – but the truly great players hurt the opposition with one devastating pass.' Graham Taylor, defending the tactics of a team containing Geoff Thomas.

☞ The advent of substitutes and large squads has allowed managers more flexibility with tactics. 'I don't drop players, I make changes.' Bill Shankly.

☞ Once the players are out there it's beyond the manager's control: 'I went down to pass on some technical information to the team like the fact the game had started.' Ron Atkinson forsakes his seat in the stand as things don't go to plan.

'I do want to play the long ball, and I do want to play the short ball. I think long and short balls are what football is all about.'

Bobby Robson

Clockwise from top left: old-style 2-3-5, 4-4-2, 90s-style Christmas tree, sweeper system with overlapping fullbacks.

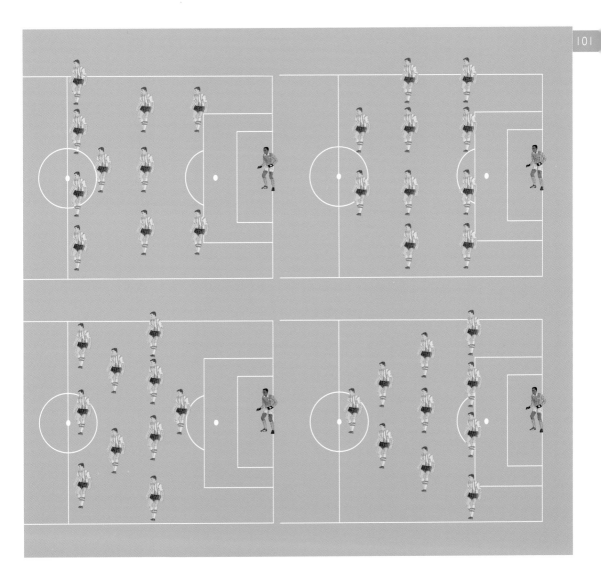

Clough, Brian

Middlesbrough, Derby County, Nottingham Forest, England

REMEMBERED BY MODERN SUPPORTERS as one of the great managers of his era, Clough was also a fine player. A phenomenal scoring record at Middlesbrough and then Sunderland was down to a sharp turn of speed and clinical finishing. Clough's playing career was cut short by a serious knee injury suffered on Boxing Day 1962, after which he concentrated on management, initially at Hartlepool, where he was joined by Peter Taylor, an old team-mate from his Middlesbrough days. The pair moved to Derby where Clough won his first league title in 1972. In October 1973, Clough resigned from Derby and joined Brighton. In July 1974, Clough was appointed by Leeds for his infamous 44 days. Elland Road just wasn't big enough for all those egos.

It was at Forest that Clough really hit the heights. Reunited with Taylor, he built a successful, well-organised side that continually managed to punch above its weight, winning two European Cups in 1979 and 1980. Clough finally left Forest towards the end of the 1992–93 season, with the club relegated, in disarray, and amid accusations of excessive drinking. It was a sad end to a glorious and charismatic career. His death in September 2004 inspired almost unprecedented respect.

- After resigning due to ill health, Peter Taylor returned to management at Derby, and promptly poached John Robertson, one of Forest's key players. He and Clough never spoke again before Taylor's death.
- Players at Derby threatened to strike when Clough left in 1973.
- Two caps was a risible return for such a fine striker.
- Forest were unbeaten for a record 42 league matches between November 1977 and December 1978.
- Forest only once finished outside the top 10 in the First Division during Clough's 18 years, prior to the relegation season.
- Was passed over for the England manager's job in the mid-70s. The FA knew they could never have handled him.

VITAL STATISTICS

Place of Birth: Middlesbrough, England

Date of Birth: 21 March 1935 **Died:** 20 September 2004

Caps: 2 (England) **Goals (International):** 0

Clubs: As Player: Middlesbrough, Sunderland;
As Manager: Hartlepool United,
Derby County, Brighton & Hove Albion,
Leeds United, Nottingham Forest

Trophies: LT 1972, 1975, 1978; EC 1979,
1980; LC 1978, 1979, 1989, 1990

MANAGER		PLAYER	
Achievement	9	Achievement	6
Tactical Awareness	9	Skill	9
Motivation	9	Teamwork	7
Team Selection/Transfers	8	Passion	8
Personality	10	Personality	7
TOTAL	**45**	**TOTAL**	**37**

LEGEND RATING

Collins, Bobby
Celtic, Everton, Leeds, Scotland

FEW PLAYERS BECOME LEGENDS at more than one club. But invite fans of Celtic, Everton and Leeds to name their greatest characters, and Bobby Collins will feature prominently in all three lists. What he lacked in stature the 'Wee Barra' made up for in passion and skill. At 5 ft 4 in he was hardly an aerial target but, when it came to balance, control and pace, he had the edge over most of his opponents. For both his major clubs his haul of silverware was less impressive than the platform he helped build. Rangers were the Glasgow force in the 1950s, but Collins threw cash-strapped Celtic a financial lifeline when Everton offered £25,000 for him in 1958. After helping Everton secure their future as a First Division club, Collins moved to Leeds in 1962, joining a team who were on the threshold of greatness. His transfer to Elland Road brought the club the Second Division title, just two years after he had almost single-handedly prevented them dropping into the Third Division. The great Revie side was built around him. He was always the architect, but seldom reaped the reward. Fortunately, the fans are still grateful.

- In 1965, Collins was the first Scot to become Footballer of the Year in England.
- Curiously, despite a 14-year international career, Collins was not selected for six years between 1959–65.
- Collins once scored a hat-trick of penalties, for Celtic against Aberdeen in 1953.
- The rest of his playing, coaching and managerial days are best forgotten. He became a nomad, flitting between England, Scotland, Ireland and Australia, but he had little success.
- In 1968 Collins and John Charles were awarded a joint testimonial by Leeds. A fitting but belated reward for a player who had left Elland Road 11 years earlier.

VITAL STATISTICS

Place of Birth: Govanhill, Scotland
Date of Birth: 19 February 1931   **Died:** n/a
Caps: 31 (Scotland)   **Goals (International):** 10
Clubs: Celtic, Everton, Leeds, Bury, Greenock Morton, Oldham Athletic
Appearances: Club (for Leeds): 168
Goals: Club (for Leeds): 25
Trophies: SLT 1954, SFAC 1954

	LEGEND RATING
Achievement	7.0
Skill	7.0
Teamwork	8.0
Passion	8.0
Personality	6.0
TOTAL	**36.0**

Commentators
Nice Work, If You Can Get It

LOVE THEM OR LOATHE THEM, commentators are an integral part of the modern football-watcher's perception of the game. Initially, in the Pathe days, and especially in Kenneth Wolstenholme's early broadcasts, commentary was simply a scientific narrative of the match, but as the art developed they became more intrusive, sharing opinions and statistical nuggets of information with their audience. John Motson became the master of the trivial aside, relishing every opportunity to embellish his reports with whimsical extras. ITV joined the fray, and Brian Moore's voice soon became as familiar as that of Motty and David Coleman.

New technology led to increased coverage, and an increase in the studio body count. Suddenly, presenters like Desmond Lynam were joined by teams of 'expert' summarisers, usually retired, or uninvolved current players. The two-commentator broadcast became ever-more popular, with a pundit sitting alongside a match commentator, sharing views and an occasional bit of banter.

All in all, football commentary and punditry has made a disappointing contribution to the game; intelligent and articulate people are shackled by fear of upsetting one faction or the other, or even a sponsor, and the result is too often bland and innocuous.

☞ The first radio broadcast was on 2 January 1927. The game? Arsenal versus Sheffield United.

☞ The first TV broadcast was in 1936, and was followed a year later by the first live TV broadcast (1938 FA Cup final, Preston versus Huddersfield). The BBC tested their 'live' technology with a test broadcast of Arsenal versus Arsenal Reserves.

☞ *Match of the Day* began in 1964, with Kenneth Wolstenholme as commentator. The first game covered was at Anfield as Liverpool beat Arsenal 2-0.

☞ The BBC's best TV commentator, Barry Davies, finally hung up his mike in October 2004. His description of a Francis Lee goal at Maine Road in the early 1970s has become the oft-repeated stuff of legend: 'Interesting ... VERY interesting ... LOOK AT HIS FACE ... JUST LOOK AT HIS FACE!'

☞ Why ex-footballers or managers? Why not people trained professionally to talk, not play? That way we could avoid the cliché and banality offered by Messrs Brooking, Charlton, Pleat, Keegan, Francis, Pleat (again, for being spectacularly awful) and Atkinson.

'Poland nil, England nil, though England are now looking better value for their nil.'

Barry Davies, 1989

John Motson, poised to deliver another statistic.

Corinthian Spirits

Amateur Football

IN THE BEGINNING they were all amateurs. The game was born from the English public-school system when J.C. Thring published its prototype rules in 1862. A glance at the early winners of the FA Cup gives a strong indication of the amateurs' power; Oxford University, Old Etonians and Old Carthusians all battled it out in the early finals. But by the mid-1880s, the balance of power had shifted, and more recognisable names began appearing on the honours board, notably the likes of Blackburn and Aston Villa.

A two-tier structure has co-existed ever since, with famous amateur sides continuing to fly the flag and provide a feeder system for the professional game. One of the best, Bishop Auckland, nurtured a certain Bob Paisley before he turned professional with Liverpool. In 1974, the term 'amateur' was officially abolished by the FA, who now class all participants in the game as 'players'. But for every park footballer, coach and manager who marvels at the wages of today's Premiership stars, the distinction remains clear enough.

☞ The individual record for FA Cup winners' medals is still shared by three amateurs. The Hon. Alfred Kinnaird, Charles Wollaston and James Forrest all won five in the competition's first 20 years.

☞ The Corinthian Casuals' missionary tours helped bring the game to Brazil: one of its biggest clubs is named Corinthians.

👍 Corinthian Casuals struck a rare blow for amateurism in 1924, knocking First Division Blackburn out of the FA Cup.

👍 The original Scottish amateurs, Queen's Park, are the only remaining example of an amateur club playing in a wholly professional league.

👍 1951. A record crowd of 100,000 attended the Amateur Cup final at Wembley to see Pegasus beat Bishop Auckland 2-1.

'*Ludere causa ludendi.*'

**Motto of original Scottish amateurs'
Queens Park. It translates as 'to play
for the sake of playing'**

The Corinthian Casuals football team. FA Amateur Cup final, 20 March 1956.

Crawford's Cracker
Colchester United 3 Leeds United 2, 1971

'THE MOST FANTASTIC RESULT you'll ever see!' For once, this was a headline that avoided hyperbole. Although not non-leaguers, Fourth Division Colchester's feat was, in relative terms, more notable than any previous Cup giant-killing. This was Leeds. Don Revie's Leeds. The best team in the country, a line-up replete with seasoned internationals and a reputation for hard-man cynicism that made them the least likely of pushovers.

Colchester had one international up their sleeve. True, Ray Crawford's two England caps had been won nine years earlier and at 34 his star was hardly in the ascendant. But all this counted for nothing as Crawford's double swept Colchester to an incredible 3-0 lead just after half-time. Normal service was partly resumed as Hunter and Giles set up a frantic finish that saw Leeds keeper, Gary Sprake, reduced to a role as a distant onlooker. But his counterpart in the Colchester goal, Graham Smith, proved equal to the bombardment and the Essex club held out to produce a result that provoked open-mouthed astonishment across the country. Revie's Leeds had their share of big-match disappointments, but none was as humiliating as this.

- Colchester hero Ray Crawford has a league championship medal, won with Ipswich in 1962.
- Manager Dick Graham had promised a free fortnight's holiday for his players and their wives if they won. He paid up.
- A triumph for experience; six Colchester players were over 30.
- Colchester lost 5-0 at Everton in the sixth round.

SCORERS   **Colchester:** Crawford 2, Simmons
               Leeds: Hunter, Giles
EVENT   FA Cup Fifth Round, Layer Road, Colchester, 13 February 1971

COLCHESTER (Man: Dick Graham)
               1. Smith G. 2. Hall 3. Cram 4. Gilchrist 5. Garvey 6. Kurila 7. Lewis
               8. Simmons 9. Mahon 10. Crawford 11. Gibbs
LEEDS   (Man: Don Revie)
               1. Sprake 2. Reaney 3. Cooper 4. Bates 5. Charlton 6. Hunter
               7. Lorimer 8. Clarke 9. Jones 10. Giles 11. Madeley

Ray Crawford (left foreground) turns away after scoring one of his giant-killing goals.

Cruyff, Johan
Ajax, Amsterdam, Barcelona, Holland

JOHAN CRUYFF'S MOTHER worked as a cleaner at Ajax's ground in Amsterdam, and the club were persuaded to give the youngster trials. One suspects they didn't regret it. He was fortunate to develop under the legendary Ajax coach Rinus Michels, but not as fortunate as Ajax were to have such an extraordinary talent born on their doorstep. Cruyff had the lot: pace and strength allied to nigh-perfect ball control, and a punishing finish with either foot. But, as is often the case with men of genius, Cruyff had a flawed side to his personality. An irritable and greedy nature saw him often at odds with authority and meant he was lost far too early to international football.

As a manager he was quixotic and opinionated too, and brought great success to Barcelona, landing them the coveted European Cup, but his tenure at the Nou Camp was plagued by clashes with key players, notably Hristo Stoichkov and the Brazilian striker, Romario. Despite his arrogance and irritability, Cruyff will be remembered as a breathtaking footballer to rank with the best in the world. Living in his native Holland, he has retired from management after developing a heart problem due to his penchant for chain-smoking.

- Cruyff destroyed Inter in the 1972 European Cup final, scoring both goals in Ajax's 2-0 win.
- Legendary sports writer David Miller dubbed Cruyff 'Pythagoras in boots', such was the geometric precision of his passing.
- After a bust-up with Ajax at the end of his playing career, Cruyff responded by joining their arch-rivals Feyenoord as player-coach, promptly winning the double for the old enemy.
- He is one of only three players to have won the European Player of the Year award three times, in 1971, 1973 and 1974 (the others were Michel Platini and Marco van Basten).

VITAL STATISTICS

Place of Birth:	Amsterdam, Holland				
Date of Birth:	25 April 1947	**Died:** n/a			
Caps:	48 (Holland)	**Goals (International):** 33	MANAGER	PLAYER	
Clubs:	Ajax, Barcelona, Los Angeles Aztecs,		Achievement 9	Achievement 9	
	Washington Diplomats, Levants, Feyenoord		Tactical Awareness 8	Skill 10	
Appearances:	Club (All Matches): 704		Motivation 6	Teamwork 10	
Goals:	Club (All Matches): 392		Team Selection/Transfers 9	Passion 9	
Trophies:	OLT 1966–68, 1970, 1972–73, 1982–84,		Personality 7	Personality 7	
	(1986, 1987); PLA 1974, (1991–94);				
	EC 1971–72, (1992); CWC 1987, 1989		**TOTAL 39**	**TOTAL 45**	

LEGEND RATING

Dalglish, Kenny
Celtic, Liverpool, Scotland

KENNY DALGLISH EMERGED as a major force with Celtic in the early 1970s, in a side that dominated Scottish domestic football. It did not take him long to establish himself in the Scottish national team or to convince Liverpool to part with a massive £440,000 to take him to Anfield as a successor for the departing Kevin Keegan. Dalglish repaid their faith in him immediately forming a deadly combination with Ian Rush. It is hard to envisage a harder player to mark – subtle, strong and two-footed, he could turn defenders any which way he wanted.

When Liverpool needed a manager to keep up the boot-room succession, they surprised many by turning to Dalglish as player-manager in 1985. Again their faith was repaid. Dalglish became the first (and remains the only) player-manager to win the League and Cup double.

Dalglish later retired as Liverpool manager, blaming cumulative stress partially brought on by the Hillsborough disaster. A year later, though, he returned to football as manager of Blackburn Rovers, whom he led to the Premiership title in 1995. More recently spells at Newcastle and Celtic, where he took up a role as technical director, both ended in acrimony and failure. But who's to say he won't be back?

- Dalglish scored Liverpool's only goal in the 1978 European Cup final against Bruges.
- He is the only player to score 100 goals for English and Scottish clubs.
- Dalglish is a superb golfer, and could have been good enough to play professionally.
- He was one of only three managers to win the English First Division with two different clubs.
- He was PFA and Football Writers' Player of the Year, 1983.

VITAL STATISTICS

Place of Birth:	Glasgow, Scotland			
Date of Birth:	4 March 1951	**Died:** n/a		
Caps:	102 (Scotland)	**Goals (International):** 30		
Clubs:	Celtic, Liverpool			

		MANAGER		PLAYER	
Appearances:	Club (League): 559	Achievement	9	Achievement	9
Goals:	Club (League): 230	Tactical Awareness	8	Skill	8
Trophies:	SLT 1972, 1973, 1974, 1977; SFAC	Motivation	8	Teamwork	9
	1972, 1974, 1975, 1977; EC 1978,	Team Selection/Transfers	7	Passion	9
	1981, 1984; LT 1979, 1980, 1982–84,	Personality	6	Personality	7
	(1986), (1988), (1990); LC 1981,				
	1982, 1983, 1984; FAC (1986), (1989)	**TOTAL**	**38**	**TOTAL**	**42**

LEGEND RATING

Day Of The Dons
Aberdeen 2 Real Madrid 1, 1983

BASED ON THE EUROPEAN pedigrees of these two clubs, this final looked like a mismatch. But this was no ordinary Scottish club side, and it was a Real side in a lean spell, struggling to make any real impact in European competition.

Alex Ferguson had forged Aberdeen into a durable and courageous team that boasted three international-class players in the shape of Gordon Strachan, Willie Miller and Alex McLeish. In winger Peter Weir, Fergie also had a talented maverick at his disposal. The rest were tough pros who would respond in a tight corner. In the quarter-final, after a grim draw in Munich, they were 2-1 down at home to Bayern in the second leg with 15 minutes to go, but came back to stun the Germans with two goals in two minutes.

The final wasn't a classic. Aberdeen were the better side throughout, but as the match wore on it began to look as if they might be edged out. But then John Hewitt came on for Eric Black, scorer of the opening goal, and within minutes he was on hand to head home after a neat move between Mark McGhee and Weir.

☞ Real's manager was none other than the legendary Alfredo Di Stefano. His coaching skills were not the equal of his playing ability, and he lasted just one season as boss.

✍ Aberdeen went on to beat European Cup winners Hamburg in the Super Cup, and reached the semi-finals of the European Cup Winners' Cup again a year later.

✍ In the following year's European Cup Winners' Cup, Mark McGhee scored a hat-trick in a 3-0 win over Ujpest Dozsa, overturning a 2-0 deficit from the first leg.

☞ Aberdeen won the double in 1984 and another title in 1985.

SCORERS	**Aberdeen:** Black, Hewitt
	Real Madrid: Juanito (pen)
EVENT	European Cup Winners' Cup final, Gothenburg, 11 May 1983
ABERDEEN	(Man: Alex Ferguson)
	1. Leighton 2. Rougvie 3. McMaster 4. Strachan 5. Miller 6. McLeish
	7. Cooper 8. Black 9. McGhee 10. Simpson 11. Weir
REAL MADRID	(Man: Alfredo Di Stefano)
	1. Agustin 2. Metgod 3. Bonet 4. Camacho 5. Juan Jose 6. Angel
	7. Gallego 8. Stielike 9. Juanito 10. Santillana 11. Isidro

Dean, William 'Dixie'

Everton, England

FOOTBALL'S MOST PROLIFIC pre-war goal machine was the original English centre forward. Lawton, Lofthouse and Milburn may have carried on the tradition, but none of them scored goals like Dixie Dean. His British record of 379 is one that will stand forever. True, today's superior marking and packed defences would have prevented this avalanche, while Dean's bustling strength would have incurred the displeasure of modern referees, but none of this should overshadow the man's talent – at times he seemed to challenge Arsenal's dominance of the league title almost single-handedly, shooting Everton to a brace of league titles and an FA Cup in six seasons.

Dean was born, raised and remained in the north-west all his life, retiring in modest circumstances before a disgracefully overdue testimonial in 1964 drew 40,000 to Goodison Park. Fittingly Dean even took his last breath at his beloved Everton's ground, passing away at Goodison after watching a Merseyside derby in 1980.

- 1928–29 season. Scored 60 goals in 39 games for Everton in the First Division, a record that still stands.
- Lived most of his life with a steel plate in his head, after fracturing his skull in a motorcycle crash as a youth.
- 1936. Overhauled Steve Bloomer's record of 352 league goals.
- Dean scored twice on his debut for England and hit hat-tricks in his second and fifth matches.
- He preferred his real name William to his life-long nickname Dixie.

VITAL STATISTICS

Place of Birth:	Birkenhead, England		Achievement	8.0
Date of Birth:	27 January 1907	**Died:** 1 March 1980	Skill	8.0
Caps:	16 (England)	**Goals (International):** 18	Teamwork	10.0
Clubs:	Tranmere, Everton, Notts County		Passion	9.0
Appearances:	Club (League): 438		Personality	6.0
Goals:	Club (League): 379			
Trophies:	LT 1928, 1932; FAC 1933		**TOTAL**	**41.0**

LEGEND RATING

Di Canio, Paolo

Celtic, Sheffield Wednesday, West Ham United

LIKE FELLOW MAVERICK Eric Cantona, Paolo di Canio's talents have been more appreciated in Britain than in his home country. Volatility and indiscipline have led successive Italian managers to ignore him, and have resulted in a lengthy exile from his homeland following precocious beginnings at Milan. The case against was most vividly illustrated in 1998 when, reacting to being issued with a red card playing for Sheffield Wednesday against Arsenal, he pushed referee Paul Durkin to the ground. The shove inflicted only bruised pride, but left another manager resigned to parting with a wayward talent.

With passion and skill complementing his sublime touch and striker's instinct, Di Canio has been a folk hero at every club from the San Siro to Celtic Park, always resurrecting a career that has appeared irretrievably damaged. His occasional indiscretions conceal a fierce commitment and passion; Di Canio is no wastrel maverick, but a hard-working team player, albeit one susceptible to extravagance. A twilight move to Old Trafford never materialised and Di Canio moved back to Italy to see out his career.

- 👍 Di Canio even takes penalties in style; his trademark chips continue to embarrass keepers.
- 👍 2000. Outrageous volley v Wimbledon wins BBC's goal of the season.
- 👍 2001. Won Fair Play award after catching the ball to allow Everton's fallen keeper to receive treatment when he might have pulled the ball down and scored.
- 👎 He has never won a trophy in Britain.
- 👉 West Ham fans chanted his name to the tune of an aria from Verdi's 'Rigoletto'.

VITAL STATISTICS

Place of Birth:	Rome, Italy		
Date of Birth:	9 July 1968	**Died:** n/a	
Caps:	0 (Italy)	**Goals (International):** 0	

Clubs:	Terrana, Lazio, Juventus, Napoli, AC Milan,	Achievement	4.0
	Celtic, Sheffield Wednesday, West Ham,	Skill	9.0
	Charlton	Teamwork	8.0
Appearances:	Club (League): 358	Passion	10.0
Goals:	Club (League): 94	Personality	9.0
Trophies:	UEFAC 1993	**TOTAL 40.0**	

LEGEND RATING

Dirtiest Cup Final Ever
Chelsea 2 Leeds United 1, 1970

THIS INFAMOUS MATCH was a bloodbath. Chelsea were the fancydan southerners, flashy and inconsistent with a reputation for boozy late nights, while Leeds were the no-nonsense, cynical professionals whose pre-match evenings were spent playing dominoes. Both teams viewed each other with contempt. At Wembley, Eddie Gray had tormented Chelsea's right back David Webb, and the tactic of switching Webb with Ron Harris for the replay had the desired effect within minutes. Gray became a limping passenger for the rest of the game. 'Chopper' had set the tone.

In a tit-for-tat response that would have brought approval from hardliners in the Middle East, Bonetti was taken out moments later, subsequently giving a commendable display on one leg. From then on, a pulsating and skilful Cup final was routinely punctuated by outbreaks of violence. Hutchinson and Charlton traded blows, while McCreadie's two-footed lunge at Bremner's neck introduced kung fu to a British audience several years before Bruce Lee. Yet for all the 'southern softies' jibes, it was Chelsea who prevailed. A goal down at half-time, they hit back through a diving header from Osgood and scrambled a winner courtesy of Webb's right ear.

☞ When Chelsea finally went ahead in extra-time, it was the first time they had led in the tie. They had pegged Leeds back at Wembley with two equalisers.

✍ Osgood's goal meant he had scored in every round.

☞ This was the first FA Cup final settled outside Wembley since it became the venue in 1923.

☞ Referee Jennings must have forgotten his pencil. Despite the violence not one player was cautioned.

☞ David Harvey was the only change from the teams who contested the first match. Gary Sprake was left out after a trademark howler had gifted Chelsea their first equaliser.

SCORERS	**Chelsea:** Osgood, Webb
	Leeds: Jones
EVENT	FA Cup Final Replay, Old Trafford, 29 April 1970
CHELSEA	(Man: Dave Sexton)
	1. Bonetti 2. Harris, R 3. McCreadie 4. Hollins 5. Dempsey 6. Webb
	7. Baldwin 8. Cooke 9. Osgood 10. Hutchinson 11. Houseman
LEEDS	(Man: Don Revie)
	1. Harvey 2. Madeley 3. Cooper 4. Bremner 5. Charlton 6. Hunter
	7. Lorimer 8. Clarke 9. Jones 10. Giles 11. Gray, E

Alan Clarke shoots for Leeds in the replay at Old Trafford.

Disasters
Footballing Tragedies

FOOTBALL ATTRACTS MORE SPECTATORS than any other sport in the world. The downside to this is that when things go wrong they go wrong in a big way. Recent advances in stadium safety seem to have eradicated most of the problems, but it took a scandalously long time for the authorities to take action. In 1946, a wall collapsed under pressure from spectators eager to watch Bolton's FA Cup quarter-final against Stoke. Thirty-three people were crushed to death. After this the luck of the authorities held until 1971, when 66 people died at Ibrox. Rangers fans were filing down a staircase, believing their team to have been beaten in the New Year derby. A last-minute equaliser caused thousands to turn back and the crush barriers failed to take their weight.

Ibrox's legacy was the Safety of Sports Grounds Act, which, although a development, failed to address the problem of old wooden structures and fire risk. In 1985, this oversight resulted in the deaths of 56 fans from a fire started by one cigarette, dropped on to rubbish under a stand at Valley Park. Though most British grounds are safer now, the mixture of weak stadium, bad policing, hooliganism and panic can result in tragedy anywhere in the world. It is inevitable that, one day, this page will require updating.

- 1982. In a chilling echo of Ibrox, 340 people died at a European Cup match in Moscow after a late goal. Russian officials claimed the death toll was 61 in an attempt to disguise poor policing.
- Locked gates and an exiting human tide have proved a fatal combination. 74 people were crushed at an Argentine game in 1968; 71 died for the same reason in Katmandu 20 years later.
- In 1964 police fired shots as a crowd 'control' exercise in Lima. Over 300 people died in the resulting panic.
- African crowd control has not kept pace with modern improvements. Three unnecessary uses of tear-gas have produced separate disasters in the last few years.
- 26 people died at Ibrox in 1902 after a stand collapsed.

'Football is not a matter of life and death – it's much more important than that.'

In the context of Heysel and Hillsborough, Bill Shankly's words have a hollow ring

The dead and wounded are carried out of the first Ibrox disaster in 1902.

Docherty, Tommy
Chelsea, Manchester United, Scotland

FOR ALL HIS BREAST-BEATING and fondness for soundbites (he could have invented the term), Tommy Docherty built only two teams of note in a multi-club career. The first was at Chelsea, where a Second Division side still reeling from the loss of Jimmy Greaves became football's embodiment of the 'swinging sixties' and brought fame and recognition to the likes of Venables, Graham and Osgood.

A decade later, after first taking them down into the Second Division, he won promotion with Manchester United and built a swashbuckling attacking team whose stars, the likes of Coppell, Hill, Pearson, Macari and the brothers Greenhoff, replaced the heroes of the Busby era in the affections of the Old Trafford fans. But then, like always with Docherty, things turned sour. Within weeks of winning the FA Cup in 1977 he was found to have been having an affair with the club physio's wife, Mary Brown, and was sacked on the spot. He later tried his luck at a bewildering assortment of other clubs, but never hit the heights of his Old Trafford days again. Now he makes his money doing what he was always best at: rattling off one-liners and telling jokes on the lucrative after-dinner circuit.

- Docherty only won two trophies as a manager, and never won the league.
- A mediocre Scotland manager, he left after a year to take the United job.
- 'I've had more clubs than Jack Nicklaus,' Docherty on his ever-lengthening employment record.
- On being told his board were right behind him: 'I want them in front of me, that way I can see what they're doing'.

VITAL STATISTICS

Place of Birth:	Glasgow, Scotland		
Date of Birth:	24 April 1929	**Died:** n/a	
Caps:	25 (Scotland)	**Goals (International):** 1	
Clubs:	As Player: Celtic, Preston North End, Arsenal;		
	As Manager: Chelsea, Rotherham United,		
	Queens Park Rangers, FC Porto, Hull City,	Achievement	4
	Scotland national side, Manchester United,	Tactical Awareness	7
	Derby County, Sydney Olympic, Preston North End,	Motivation	6
	Wolverhampton Wanderers, Altrincham	Team Selection/Transfers	9
Appearances:	Club (All Matches): 427	Personality	7
Goals:	Club (All Matches): 91		
Trophies:	LC 1965; FAC 1977	**TOTAL**	**33**

LEGEND RATING

Doncaster Belles
Pioneers Of The Women's Game

THE DONCASTER BELLES have been a force in women's football in England since they were formed in 1969 by a group of women who sold 'Golden Goal' tickets for Doncaster Rovers. They won the Notts League a remarkable 11 times in 13 seasons between 1977 and 1989 and were without doubt the biggest women's club in the land during the 1980s and early 1990s. During a golden 12-year period they won the Women's FA Cup six times and were runners-up five times. In 1983 the entire Belles side represented England in Holland for the European Championships. The Belles lifted the first-ever national title in 1992, a feat they repeated in 1994, but in more recent seasons they have had to take a back seat to the likes of Arsenal and QPR. The Belles are one of the few women's clubs not to be directly affiliated to their male professional counterparts. They previously shared a humble ground with Brodsworth Welfare of the Northern Counties east league but recently moved to a new £1.8 m stadium with a 4,000 capacity and corporate entertaining facilities.

☞ Popular BBC TV series *Playing The Field* was inspired by author Pete Davies' book on the Doncaster side, *I Lost My Heart To The Belles*, that detailed events in the season after they won the double in 1994.

☞ Half the England midfield is made up of Belles – Burke, Exley and Hunt with Walker up front. Three ex-Belles are also regular members of the squad.

☞ Doncaster Belles are the last team in the 10-strong FA Women's Premier League to still have a woman at the helm. Manager Julie Chipchase is in her third season.

☞ Record Belles goalscorer Karen Walker carries the nickname of 'Wacker'. She has 61 England caps.

'We just don't like males and females playing together. I like feminine girls. Anyway it's not natural.'

Ted Croker, FA Chief Executive (and Sexist), 1988

Don't Expect It To Happen Again
Liverpool 4 Newcastle United 3, 1996

IN 10 YEARS of the Premier League, there had never been a game quite like it. With the season approaching its climax, both teams were straining for the Champions League, while Newcastle were also slugging it out with Man United for the title.

Under the circumstances a cagey, low-scoring affair would have been understandable. Instead, both teams came at each other from the off, and after an extraordinary opening 15 minutes Newcastle were 2-1 to the good, having overturned Robbie Fowler's second-minute strike. A sense of normality returned for the following 30 minutes but half-time only served to recharge the batteries. Fowler slid in an equaliser 10 minutes after the restart, only for Asprilla to restore Newcastle's lead within another two. A spectator for 68 minutes, Stan Collymore woke up sufficiently to turn in McAteer's cross to level the scores again. A draw seemed the fair result, but Ian Rush had other ideas. His appearance as an 82nd-minute substitute spurred Liverpool for one last effort and two minutes into injury time Anfield's greatest goalscorer turned provider, combining with John Barnes to set up an unmarked Collymore for the winner. Fairytale stuff.

☞ 'If they score three, we'll score four.' Keegan's words earlier in the season characterised Newcastle's approach and so nearly proved prophetic.

☞ For Newcastle it was another away defeat in a stuttering run that cost them the title. They had been 12 points ahead at the turn of the year.

☞ Best moment of the match? Asprilla nutmegging Ruddock before scoring Newcastle's third.

☞ Radio Five Live's captain smugness, Alan Green, before the corresponding fixture the following season: 'Welcome to a packed Anfield. And do yourselves a favour folks: don't expect 4-3. That happens once every 10 years.' You've guessed it....

SCORERS	**Liverpool:** Fowler (2), Collymore (2)
	Newcastle: Ferdinand, Ginola, Asprilla
EVENT	FA Premiership, Anfield, 3 April 1996
LIVERPOOL	(Man: Roy Evans)
	1. James 2. Wright 3. Scales 4. Ruddock 5. McAteer 6. Redknapp
	7. Barnes 8. McManaman 9. Jones 10. Fowler 11. Collymore
NEWCASTLE	(Man: Kevin Keegan)
	1. Srnicek 2. Watson 3. Howey 4. Albert 5. Beresford 6. Beardsley
	7. Lee 8. Batty 9. Ginola 10. Ferdinand 11. Asprilla

Michael Owen leaves Newcastle's Steve Watson floundering.

Drake, Ted
Arsenal, England

WHEN HERBERT CHAPMAN decided he needed a replacement for his centre forward Jack Lambert, he had only one target in mind: Ted Drake, the barnstorming Southampton striker. And so, for the princely sum of £6,500, Drake moved to Arsenal, becoming the latest piece in Chapman's ever-shifting jigsaw. The attacking line-up in the 1934–35 season read thus: Bastin, Jack, Drake, James and Hulme. Like Lambert, Drake was strong and fearless, often playing through injuries that would have ruled out lesser men. In 1935 Arsenal beat Aston Villa 7-1, a game in which Drake had nine attempts at goal. One was saved, one hit the bar and he scored with the other seven.

The vagaries of international selection in those days meant he played only five times for England; it is testimony to his striking instincts that he still managed to notch six goals. After the war Drake tried his hand at management, and enjoyed a nine-year spell at Chelsea, during which he led the club to its only league title, in 1955. A tall, handsome, athletic man, but without excessive vanity, Drake would have been a marketing manager's dream had he played today.

- Scored the only goal in the 1936 FA Cup final.
- In 1963 Drake became a member of the first ever pools panel, convened in the 'big freeze' of that winter.
- Drake's tackle on Italy's Luisito Monti sparked off the 'Battle of Highbury,' a bruising encounter between Italy and England in 1934. England won 3-2, Drake scored.
- He scored 42 league goals in his first season at Arsenal, including four in a match on four occasions.
- His seven goals against Aston Villa (see main text) were made even more remarkable by the fact that Drake played with a heavily-strapped knee.

VITAL STATISTICS

Place of Birth:	Southampton, England		
Date of Birth:	16 August 1912	**Died:** 30 May 1995	
Caps:	5 (England)	**Goals (International):** 6	
Clubs:	Southampton, Arsenal		
Appearances:	Club (All Matches for Arsenal): 184		
Goals:	Club (All Matches for Arsenal): 139		
Trophies:	LT 1935, 1938, (1955); FAC 1936		

LEGEND RATING	
Achievement	7.0
Skill	8.0
Teamwork	7.0
Passion	9.0
Personality	6.0
TOTAL	**37.0**

Dream Dragons
The Wales Dream Team

HARDLY SCINTILLATING IS IT? Welsh football has had its moments, but they have tended to come when a team made up mainly of ordinary players has elevated itself by dint of endeavour and passion. The squad of 16 below contains no more than half a dozen world class players, and neither Giggs nor Rush produced their best for Wales. This team is not reflective of the players with the most caps, otherwise the midfield might comprise Peter Nicholas, Brian Flynn, Barry Horne and Mickey Thomas, if he's out of jail.

At least the keeper is world class, and Kevin Ratcliffe was a hugely under-rated defender. John Charles would start at the back, but could also bolster the attack. Two decent wingers, Meredith from the early part of the last century, and the whippet-like Cliff Jones from Spurs double-winning side, might create some problems, and leave Giggs to try and cause damage wherever. Hughes would give anyone a hard game, even if he wasn't a prolific scorer, and Rush, in this company, might do what he never really did for Wales.

⚜ Fred Keenor was captain of the Welsh team which won the Home Internationals in the 1920s, and also captained the Cardiff City side which won the 1927 FA Cup. He would provide a muscular heart to the midfield alongside the seemingly timeless Gary Speed.

⚜ Mike Smith oversaw a Welsh team that achieved more than its collective parts suggested it was capable of – which was more than many of his better known successors managed.

☞ We went for a 3-4-1-2 to avoid picking Joey Jones.

☞ John Charles' brother, Mel, was also up for selection, as were a few other Jonesies apart from Cliff. As were Mark Aizlewood, Glynn Hodges, Clayton Blackmore, Kenny Jackett and Eric Young. We didn't pick them either. Not because they had brothers but because they weren't very good.

Manager: Mike Smith (80s)

3-4-1-2

Neville Southall (80s/90s)

Kevin Ratcliffe (80s) Mike England (70s) John Charles (60s)

Billy Meredith (00s/10s) Fred Keenor (20s)
Gary Speed (90s/00s) Cliff Jones (C) (50s/60s)

Ryan Giggs (90s)

Mark Hughes (80s/90s) Ian Rush (80s)

Subs: Jack Kelsey (G) (50s) Len Allchurch (D) (50s)
Ivor Allchurch (50s) Trevor Ford (F) (40s/50s) Ted Vizard (W) (20s)

John Charles, the greatest Welsh player of all, against Hungary in the 1958 World Cup.

Dreaming in Red

Liverpool's All-Time XI

IT WAS SURPRISING, when we started to examine the Liverpool players of the last 35 years as individuals, how few of them stood out as genuine world-class performers. The likes of Tommy Smith, Brian Hall, Phil Neal, Sammy Lee and Jimmy Case were crucial parts of the Anfield jigsaw, but taken out of that context were relatively unremarkable players.

But an endless cycle of international players in recent years was not allowed to blur the fact that it was the more prosaic home-grown talents – the likes of fullbacks Lawler and Hughes that brought Liverpool their vast array of trophies over two decades. Those two, with Lawrenson (narrowly over Ron Yeats) and Hansen – probably the best ever pairing in English club football – and the redoubtable Clemence in goal make up a formidable back five.

The midfield choices ignored the claims of St John, McDermott and Molby, but allies work-rate to skill, the selection of Liddell, acknowledges the other great Liverpool teams in the early part of the last century.

Keegan and Dalglish could interchange, and Rush would surely relish service of the quality this team could provide. If he didn't, there's always Roger Hunt or Michael Owen to replace him!

☞ The Kop, originally standing on a mound of ashes and cinders, was named after the Spion Kop, a hill successfully defended by the Boers in the Boer War.

☞ Club anthem 'You'll Never Walk Alone' came from a hit by Merseybeat singer Gerry Marsden. The phrase is now carved into the wrought-iron gates at the ground.

☞ No Heighway, Toshack, Aldridge, Beardsley, Barnes, Fowler. Simply no room at the inn.

☞ Only Gerrard from the current crop – though in three or four years Hyppia and Kewell may push for consideration.

☞ 'Mind you, I've been here during the bad times too – one year we came second.' Bob Paisley

---

Manager: Bill Shankly (60s/70s)

4-4-2

Ray Clemence (70s/80s)

Chris Lawler (60s/70s) Mark Lawrenson (80s)
Alan Hansen (70s/80s) Emlyn Hughes (C) (70s)

Kevin Keegan (70s) Graeme Souness (80s)
Steven Gerrard (00s) Billy Liddell (40s)

Kenny Dalglish (70s/80s) Ian Rush (80s)

Subs: Elisha Scott (G) (20s) Ron Yeats (D) (60s) Roger Hunt (F) (60s)
Ian Callaghan (M) (60s/70s) Michael Owen (F) (90s/00s)

Duff, Damien

Blackburn Rovers, Chelsea, Republic Of Ireland

AMIDST ALL THE KERFUFFLE of Roy Keane's exit from the 2002 World Cup Finals, many journalists passed the opinion that Ireland had lost their only world-class player. They were wrong. For a year or two, the stocky Blackburn Rovers winger, Damien Duff, had been tormenting Premiership right backs, providing a stream of crosses for his forwards, and notching a few goals himself.

Able to go either way, with great balance and a sporty extra gear, Duff was the envy of many of the Premiership big-boys, always on the lookout for a lock to pick stubborn defences. His performances, post-Keane, in the 2002 World Cup, did nothing to damage that reputation. After exciting in the group matches, especially in the vital draw with Germany, he was simply outstanding in the defeat by Spain on penalties. That form carried on into Blackburn's excellent 2002–03 season in the Premiership, a season that made an approach from one of the Champions League clubs inevitable.

In an injury-hit first season at Chelsea, Duff's talent was more evident in how much the team missed him than for his dangerous contributions when he was fit. Without him, Blackburn, too, looked a shadow of the team they were the previous season. The best should be yet to come.

☞ On his U-21 Ireland debut, the team were housed in a basic hotel in poverty-stricken Moldova. Duff responded by sleeping for 12 hours while the others complained.

☞ Chelsea had to pay £17 m for Duff's services, then a club record; this figure triggered a break clause in his contract at Blackburn.

☞ In the 2002 World Cup, Mick McCarthy used Duff as a support striker rather than a winger. A debate still goes on as to where he is most effective.

☞ Summer 2004. Duff publicised his displeasure at Chelsea's signing of Dutch winger and first-team threat Arjen Robben. Both players, when fit, have been included in the starting line-up.

VITAL STATISTICS

Place of Birth: Ballyboden, Ireland
Date of Birth: 2 March 1979 **Died:** n/a
Caps: 57 (R. Ireland) **Goals (International):** 6
Clubs: Blackburn Rovers, Chelsea
Appearances: Club (League): 245
Goals: Club (League): 40
Trophies: LT 2005; LC 2002, 2005

LEGEND RATING	
Achievement	6.0
Skill	9.0
Teamwork	7.0
Passion	7.0
Personality	7.0
TOTAL	**36.0**

Edwards, Duncan
Manchester United, England

FROM THE MOMENT Duncan Edwards died in Munich, losing a desperate battle for life two weeks after seven team-mates had perished on the runway, his status as a footballing immortal was assured. Only 21 years of age when he died from his injuries, his achievements at the heart of the famous Busby Babes team were the pipe dreams of most players 15 years his senior. Wistful debates have continued for over 40 years as to what he might have achieved, but Sir Duncan Edwards with a World Cup winner's medal and a century of England caps is a realistic, some might say even conservative, projection.

Edwards was earmarked for stardom at an early age, excelling for England's under-14s and creating a queue for his signature that saw the wily Matt Busby at its head. He was equally at home at centre half or half back but his physique, strength and authority (unprecedented in a teenager) meant he could operate pretty much wherever Busby wanted him to. All deaths at Munich were individual tragedies of equal measure, but Edwards' loss was the biggest for English football.

- 1953. Edwards made his professional debut for Manchester United aged only 16 years 185 days.
- 1955. Became England's youngest debutant of the century at 18 years 183 days. Scotland are trounced 7-2.
- He played for England at five different levels.
- He won two league titles before his 21st birthday.
- Had he lived, Edwards would now be a pensioner, having reached 65 in October 2001.

VITAL STATISTICS

Place of Birth:	Dudley, England	
Date of Birth:	1 October 1936	**Died:** 21 February 1958
Caps:	18 (England)	**Goals (International):** 5
Clubs:	Manchester United	
Appearances:	Club (League): 175	
Goals:	Club (League): 21	
Trophies:	LT 1956, 1957	

LEGEND RATING	
Achievement	7.0
Skill	8.0
Teamwork	9.0
Passion	9.0
Personality	7.0
TOTAL	**40.0**

Eleven Lions In Their Shirts
The England Dream Team

WE WERE TEMPTED BY 3-5-2 due to lack of great fullbacks, but that would not be England, so 4-4-2 it is. Unfortunately, this means we had to omit one of three great centre halves, the much-capped Billy Wright. Leaving out Moore was unthinkable, and the monolithic Duncan Edwards adds much-needed strength and attacking power. Eddie Hapgood switches to the right – he was the best of the pre-war, old-fashioned fullbacks. Ashley Cole is a controversial inclusion, but he was outstanding at Euro 04, improves every year, and is still a few years short of the footballer's 'peak'. Roger Byrne, Terry Cooper and Stuart Pearce miss out.

Oh, those wingers! Only Brazil can boast a pair to match this; their genius relegates Beckham, with his expert deliveries, to the bench. Robson's tackling and stamina allow Charlton to push behind the front pairing and use his explosive shooting.

We opted for the big man/quick man combination up front, with Lineker shading Greaves and Jackie Milburn in the quick-man stakes. Dean was a towering presence, creating as well as scoring goals with his aerial power. But then, to be fair, so would Drake, Lawton, Lofthouse or Tommy Taylor. Decisions, decisions....

☞ We would like to point out that we mean Billy Wright, as opposed to Mark Wright or, indeed, Ian Wright playing out of position.

☞ The assumption that all players are operating at the peak of their career means only one of Bryan Robson's legs is currently broken.

👋 Dean would need to be briefed on law-changes as smacking the keeper into the net is simply not done any more, chaps!

☞ Alf Ramsey would only be given the job if he signed a contract agreeing to play wingers.

👋 Charlton would take the penalties, as Le Tissier didn't make the 16, and Beckham, if used, would be spoilt for choice over who to pick out from set pieces.

👋 Unproven or not, Wayne Rooney remains the most prodigious raw talent in the game, possibly in English football history.

Manager: Alf Ramsey

4-4-2

Gordon Banks (60s)

Eddie Hapgood (30s) Duncan Edwards (50s)
Bobby Moore (C) (60s) Ashley Cole (00s)

Stanley Matthews (40s/50s) Bobby Charlton (60s)
Bryan Robson (80s) Tom Finney (50s)

Gary Lineker (80s/90s) Dixie Dean (20s/30s)

Subs: Peter Shilton (G) (70s/80s) Billy Wright (D) (50s) David Beckham (W) (90s) Wayne Rooney (F) (00s) Jimmy Greaves (F) (60s)

Emerald Eleven
The All-Ireland Dream Team

IN CASE YOU'RE LOOKING for some sectarian motivation for an All-Ireland team, there is none, it was just a fun exercise. The surprise for those aware of only recent pedigree is the presence of five Ulstermen in the first XI. Pat Jennings was one of the half-dozen finest goalkeepers in history, so stands unchallenged. As do the schemer, Danny Blanchflower, and the incomparable George Best. Martin O'Neill may yield his right-wing berth to Damien Duff in time, and the choice between Dougan and Stapleton, both effective target men who scored their fair share of goals, was the toughest one. Stapleton would enjoy the supply from Best and the gifted left foot of Liam Brady. The wingers would enjoy the possession won by the awesome power of Keane in the centre. The defence is from the South (or Preston, in Lawrenson's case). Lawrenson was quick and strong, McGrath dominant and always composed, dodgy knees permitting. Johnny Carey was a key member of the Busby Babes and Dennis Irwin a stalwart of a later great Manchester United team.

This is a genuinely talented team. The real key to the successes achieved by both Irish teams has been the commitment of those less gifted in support of these quality players.

👍 Billy Bingham gets the nod as manager. His achievements with limited resources were outstanding, and, unlike the most successful Republic manager, Jack Charlton, he is Irish.

👍 The backup midfield is top quality – Giles and Duff are world class, and there's no place for players as good as Kevin Sheedy, Ronnie Whelan and Norman Whiteside.

👎 No place for John Aldridge – prolific at club level but consistently off target for his country. Robbie Keane is more unfortunate to miss out; he performs better for the Republic than for his clubs; his partnership with Niall Quinn was a classic big-and-little combination.

Manager: Billy Bingham* (60s/70s)

4-1-4-1

Pat Jennings* (forever)

Johnny Carey (50s) Mark Lawrenson (80s) Paul McGrath (80s/90s)
Dennis Irwin (90s)

Martin O'Neill* (70s/80s)

Danny Blanchflower* (C) (50s/60s) Roy Keane (90s) Liam Brady (80s)
Derek Dougan* (60s/70s)

George Best* (60s/70s)

Subs: Packy Bonner (G) (90s) Terry O'Neill* (D) (90s) Johnny Giles (M) (60s/70s)
Damien Duff (W) (00s) Frank Stapleton (F) (70s)
* indicates a Northern Ireland player

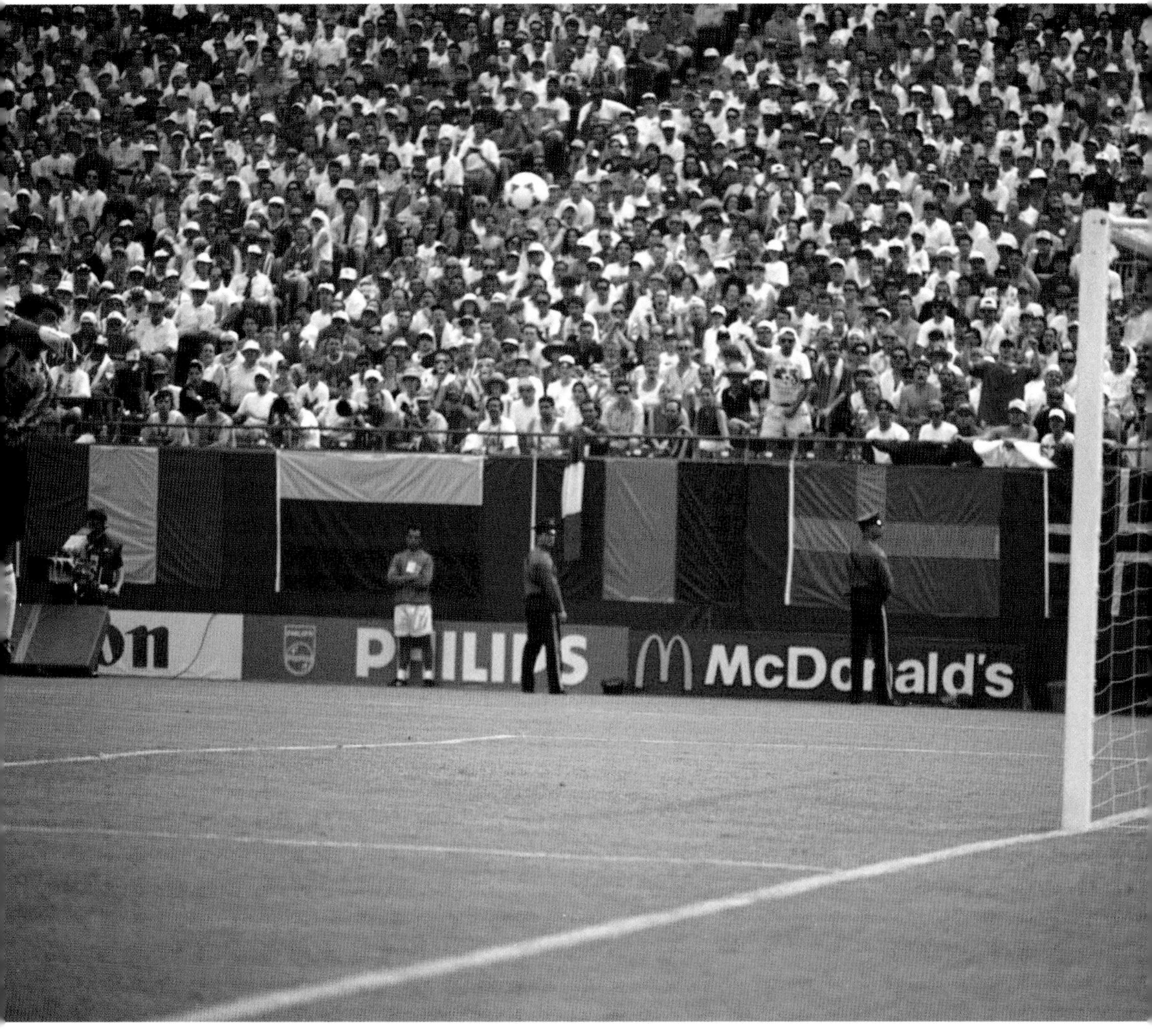
PHILIPS
McDonald's

England Expects
England At The 2006 World Cup

A LOT OF NONSENSE has been talked about England's chances in the World Cup in Germany. The tabloids have veered between manic optimism and dismissive insults. Neither is appropriate. England at full strength are a very good side, but may ultimately lack the self-belief needed to win the World Cup.

The back four is super-solid. The cover in the centre is excellent – many countries would love to have a Gareth Southgate or Michael Dawson and they won't even travel. Gary Neville and Ashley Cole are excellent and their autumn injuries are a blessing, not a hindrance; it means they will be less fatigued. If either gets injured, use Jamie Carragher – Luke Young would get crucified in a World Cup. The midfield is riddled with talent as long as it can be fitted together. Beckham must play on the right, Shaun Wright-Phillips isn't ready, and Steven Gerrard is needed to play in the defensive midfield position. If Gerrard can't or won't play there, leave him out and use a Spurs player – Michael Carrick, not Ledley King. The trump card is Rooney, currently the second-best player in the world. It must be assumed that he will miss at least one match through suspension – just give the role to Joe Cole and play a sub on the left. Jermaine Defoe and Peter Crouch are 'last twenty' options. Crouch's strength of character should not be underestimated; to ride the abuse he received in the autumn was immensely creditable.

☞ Centre half: leave out Rio Ferdinand. He is a lesser player than he was in 2002, largely through his own presumptuousness. Pick the guy's who won't let you down.

☞ Left midfield: must be Joe Cole. He will have had a light workload at Chelsea, but now knows he is a class player, and will prove it. Stewart Downing, if fit, can cover.

☞ Reserve goalkeepers: forget the error-prone David James and Robert Green, take Nigel Martyn for experience and Jamie Ashdown for talent – if he can look good at Portsmouth, he's ready.

☞ Please, please, can we dispense with Owen Hargreaves, Alan Smith and Kieran Dyer? Not good enough, too physical and too weak-minded, respectively. Jermaine Jenas has matured at Tottenham and Kevin Nolan will bring some of Bolton's resolve and an eye for goal.

Manager: Sven-Goran Eriksson

4-4-1-1

Best XI: Paul Robinson Gary Neville Sol Campbell John Terry
Ashley Cole David Beckham Steven Gerrard Frank Lampard
Joe Cole Wayne Rooney Michael Owen

Rest of Squad: Nigel Martyn Jamie Ashdown Jamie Carragher
Rio Ferdinand Ledley King Shaun Wright-Phillips Kevin Nolan
Michael Carrick Jermaine Jenas Stewart Downing
Jermaine Defoe Peter Crouch

England v Spain friendly, 2004. Raul is kept off the ball by Ashley Cole and John Terry.

Eriksson, Sven-Goran

IFK Gothenburg, Benfica, Lazio, England

UNASSUMING, softly spoken and seemingly dispassionate, Sven-Goran Eriksson has many qualities you would not expect to find in a football manager. He also possesses plenty of common sense, which appears to have stood him in good stead.

An unremarkable playing career was ended early by a knee injury; he then commenced a coaching career that has taken in a number of the biggest clubs in Europe. Then the bombshell: for the first time in history, England appoint a foreigner as manager of the national team! Despite opposition from the sceptics – not all of them for moronic nationalistic reasons – Eriksson quickly settled into his new role. With better tactics and discipline, the same squad that failed at home to Germany in a World Cup qualifier tore the same opposition apart in Munich, winning 5-1 and sending a minor tremor through European football.

The team have continued to qualify for major finals without taking the tournament by storm – the nature of a strong side's challenge for the 2006 World Cup will be the final measure of Eriksson's worth in the eyes of a persistently critical media.

- A five-year spell at Sampdoria was something of a mid-career hiccup for Eriksson, as he failed to galvanise the unfashionable side.
- Eriksson has endured the time-honoured English tradition of trial-by-tabloid. Lurid stories about his private life don't appear to have greatly disturbed his equanimity.
- As manager of IFK Gothenburg, he becomes the first man to win a European trophy with a Swedish club side, capturing the UEFA Cup in 1982.
- Eriksson's appointment appears to have coincided with a decline in the influence of Howard Wilkinson on the England scene. Attaboy Sven!

VITAL STATISTICS

Place of Birth:	Torsby, Sweden	
Date of Birth:	5 February 1948	**Died:** n/a
Caps:	0	**Goals (International):** 0
Clubs:	As Player: KB Karlskoga; As Manager: Degerfors IF, IFK Göteburg, Benfica, AS Roma, Fiorentina AC, Sampdoria, Lazio, England national side	
Trophies:	SA 2000; SLT 1981; PLT 1983, 1984, 1991; UEFAC 1982; CWC 1999; ESC 1999	

Achievement	8
Tactical Awareness	9
Motivation	8
Team Selection/Transfers	8
Personality	7
TOTAL	**40**

LEGEND RATING

FA Cup
The Blue Riband

ON 16 OCTOBER 1871, 13 teams entered a knockout competition dreamt up by FA secretary Charles Alcock. It thrives today with the same name, the Football Association Challenge Cup.

Little did Alcock know what he had started. The first final was played in front of 2,000 spectators at the Kennington Oval. As the competition grew in stature, so did the venues, until the twin towers of the newly built Wembley became the permanent home for finalists in 1923. Even then, the Cup's popularity was underestimated; the first final was not all-ticket and over 200,000 turned up, leaving a white horse called Billy to shepherd spectators off the pitch.

The Graf Zeppelin's visit in 1930 ... Bert Trautmann massaging his broken neck in 1956 ... Jim Montgomery's miraculous save for Sunderland in 1973 ... the final has produced memories that have endured through generations, passed on from father to son. Once it was the dream of every minnow to reach the final. That has long passed but the Cup's value to the lesser lights should not be underestimated; one tie against a top division club can bring more revenue than they would usually amass in an entire season. Other competitions come and go, but the oldest and best will always be known, quite simply, as The Cup. And long may it continue.

☞ Ten venues have staged the FA Cup final. In 1920 the final was scheduled for Stamford Bridge. Chelsea were knocked out in the semi by Aston Villa, saving the FA from the potentially embarrassing situation of having to rewrite their rule book (the final is supposed to be played on a neutral ground).

👍 The best final? It has got to be 1953 when, inspired by Stanley Matthews, Blackpool recovered from 3-1 down to win in the last minute.

☞ There have been four trophies. The first cost £20 to make but was stolen in 1895. The present design was created for the 1911 final by Italian silversmiths in Bradford, Messrs Fattorini and Sons. Appropriately, Bradford were its first winners.

'The Crazy Gang have beaten the Culture Club.'

John Motson describing Wimbledon's surprise victory over Liverpool in the 1988 final

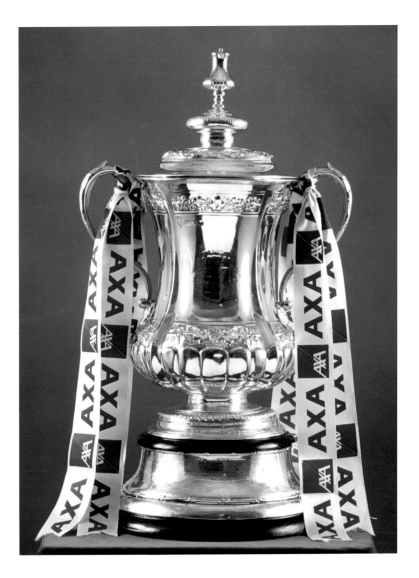

Fashion Victims, Part 1

Hair

THE CATEGORY WINNERS IN THE 'SILLIEST HAIR IN FOOTBALL' AWARDS ARE AS FOLLOWS:

CATEGORY	GOLD	SILVER	BRONZE
Mullet	Brian Kilcline	Kevin Keegan	Chris Waddle
Comb-Over	Ralph Coates	Sir Bobby Charlton	Uwe Seeler
Perm	Tommy Caton	Bob Latchford	Terry McDermott
Dreadlocks	Jason Lee	Henrik Larsson	Tony Daley
Ponytail	Roberto Baggio	David Seaman	Darren Peacock
Beard	Trevor Hockey (aka Chewbacca)	Abel Xavier	Alexei Lalas
Dyed	Taribo West	Ian Wright	Romania, 1998
Outrageous	Abel Xavier	Carlos Valderrama	Alexei Lalas
Girlie	Charlie George	Barry Venison	Mario Kempes
AND THE WINNER IS:	**Abel Xavier**	**Jason Lee**	**Alexei Lalas**

✎ Xavier scores in two categories: outrageous hair and silly beard. He could easily have featured in dyed. Overall, a worthy winner.

☞ Jason Lee appeared confused and hurt when his coiffured 'pineapple' was met with derision from the terraces. His manager saw fit to defend him against a barrage of abuse from comedy duo Baddiel & Skinner, but that hair was indefensible.

☞ The 1970s was a shocking decade for haircuts in football. Starting with Charlie George looking like a big girl's blouse, the decade moved into bubble perms, ending with the mullet.

✎ The influence of style icons like Gullit and Batistuta has spawned a generation of wannabees. White men in dreads and sweaty Englishmen attempting windswept Latin locks. Yeeuch!

KEY

Mullet: grievous 1970s rear overhang.
Comb-over: bald and in denial.
Perm: deliberate attempt to look like a show dog.
Dreadlocks: cool on Ruud, but pineapples were never in.
Ponytail: old and in denial.
Beard: aerodynamically unsound, visually absurd.
Dyed: last resort of the immature.
Outrageous: says it all.
Girlie: 'La la la, superstar, he looks like a woman and he wears a bra.'

The Pineapple and Jesus go head-to-head with the daddy of them all.

Fashion Victims, Part 2
Silly Strips

IT WAS EASIER in the old days. Back then it was safe to rally your team with cries of 'Come on you blues/reds/whites.' Now it's not so simple. 'Come on you azures with the sienna trim, epaulettes and unfeasibly large logo,' just doesn't have the same ring to it does it? In the last 25 years, football kits have gone from simple, functional designs to the sort of garish tat normally peddled by the likes of Zandra Rhodes. The decline started in the late 1970s when manufacturers' logos joined club badges as a staple decoration on your standard jersey; these grew from discreet chest emblems to covering entire sleeves. Once clubs realised that fans would line up like sheep to part with £50 ever other year for a shirt with a minutely modified collar, filthy lucre instantly kicked tradition into touch. Nowadays, a successful performance in the club shop is more important than a Cup run. Manchester United have become the world's richest club by selling not just strips, but lampshades, duvet covers and credit cards. Traditionalists and parents may moan, but the biggest culprits are not the clubs but the fans. There is no law that states we have to buy a replica shirt, no one puts a gun to our heads. Guns to heads? Now there's an idea. Anyone know the way to Umbro's design department?

- Worst away-kit offenders? Chelsea. Jade green was offensive enough, while the 'tangerine and graphite' efforts in the mid-1990s were enough to trigger epilepsy.
- Manchester United famously changed their kit at half-time following a disastrous 45 minutes at the Dell. Alex Ferguson claimed their new grey strip made the players difficult to see.
- The pioneers of the silly strip were Coventry, who as early as the 1970s appeared in a chocolate-brown away kit.
- Shiny kits in the 1980s were a big mistake. The sight of Jan Molby and Paul Stewart squeezing their ample torsos into them rendered pre-match pies even more indigestible.

'For those of you watching in black and white, Spurs are the team in yellow.'

John Motson describes Tottenham's away strip

Clockwise from top left: Arsenal, Norwich, Chelsea and Forest employed the same two-year-old designer.

Ferdinand, Rio

West Ham United, Leeds United, Manchester United, England

THIRTY YEARS AGO, England's strength in depth was goalkeepers, whilst the departing Bobby Moore left a void in central defence. Today, the opposite is true, with the player originally dubbed 'the new Bobby Moore' ably filling the great man's boots.

Rio Ferdinand was destined for the big time at a young age, when he came through the 'academy' at Upton Park to make his Premiership debut at 17 years old. Unflappable and assured, he quickly appeared to be the ball-playing centre back that English fans had assumed was the preserve of continental clubs. Signed in 2000 for a king's ransom by Leeds, his departure (for another mammoth fee) two years later confirmed reports of financial meltdown at Elland Road. His value at Old Trafford has been proven by his absence, not least by the unenforced lay-off in 2004. Ferdinand had been charged following his failure to attend a routine drugs test in September 2003. Citing forgetfulness, he passed the same test 48 hours later but by then the damage was done. An eight-month suspension cost him an FA Cup winner's medal and a place at Euro 2004. United's league form, irresistible at the start of the season, faded badly and they surrendered their title to Arsenal.

☞ Ferdinand's transfer fees, of £18 m and £30 m, both broke the British record.

⚗ Ferdinand's finest form was at the 2002 World Cup. He and Sol Campbell formed the best central-defensive partnership in the tournament. The exit against Brazil wasn't all bad news; Simon le Bon had promised to re-record Duran Duran's 'Rio' if England won the trophy.

☝ In October 2003, in the wake of Ferdinand's drugs-test controversy, England dropped him before a Euro 2004 qualifier against Turkey, a decision that caused a revolt and near-strike by his team-mates.

☞ Ferdinand comes from a footballing dynasty. His cousin is ex-England international Les Ferdinand, while brother Anton is following in his footsteps as a central defender at West Ham.

VITAL STATISTICS

Place of Birth: Peckham, England
Date of Birth: 7 November 1978 **Died:** n/a
Caps: 42 (England) **Goals (International):** 1
Clubs: West Ham United, Leeds United, Manchester United
Appearances: Club (League): 278
Goals: Club (League): 4
Trophies: LT 2003

Achievement	6.5
Skill	9.0
Teamwork	7.0
Passion	7.5
Personality	6.0
TOTAL	**36.0**

LEGEND RATING

Ferguson, Alex
Aberdeen, Manchester United, Scotland

RUTHLESS AS A PLAYER and driven as a manager, Alex Ferguson's record is one that only Bob Paisley can match. His background from the school of hard knocks in Govan served him well, requiring a commitment and self-discipline that he has always demanded, and received, from his players. Strange that such a professional started his footballing life with archetypal amateurs Queens Park, but it was as Aberdeen manager that he really made his mark. For six years the Old Firm dominance was interrupted as three titles and a European trophy arrived at Pittodrie. Manchester United, desperate to escape Liverpool's shadow, broke the bank, and Aberdonian hearts, to get their man. Although his 18-year tenure is the Premiership's longest, the first trophy did not arrive for four years amid mutterings that the Midas touch had vanished.

In 1993 he landed United's first title for 26 years and their subsequent run of success ought to have made his depature unthinkable. Arsenal's recent rise and the near-legal spat in 2003–04 with United's major shareholder, J.P. McManus, over the stud rights of the racehorse Rock of Gibraltar threatened an acromonious departure. An uneasy truce was declared when Ferguson signed a rolling one-year contract. If he goes, it will be on his terms.

- A tearaway player, Ferguson was sent off seven times in the days when once was a rarity.
- 1978. St Mirren sacked Ferguson for the only time in his career after 'unpardonable swearing at a lady on club premises'. The hair-drying technique was honed later.
- 1989. United fans called for Ferguson's head after a 5-1 defeat to local rivals City.
- 1999. Knighted following United's unique treble of League, FA Cup and European Cup.
- 2001. Won his seventh English league title to beat Bob Paisley's record.

VITAL STATISTICS

Place of Birth:	Glasgow, Scotland
Date of Birth:	31 December 1941 **Died:** n/a
Caps:	0 **Goals (International):** 0
Clubs:	As Player: Queens Park, St Johnstone, Dunfermline, Rangers, Falkirk, Ayr United; As Manager: East Stirling, St Mirren, Aberdeen, Scotland national side (as caretaker manager), Manchester United
Trophies:	SLT 1980, 1984–85; SFAC 1982–84, 1986; CWC 1983, 1991; FAC 1990, 1994, 1996, 2004; LC 1992; LT 1993, 1994, 1996, 1997, 1999–2001, 2003; EC 1999

LEGEND RATING	
Achievement	10
Tactical Awareness	9
Motivation	10
Team Selection/Transfers	9
Personality	8
TOTAL	**46**

Fever Pitch
Football Writing

THERE HAVE ALWAYS BEEN good football books. Hunter Davies' *The Glory Game* (1972) and Eamon Dunphy's *Only A Game* (1976), are examples of superb tomes published pre-Nick Hornby. Yet these books were released almost apologetically by publishers, as if they could never truly bring themselves to believe that football supporters actually had the ability to read. Hornby changed all that. *Fever Pitch* (1992) redefined football publishing. People with no interest in the game read and – often to their great surprise – even enjoyed it, impressed by Hornby's passion and insight. This was no journalist recounting his views from the press box, no retired player explaining why a fat has-been wasn't picked for the Cup final. This was a true fan, a terrace sweat, living out the triumph and the torture of the national game. Inevitably, the accelerating bandwagon was leapt upon enthusiastically, with publishers falling over themselves to print the memoirs of every two-bob sports journalist they could get their hands on. Wanabe Hornby's were rife, and the world was inundated with entries for soccer's 'Pseuds' corner'.

☞ *The Glory Game* is Hunter Davies' account of a year behind the scenes at Tottenham. An early insight into professional football, it remains an absorbing read.

☞ Recent footballing biographies have been written with greater care and consideration in the light of Hornby's achievement. Alex Ferguson's autobiography, by Hugh McIlvanney, and Tony Adams' searching *Addicted*, were bestsellers.

☞ Lesser players produce fascinating insights too. Gary Nelson's *Left Foot Forward*, and Steve Claridge's *Tales From The Boot Camp* are fine examples of this sub-genre.

☞ Splenetic and acerbic, *Only A Game* is a journeyman footballer's exploration of the whys and wherefores of the game.

'A feminist colleague of mine literally refused to believe that I watched Arsenal, a disbelief that apparently had its roots in the fact that we once had a conversation about a feminist novel.'

Nick Hornby

FEVER
P*I*TCH

Nick Hornby

'Funny, wise and true'
RODDY DOYLE

Finney, Tom
Preston North End, England

'TOM FINNEY WOULD HAVE been great in any team, in any match and in any age … even if he had been wearing an overcoat,' So said Bill Shankly. Speculation as to how the great players of the 1940s and 1950s would have fared in the modern game is a favourite subject of bar-room, but it would take a brave man to dispute Shankly's assessment of his former Preston team-mate. There is no doubt that Finney's dribbling ability was the equal of his contemporary, Stanley Matthews, and many have argued that his reading of the game, and his shooting, were far superior. Whether he was better than Matthews will always be a matter of opinion.

After the war, Finney became the star of a great England side. His performances in a 10-0 demolition of Portugal and 4-0 thrashing of reigning World Champions Italy, were highlights of his early career. He continued playing for England until the age of 36, and his 30 goals for his country remained a record for many years. The maximum wage ruling meant Finney never earned the financial rewards his talents probably merited. It also tied him to Preston, which meant his medal collection was nothing to write home about either.

- Aged 40, Finney made a belated appearance in Europe. At the invitation of George Eastham he played for Irish club Distillery against Benfica in 1963. Distillery emerged with a heroic 3-3 draw.
- He was named Football Writers' Player of the Year in 1954 and 1957, the first player to win the award twice.
- Finney received an OBE in 1961 and a belated knighthood in 1999.
- Like Stanley Matthews, he was never booked in his career.
- Finney blew his one chance to win the FA Cup, having an uncharacteristically poor game in the 1954 final. North End lost 3-2.

VITAL STATISTICS

Place of Birth:	Preston, England	
Date of Birth:	5 April 1922	**Died:** n/a
Caps:	76 (England)	**Goals (International):** 30
Clubs:	Preston North End	
Appearances:	Club (League): 433	
Goals:	Club (League): 187	
Trophies:	None	

Achievement	6.0
Skill	10.0
Teamwork	9.0
Passion	8.0
Personality	7.0
TOTAL	**40.0**

LEGEND RATING

Five Times Champions!
Real Madrid 7 Eintracht Frankfurt 3, 1960

IT WAS A TREAT for the fans in Glasgow and is widely touted as the finest-ever display by a club side. Frankfurt, physical and formidable, arrived to challenge the mighty Real. Gone for Real were the smooth skills of Kopa and Rial, but they still had the two giants Puskas and Di Stefano who, even if the rest of the team were misfiring, could usually be relied upon to produce something special. At 1-0 down after 20 minutes the Spanish team began to find their rhythm, and soon it was clear that both Madrid's great players were on top form – which was just as well because Santamaria and his defence were being made to look ponderous by the quick German forwards.

By half-time Di Stefano had scored twice and Puskas once. Puskas completed a hat-trick before the hour to make it 5-1, and then two more goals for each side in a breathless four-minute spell completed a fine night's entertainment. It was to be the last of Real Madrid's run of five consecutive European Cup trophies. What a way to end an era.

☞ Some claim Frankfurt were poor opposition, but Rangers probably wouldn't agree; in the semi-finals they went down to them 12-4 on aggregate.

☞ It was to be 14 years before another German team reached the final, Bayern Munich winning the first of their three consecutive victories in 1974.

☞ The Germans were also criticised for their tactics, but surely the only way to beat Real was to attack their vulnerable defence; it was hugely optimistic to hope for a clean sheet against that forward line.

✎ While they never attained this level again, Real reached three further finals in the 1960s, winning in 1966.

SCORERS	**Real Madrid:** Di Stefano 3, Puskas 4
	Eintracht Frankfurt: Kress, Stein 2
EVENT	European Cup Final, Hampden Park, Glasgow, 18 May 1960, a crowd of 134,000!
REAL	(Man: Miguel Munoz)
	1. Dominguez 2. Marquitos 3. Pachin 4. Vidal 5. Santamaria 6. Zarraga 7. Canario 8. Del Sol 9. Di Stefano 10. Puskas 11. Gento
FRANKFURT	(Man: Paul Osswald)
	1. Loy 2. Lutz 3. Hofer 4. Weilbacher 5. Eigenbrodt 6. Stinka 7. Kress 8. Lindner 9. Stein 10. Pfaff 11. Meier

Di Stefano celebrates, the Frankfurt defence look on helplessly.

Flair And Failure
The Demise Of The Gifted In The 1970s

THE 1970s, an otherwise dour period for English football, was enlivened by a handful of rebellious and talented individuals. They never seemed to feature much in the England set-up – perhaps that was why England were so poor – because Ramsey and Revie were mistrustful of their maverick talents.

Frank Worthington (eight caps), the strutting Elvis dress-a-like, won most of his caps under Joe Mercer. The conceited but gifted Alan Hudson (two caps) played two matches under Revie (both wins) and was discarded. Stan Bowles (five caps), a god at Loftus Road, was barely an apostle for England, much like his predecessor Rodney Marsh (eight caps). The most capped of the 1970s entertainers was Tony Currie (17 caps), but his international career was spread over seven years. All these players, gifted as they were, invited criticism over their attitude. Hudson's career declined early, and Marsh always promised more than he delivered. By contrast, Bowles and Worthington, for all their flamboyance and apparent nonchalance, were fit and diligent players, with Worthington playing league football into his late 30s.

- Bowles scored 11 goals in QPR's UEFA Cup campaign in 1976–77, playing brilliantly throughout the tournament. Three years later he walked out on Brian Clough and Nottingham Forest, and became a forgotten man.
- Hudson's first cap was against World Cup holders West Germany in 1975. He orchestrated a 2-0 win, showing awesome confidence for a debutant. A 5-0 win over Cyprus followed, and then oblivion.
- Asked which opponent he most feared, Worthington's answer was: 'My wife.' His autobiography was entitled *One Hump Or Two*. Frank was an entertaining footballer with a host of clubs, and remains an idol at Huddersfield, Leicester and Bolton.

'I never seem to miss England quite enough. I might only be operating at about 30 per cent of my potential as a manager, but the lifestyle makes up for the rest.'

Rodney Marsh, comfortably ensconced at Tampa Bay Rowdies, reveals why he was such a perennial underachiever

Not Elvis with a beard, but the irrepressible Frank Worthington.

Flower Of Scotland
The Scotland Dream Team

THE KEEN-SIGHTED AMONG YOU will probably notice that we have not selected a goalkeeper. We make no apologies for this, reasoning that this team would have more chance of preventing goals with Alan Hansen as a sweeper cum rush-goalie than if we had selected any of the other clowns that have worn the Scottish number one jersey down the years. It also allows us to atone for the errors of various Scots managers and actually pick Hansen, who makes up a revolutionary back four with McLeish, Miller and Young. Apologies to John Greig, Martin Buchan, Richard Gough and Tom Boyd, who don't even make the 16.

The presence of the biting Bremner in midfield adds to the defensive cover, Baxter supplies enigmatic vision and Alex James combines ceaseless industry with neat footwork. On the wing Jimmy Johnstone provides flair out wide, so no place for Archie Gemmill who sits on the bench, ahead of other contenders Strachan and Souness.

The forward line picked itself. Skill, strength, imagination, pace and finishing – and that's just Kenny Dalglish! Craig Brown got a sympathy vote as manager, as he deserves the chance to work with some decent players. And because none of the truly great Scottish players have managed Scotland, at least not effectively.

- George Young, the Rangers defender, won over 50 caps immediately after the war, and was the mainstay of Rangers' famous 'Iron Curtain' defence.
- Unlucky omissions? Talented wingers like Lennox, Cooke, Morgan and Robertson. Alex Jackson (a 1920s striker), Ally McCoist and also Danny McGrain, a fine attacking fullback.
- Deserving omissions? Paul McStay and Maurice Malpas – 77 and 55 caps respectively but neither fulfilled his potential.
- No current players make this team. Never before have Scotland had such a dearth of international-class players. Only Darren Fletcher of the current squad is a regular pick for a top Premiership side.

Manager: Craig Brown (90s)

4-4-3

Alan Hansen (70s/80s) George Young (50s)
Alex McLeish (80s) Willie Miller (80s)

Jimmy Johnstone (60s/70s) Billy Bremner (C) (60s/70s)
Jim Baxter (60s) Alex James (20s/30s)

Kenny Dalglish (70s/80s) Hughie Gallacher (20s/30s)
Denis Law (60s/70s)

Subs: Dave Mackay (D/M) (60s/70s) Billy McNeill (D) (60s)
Archie Gemmill (M) (70s/80s) Billy Liddell (F) (00s) Andy Gray (F) (80s)

Football's Coming Home
England 4 Holland 1, 1996

ENGLAND'S LAST GAME in the opening phase of Euro 96 promised to be a tight affair, as the two best teams in the group met with Terry Venables' men needing only a draw to progress to the quarter-finals. The first half was tight, with Alan Shearer's penalty the only difference between the teams, but the second period left fans open-mouthed as, in a glorious 11 minutes, England tore one of Europe's finest sides to shreds. The newly discovered combination of Sheringham and Shearer ran riot.

Holland's night was summed up by Van der Sar's fumble from Anderton's shot that allowed Sheringham to score England's fourth, although, in truth, the Dutch keeper didn't know what had hit him. With Gascoigne at his impish best, McManaman raiding down the flanks and Anderton finding space galore, England were irresistible, for once performing with the uninhibited style that has characterised so many of their successful club sides. If the Gazza-inspired victory over Scotland in the previous game had revived the hosts' expectations, this result raised them to euphoric levels.

☞ At 4-0, England had inadvertently thrown Scotland a lifeline. Only Patrick Kluivert's late consolation for Holland prevented the Scots pipping the Dutch to a quarter-final place.

👆 This game formed part of Shearer's finest spell for England; he finished as top scorer in the tournament.

👆 As if this wasn't exciting enough, both England's quarter-final against Spain and semi-final versus Germany went to penalties.

👆 This result was sweet revenge for England, who had been eliminated by the Dutch during qualifying for the 1994 World Cup.

👇 Euro 96 was to end for England in familiar fashion, losing to Germany on penalties.

SCORERS   **England:** Shearer 2 (1 pen), Sheringham 2
             Holland: Kluivert
EVENT   Group Stage, European Championship Finals, Wembley, 18 June 1996

ENGLAND   (Man: Terry Venables)
             1. Seaman 2. Neville, G 3. Pearce 4. Ince (Platt) 5. Adams 6. Southgate
             7. Gascoigne 8. Shearer (Barmby) 9. Sheringham (Fowler) 10. Anderton
             11. McManaman
HOLLAND   (Man: Guus Hiddink)
             1. Van der Sar 2. Reiziger 3. Blind 4. Seedorf 5. De Boer (Kluivert)
             6. Bergkamp 7. Hoekstra (Cocu 72) 8. Winter 9. Witschge (De Kock)
             10. Bogarde 11. Cruyff

Goal scorer Sheringham (centre) receives the congratulations of (from left) Anderton, Gascoigne and McManaman.

Foulke, Bill

Sheffield United, Chelsea, Bradford City

AT 6 FT 3 IN AND WEIGHING over 22 stones, Bill Foulke attracted the inevitable nickname 'Fatty,' but few were brave enough to use it to his face. After shooting to prominence in the Edwardian era, Foulke was not averse to chucking his considerable girth around, paying little heed to the ethics of the Corinthian age with his on-field antics. In an act of pique that would have upstaged even today's prima donnas, he once famously walked off the pitch during a match claiming that his defence wasn't trying hard enough. Opposing strikers who incurred his wrath were sometimes picked up and thrown into the goal, but his temper and stature belied a surprising agility and skill. While it's fair to say he would never have got near a professional club in the modern era (dieticians and fitness trainers would have packed him off to the nearest park team), the game's history would be poorer for his absence. So too would the sepia-toned team photographs from his playing days, depicting Foulke freakishly dwarfing his team-mates.

- ☞ He cost Sheffield United £19 when signed from his local colliery team in Derbyshire.
- ✍ Despite his size, Foulke was a talented all-rounder, and also played county cricket for Derbyshire.
- ☞ Foulke was only 1 lb lighter than both Chelsea's fullbacks put together.
- ☞ Foulke's strength was legendary; he once delayed a game by accidentally breaking the crossbar.
- ☞ 1905. Played in Chelsea's first-ever league game.

VITAL STATISTICS

Place of Birth:	Sheffield, England	
Date of Birth:	12 April 1874	**Died:** 1916
Caps:	1 (England)	**Goals (International):** 0
Clubs:	Sheffield United, Chelsea, Bradford City	
Appearances:	Club (League): 347	
Goals:	Club (League): 0	
Trophies:	FAC 1899, 1902; LT 1898	

LEGEND RATING	
Achievement	4.0
Skill	6.0
Teamwork	7.0
Passion	8.0
Personality	9.0
TOTAL	**34.0**

No prizes for spotting our hero.

Gallacher, Hughie
Newcastle United, Chelsea, Scotland

FOR A MAN STANDING ONLY 5 ft 5 in tall, Hughie Gallacher was a mighty package; stocky, strong and quick, his low centre of gravity allowed him to evade centre halves as easily as a mouse escapes the attentions of a three-legged cat. He could also dribble, tackle and packed a shot that could leave a dent in a ship's hull. And more often than not, he delivered. All this made him not just a crowd favourite, but an idol. From his amateur days in his native Scotland he played for 10 clubs, never giving less than total commitment to them all. His glory days were at Newcastle, where he delivered the Magpies the league title in his first full season. Not surprisingly, his sale to Chelsea for a then-massive £10,000 caused mass-protests on Tyneside. Gallacher continued to shine at Stamford Bridge, immediately overshadowing the Blues' top scorer George Mills, but by the late 1930s his star began to dip below the horizon and he retired in 1939. He dabbled in sports journalism but, without the structure and camaraderie that football provided, his life lost its purpose and in 1957 he created his own tragic headline by taking his own life.

- In 174 games for Newcastle, his strike rate was 82 per cent.
- Gallacher's first game for Chelsea was away to his previous club, Newcastle. The record 68,386 crowd was all down to the wee man, with thousands more locked out.
- At Airdrie, he was a one-man team. They finished runners-up in four successive seasons and won the Scottish Cup in 1924. They have never threatened since.
- Gallacher put club before country, once ruling himself out of Scotland's team against England so he could play in a vital fixture for Newcastle.
- In 1928 Gallacher was one of the legendary 'Wembley Wizards' that humiliated England 5-1.

VITAL STATISTICS

Place of Birth:	Bellshill, Scotland		
Date of Birth:	2 February 1903	**Died:** 1957	
Caps:	19 (Scotland)	**Goals (International):** 22	
Clubs:	Queen of the South, Airdrieonians,		
	Newcastle United, Chelsea, Derby County,		
	Notts County, Grimsby Town, Gateshead		
Appearances:	Club (League): 541		
Goals:	Club (League): 387		
Trophies:	LT 1927		

Achievement	6.0
Skill	9.0
Teamwork	7.0
Passion	8.0
Personality	8.0
TOTAL	**38.0**

LEGEND RATING

Nice shot of Hughie, but you can't take your eyes off of those coppers: what a pair!

Game Of Two Halves

Tottenham Hotspur 3 Manchester United 5, 2001

IT IS OFTEN SAID that football is a game of two halves, and on a bright London afternoon in September 2001, Tottenham and Man Utd endorsed the accuracy of this cliché in a match that will be talked about until young men are old. Spurs, keen to capitalise on United's uncertain start to the season, began brightly and took a 2-0 lead with goals from Dean Richards and Les Ferdinand. United were a shambles in defence and it was no surprise when, two minutes before half-time, Spurs claimed a third goal through Christian Ziege.

The heat from Alex Ferguson's team talk must have curdled the milk in the half-time tea. His practical response was to switch Irwin with Silvestre for more pace on the left flank, with Solskjaer providing a third attacker at Butt's expense. The effect was dramatic. Once Cole's header had reduced the deficit in the first minute after the break, Spurs played as if hypnotised. Blanc scored from a corner, and then Van Nistelrooy's head restored parity. United sensed Tottenham's anxiety and went for the kill. Solskjaer and Scholes combined sweetly for Veron to put them ahead 4-3 then, with four minutes remaining, Beckham hammered an emphatic swerving shot past a shell-shocked Sullivan to complete the greatest turnaround in Premier League history.

- For £8 m new signing Dean Richards, it was a bitter-sweet debut. His move from Southampton produced a goal after eight minutes. If only it was a game of one half.
- For Teddy Sheringham, the game was a particular embarrassment. He had moved back to Spurs from United in the close season and was team captain for the day.
- One Spurs fan watched the second half with horror. He had bet £10,000 on a home win at half-time. The odds were 1-16.
- Hoddle was forthright: 'It looks like a Jekyll and Hyde performance from both sides.' Unfortunately it was his players who swallowed the wrong potion at half-time.

SCORERS	**Tottenham:** Richards, Ferdinand, Ziege
	Manchester United: Cole, Blanc, Van Nistelrooy, Veron, Beckham
EVENT	FA Premier League, White Hart Lane, 29 September 2001
TOTTENHAM	(Man: Glenn Hoddle)
	1. Sullivan 2. Richards 3. King 4. Perry 5. Taricco 6. Ziege 7. Freund
	8. Anderton 9. Poyet 10. Ferdinand 11. Sheringham
MAN UTD	(Man: Alex Ferguson)
	1. Barthez 2. Neville, G 3. Irwin (Silvestre) 4. Johnsen 5. Blanc 6. Beckham
	7. Butt (Solskjaer) 8. Veron 9. Cole 10. Van Nistelrooy 11. Scholes

Beckham celebrates becoming the game's eighth (and final) scorer.

Game Of Two Halves
AC Milan 3 Liverpool 3, 2005

THIS WAS A TRULY REMARKABLE GAME of football. It would have been extraordinary if Liverpool in their pomp had recovered from a 3-0 half-time deficit against a star-studded AC Milan, but for this Liverpool side it was nothing short of a miracle.

The first half went true to form; Milan's passing and movement, especially from the Brazilian magician, Kaka, ran Liverpool ragged. The English team had no attacking response as their link player, Kewell, bizarrely selected after a woeful season, was unfit and hopelessly out of touch.

A half-time change made all the difference. Didi Hamann replaced the unlucky Steve Finnan and immediately the space closed around Milan's creative players. Instead the space was filled by Steven Gerrard and Xavi Alonso. Alonso was neat and purposeful, never wasting possession and Gerrard was simply immense; lung-bursting runs and surges driving huge wedges into the Italians' defensive formation.

Three goals in 10 minutes, plus a couple of fine interventions from Jamie Carragher and a terrific double save from Shevchenko by the much-maligned Jerzy Dudek ensured extra-time and penalties. Liverpool's nerve held, and the glory years returned to Anfield – a fifth European title meant this time they got to keep the trophy.

☞ Liverpool were kidding nobody that they were the best team in Europe. They had finished fifth in the Premiership, let down by miserable away form and lazy performances from star performers in the 'lesser' fixtures.

✐ Dudek's reward for his heroics was to be relegated to third choice behind Jose Reina and young Scott Carson. Reina looks no more convincing than the occasionally flaky Polish number one.

✐ Shevchenko, European Footballer of the Year, missed the crucial penalty with a feeble effort. To be fair, Pirlo and Serginho had already missed, while only Riise had failed for Liverpool.

✐ Hamann's performance was crucial in securing Liverpool a foothold. He even scored his penalty in the shoot-out. After signing a new contract he again finds himself behind lesser players in the Anfield pecking order.

SCORERS	**AC Milan:** Maldini, Crespo (2)
	Liverpool: Gerrard, Smicer, Alonso
EVENT	Champions League final, Ataturk Stadium, Istanbul, 25 May 2005
AC MILAN	(Man: Carlo Ancelotti)
	1. Dida 2. Cafu 3. Stam 4. Nesta 5. Maldini 6. Gattuso (Rui Costa)
	7. Seedorf (Serginho) 8. Pirlo 9. Kaka 10. Shevchenko 11. Crespo (Tomasson)
LIVERPOOL	(Man: Rafa Benitez)
	1. Dudek 2. Finnan (Hamann) 3. Carragher 4. Hyypia 5. Traore 6. Luis Garcia
	7. Alonso 8. Gerrard 9. Riise 10. Kewell (Smicer) 11. Baros (Cissé)

Liverpool pose for pictures with the European Cup.

Gascoigne, Paul
Tottenham Hotspur, Lazio, Rangers, England

IT IS A SAD FACT that the most talented footballer of his generation has also been the most self-destructive. 'He wears a No 10 jersey. I thought it was his position but it turns out to be his IQ,' said George Best in 1992 – and Georgie knew a drunken waster when he saw one. Gascoigne's excesses ranged from endearingly playful to crass and unpalatable, but his football, when fit, was sublime.

Blessed with superb control, Gascoigne also had a deceptive change of pace, a terrific shot, and great vision. He could turn a game in an instant, against opponents of the highest quality. The stunning free kick he crashed past David Seaman in the 1991 FA Cup semi-final and the cheeky goal against Scotland in Euro 96 stand out as two of his finest moments.

Despite his poor fitness and dodgy temperament, clubs queued up to sign him. Newcastle, Spurs, Lazio and Rangers all saw glimpses of Gascoigne at his most inspired. Later, at Middlesbrough and Everton, the physio saw a lot more of Gazza than the fans.

- 1990. Sports Personality Of The Year after fine performances in the World Cup, including well-documented tears after earning the booking which would have kept him out of the final.
- The reckless tackle that saw him carried off with a broken leg in the 1991 Cup final delayed his move to Italy by a year and cost Spurs about £2 m in transfer fees.
- Once asked if he had a message for Norway prior to a World Cup qualifier, Gazza replied, 'F*** off!'
- Gazza's best mate and drinking buddy, Jimmy 'Five-Bellies' Gardner became a short-lived, cult micro-celebrity.
- Gascoigne's recent attempts to resurrect his career abroad and in England have made an unedifying spectacle.

VITAL STATISTICS

Place of Birth:	Gateshead, England	
Date of Birth:	27 May 1967	**Died:** n/a
Caps:	57 (England)	**Goals (International):** 10
Clubs:	Newcastle United, Tottenham, Lazio, Rangers,	
	Middlesbrough, Everton, Burnley, Boston United	
Appearances:	Club (All Matches): 413	
Goals:	Club (All Matches): 108	
Trophies:	FAC 1991; SLT 1996, 1997; SFAC 1996	

LEGEND RATING

Achievement	7.0
Skill	9.0
Teamwork	8.0
Passion	9.0
Personality	7.5
TOTAL	**40.5**

Gazza's Tears
England 1 West Germany 1, 1990

IT COULD HAVE ALL been so different. Their best World Cup showing since 1966 had seen England edge past an unlucky Belgium with a last-gasp winner in the second round then, thanks largely to Gary Lineker's prowess from the penalty spot, narrowly defeat African challengers Cameroon in the quarter-finals. But in the semi-final they met their nemesis, the Germans.

Germany began as favourites but were more than equalled by England in a tense encounter. The match is probably most famous for Gascoigne's tears, the young midfielder breaking down after receiving a booking that, had England won, would have kept him out of the final. On the hour, Germany got lucky when Brehme's free kick, seemingly innocuous, took an extravagant deflection off Paul Parker and looped agonisingly over Shilton into the net. It looked to be enough, but with 10 minutes left Lineker eluded his marker to place a low shot across Illgner for the equaliser.

Both teams hit the woodwork in extra-time but could not break the deadlock, so a penalty shoot-out ensued. The tension was unbearable. After six successful kicks, England faltered, Stuart Pearce firing into Illgner's legs. Waddle fired his kick high into the blackness of the Turin night. Their pride was intact, but England were out.

☞ Penalty shoot-out: England: Lineker, Beardsley, Platt, Pearce (missed), Waddle (missed). Germany: Brehme, Matthaus, Riedle, Thon.

☞ 'Football is a game played by 22 players. And then Germany win'. Lineker's quote reflected the Indian sign Germany appeared to hold over England.

☞ Gascoigne was reportedly so upset that he accidentally climbed aboard the German team coach after the game.

☞ The day before, the first semi-final had produced an identical result. Italy lost 4-3 on penalties to Argentina after a 1-1 draw.

☞ Lightning was to strike for a second time six years later. England lost a second semi-final on penalties to Germany in Euro 96.

SCORERS	**England:** Lineker
	Germany: Brehme
EVENT	World Cup semi-final, Turin, 4 July 1990
ENGLAND	(Man: Bobby Robson)
	1. Shilton 2. Parker 3. Walker 4. Butcher 5. Wright 6. Pearce 7. Gascoigne
	8. Platt 9. Lineker 10. Beardsley 11. Waddle
GERMANY	(Man: Franz Beckenbauer)
	1. Illgner 2. Brehme 3. Kohler 4. Augenthaler 5. Buchwald 6. Berthold
	7. Hassler 8. Thon 9. Matthaus 10. Klinsmann 11. Voller

Geordie Boys
The Newcastle United Dream Team

NEWCASTLE UNITED HAVE had a strange history. A dominant side in the first half of the twentieth century, especially in the FA Cup, they have spent the last 50 years under-achieving, occasionally gloriously, often embarrassingly.

This squad pays respect to all of the eras, successful or frustrating. Jimmy Lawrence, Colin Veitch and Peter McWilliam won three titles in the early part of the century, and Stan Seymore's wing-play helped Hughie Gallagher bring the title home in 1927. Mitchell and Milburn performed similar feats immeadiately after the war as the title went to St James's Park in 1948. Frank Brennan and Bobby Cowell were the solid defensive base for Milburn's heroic goalscoring feats. David Craig and Bobby Moncur were virtually ever-present as Newcastle struggled in the 1960s, and enjoyed better days when Malcolm Macdonald started tearing defences apart in the 1970s. Another decline followed, despite the the skills of Beardsley, Gasgoigne and Chris Waddle, and the side was in the midst of a disastrous descent until Kevin Keegan galvanised them in the early 1990s. Keegan's unique brand of all-out attacking football won the hearts of many neutrals as they, fruitlessly in the end, challenged the might of Manchester United. Best to draw a veil over recent years.

☞ Three Geordie omissions: Frank Hudspeth, holder of the most outfield appearances for the club (1910–29); Joe Harvey, player and manager across five decades; and Malcolm Macdonald's striking partner, John Tudor.

☝ Malcolm 'Supermac' Macdonald once scored all five goals in an England win over Cyprus. Sadly, he was never the same player after he left Newcastle for Arsenal.

☞ Seven Geordie boys feature in the 16. The Toon Army has always reserved its loudest applause for the local talent.

☞ Stan Seymour's connection with the club lasted from his debut in 1920 until his death in 1978. After his playing career was over he joined Newcastle as a vocal director with a strong, often dominant, voice in team affairs.

Manager: Kevin Keegan

4-2-4

Jimmy Lawrence (1900s)

David Craig (60s) Frank Brennan (40s/50s)
Bobby Moncur (C) (60s/70s) Colin Veitch (1900s)

Paul Gascoigne (80s) Peter Beardsley (90s)

Alan Shearer (90s/00s) Jackie Milburn (40s/50s)
Malcolm Macdonald (70s) Bobby Mitchell (40s/50s)

Subs: Shay Given (G) (00s) Bobby Cowell (D) (40s/50s)
Peter McWilliam (M) (1900s) Stan Seymour (W) (20s)
Hughie Gallacher (F) (20s)

Gerrard, Steven

England, Liverpool

LIVERPOOL HAVE HAD SOME key players in the past; Keegan and Dalglish were regarded as the hub of their respective teams, and Souness was hard to replace. Never before, though, have the fortunes of the club been so dependent of the form and fitness of one man. Steven Gerrard has consistently delivered high-level performances worthy of the famous red shirt, whilst many of his colleagues looked to their manager to excuse their lame performances. Gerrard's loyalty to the club is deserving of praise; witness the obvious torment he was going through when the on/off transfer to Chelsea was filling the back pages.

No wonder Chelsea coveted Gerrard; any club or country in the world would find room for a player with his vision, stamina and pace. Those long, coltish legs bely a good touch and the shuddering tackles are untypical of a player with Gerrard's passing ability and goalscoring flair.

It only remains for Gerrard to deliver the same level of performance for England. With Frank Lampard in irresistible form, Gerrard has had to accept the holding role in midfield. Someone should tell him it's not demotion – he has all the attributes required to play in that key position.

- Gerrard played in all three of Liverpool's Cup finals in 2001. He scored one of the goals in the epic against Alaves.
- Gerrard scored with a 30-yard skimmer in England's 5-1 win in Munich in 2001, part of a colossal performance that announced his presence as a potential world-class player.
- In his early years, Gerrard suffered the occasional bout of red mist, and earned a red card or two for appallingly ill-judged tackles. That element of his game seems to be under control.
- PFA Young Player of the Year, 2001.

VITAL STATISTICS

Place of Birth:	Merseyside, England	
Date of Birth:	30 May 1980	**Died:** n/a
Caps:	38 (England)	**Goals (International):** 6
Clubs:	Liverpool	
Appearances:	Club (League): 206	
Goals:	Club (League): 28	
Trophies:	LC 2001; FAC 2001; UEFAC 2001; EC 2005	

LEGEND RATING	
Achievement	6.5
Skill	7.5
Teamwork	9.0
Passion	9.0
Personality	7.0
TOTAL	**39.0**

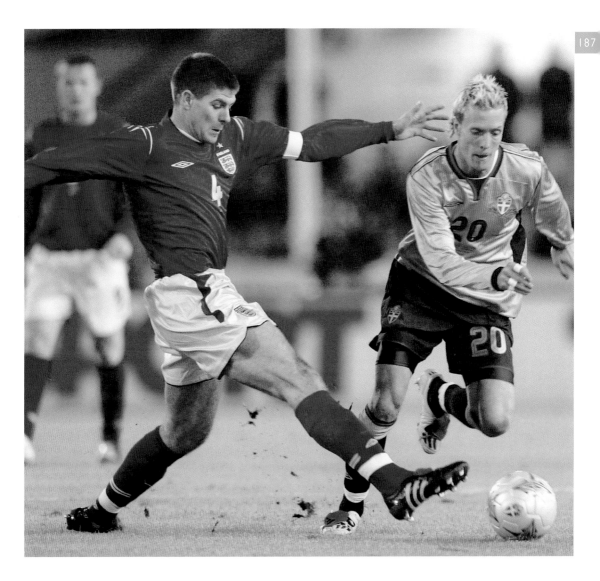

Giant Killers

Davids and their Goliaths

CRAWFORD'S QUOTE SAYS IT ALL. For small clubs, struggling on meagre attendances with only the occasional local derby to lift the gloom, a major Cup scalp is talked about for years. Down the ages, the recipe for a giant-killing has remained the same. Combine a mudheap of a pitch, a freezing winter's afternoon and a ramshackle stadium jammed to the corner flags, and add complacent opposition who would rather be playing golf. Then sit back and watch the temperature rise. Yeovil Town and their famous sloping pitch created one of the biggest upsets, removing Sunderland in 1949. But the Mackems are just one of Yeovil's 17 league scalps – a record for a team outside the top four divisions. Scoring a goal in a Cup upset is a guaranteed ticket to enduring celebrity, even if it's the only achievement of note in your entire career. Ronnie Radford and Ricky George are still D-list celebrities more than 30 years after their strikes for Hereford knocked out Newcastle. Roy Essandoh answered an Internet advertisement to sign for Wycombe, scored the only goal to knock out Leicester in the 2001 quarter-final and promptly vanished. For technical ability, a clash between the world's best wins hands down. But for sheer excitement, nothing tops a Cup giant-killing.

☞ In the days before automatic promotion, many clubs achieved league status on the back of their giant-killing exploits. Peterborough, Hereford and Wimbledon all won promotion to the professional ranks this way.

☞ Most giant killers win at home. Altrincham were the last non-leaguers to win at a top-flight ground, upsetting Birmingham 2-1 in 1986.

☞ FA Cup giant killers rarely progress to the later stages but the League Cup has produced two Third Division winners – QPR and Swindon.

☞ Colchester are responsible for two of the biggest shocks. Apart from the Leeds game, they removed First Division Huddersfield, as a non-league side in 1948.

☞ No English team has matched Calais; in 2000 the amateur side from the French fourth tier took out two Division One teams on their way to the final, where a narrow defeat by Nantes ended the dream.

☞ International shocks are rarer still. The USA's win over England in the 1950 World Cup was a shock of seismic proportions.

'This was the match of a lifetime and a day I will never forget.'

Colchester hero Ray Crawford after their epic FA Cup win over Leeds in 1971

Top non-league giant-killers Yeovil Town fail on this occasion at home to Arsenal.

Giggs At The Gallop
Arsenal 1 Manchester United 2, 1999

TOWARDS THE END OF AN exhausting season, the last thing these two teams needed was for their FA Cup semi-final to extend to a replay, especially one that went to extra-time. But it did. And then the fun really started. Beckham had opened the scoring after 18 minutes, and Bergkamp's deflected second-half shot had squared things.

After Keane was dismissed the Arsenal pressure was relentless, and Gary Neville brought down Parlour in injury time – penalty. Schmeichel, not for the first time, came to United's rescue, saving Bergkamp's tame effort. In extra-time Arsenal continued to turn the screw against 10-man United, but it was the Old Trafford men who stole victory. Deep into injury time Ryan Giggs, who had been introduced as a sub just past the hour, collected the ball in his own half and sprinted forward. He evaded Vieira, swerved past Dixon, deceived Keown, brushed off another challenge from Dixon and thrashed the ball past the suddenly exposed Seaman. Giggs had the courage to take the game into his own hands and the skill to skip through the country's meanest defence. Pure and undiluted genius.

☞ This was one of two crucial matches in United's drive for the Treble; the other being the European Cup final. Both were games of memorable late drama and emotion.

☞ Jesper Blomqvist was bought as cover for the injury-prone Giggs. Ironically, the Welshman's fitness has since improved while Blomqvist has had to resurrect his career at Everton after 18 months out with a knee injury.

☞ It was a game of two remarkable goals. For the opener David Beckham drove a 30-yard dipper over David Seaman after a perfect tee-up from Teddy Sheringham.

☟ The FA Cup final against Newcastle was an anti-climax. Newcastle froze, and United won at a canter.

SCORERS	**Arsenal:** Bergkamp
	Manchester United: Beckham, Giggs
EVENT	FA Cup semi-final replay, Villa Park, 14 April 1999
ARSENAL	(Man: Arsène Wenger)
	1. Seaman 2. Dixon 3. Winterburn 4. Parlour 5. Adams 6. Keown
	7. Ljungberg 8. Bergkamp 9. Anelka 10. Vieira 11. Petit
MAN UTD	(Man: Alex Ferguson)
	1. Schmeichel 2. Neville, G 3. Neville, P 4. Butt 5. Johnsen 6. Stam
	7. Beckham 8. Keane 9. Solskjaer 10. Sheringham 11. Blomqvist

Giggs caps an incredible run by shooting the winner past Seaman.

Giggs, Ryan
Manchester United, Wales

THE PARALLEL GROWTH of Ryan Giggs and Manchester United since 1991 is no coincidence. Emerging as a winger of raw pace and superb control, he became both key match-winner and entertainer within a season. Injuries may have reduced the directness over the years, but Giggs developed a fine sense of team-play and has remained a key player for United; only Keane and Cantona can claim to have exerted more influence over the country's dominant team.

Giggs' finest moments have all come at club level; eight titles and a European Cup represent one of the biggest hauls of an English club career. The quartet of Beckham, Keane, Scholes and Giggs may be the finest midfield to play club football in this country. Having settled a contract wrangle, it seems Giggs may well play out his time as an avuncular presence in a new generation at Old Trafford.

His international record is spotty; his unavailabilty for his country is legend, a player his age would normally have 80 or so caps, not 55. Failure to qualify for Euro 2004 surely saw the end to Giggs' chances of gracing a major international tournament.

Giggs, despite pop-star looks and an occasional celebrity girlfriend, has provided no fuel for the fires of the tabloid press. A dignified and respectful man, he seems a breed apart from the brash, crowing youngsters of the twenty-first century.

- Giggs made his professional and full international debut at 17; he had played for England schoolboys but adopted his mother's Welsh homeland; what would England have given for a decade of Giggs filling their problematic left-midfield slot?
- In 1999, his best goal and one of the finest ever, a 50-yard slalom through England's meanest club defence wins United the FA Cup semi-final v Arsenal.
- A great disciplinary copybook was blotted when Giggs was sent off for the first time in his career, as Welsh captain.

VITAL STATISTICS

Place of Birth:	Cardiff, Wales			
Date of Birth:	29 November 1973	**Died:** n/a	Achievement	9.0
Caps:	55 (Wales)	**Goals (International):** 11	Skill	9.0
Clubs:	Manchester United		Teamwork	8.5
Appearances:	Club (League): 451		Passion	8.5
Goals:	Club (League): 92		Personality	8.0
Trophies:	LC 1992; LT 1993, 1994, 1996, 1997, 1999, 2000, 2001, 2003; FAC 1994, 1996, 1999, 2004; EC 1999		**TOTAL 43.0**	

LEGEND RATING

Giles, Michael John, 'Johnny'
Leeds United, Republic Of Ireland

DON REVIE PAID Manchester United £35,000 for the young Irishman Johnny Giles in 1963. Revie had obviously seen something Sir Matt Busby had missed, and quickly converted Giles from outside right to central midfield where, within a few years, he developed into the complete midfielder. A superbly accurate passer with great vision allied to a tough streak – the Leeds side of that era took no prisoners – he was rarely injured and became a key member of a great midfield: Bremner's aggression, Lorimer's explosive shooting, Gray's dribbling, and, at the core, Giles, prompting and coaxing those around him.

In 1973 Giles was introduced to management when he was appointed player-manager of the Republic of Ireland. He introduced a young Liam Brady and David O'Leary to international football, but his squad lacked the depth that Jack Charlton was to enjoy in the following decade. He remained in the post until 1980, by which time he'd had enough of management, having earlier endured a tough couple of years at West Bromwich Albion.

☞ He made his debut for the Republic at 18 years old, scoring after 16 minutes against Sweden.
☞ Giles is Nobby Stiles' brother-in-law.
👍 He missed one penalty in his career, and scored 78.
☞ Crucially, Giles missed the European Cup Winners' Cup final in 1973 when Leeds were robbed by AC Milan.
☞ Giles on management: 'The government should issue a health warning to managers: the only certain thing is the sack.'

VITAL STATISTICS

Place of Birth: Dublin, Ireland
Date of Birth: 1940 **Died:** n/a
Caps: 59 (R. Ireland) **Goals (International):** 5
Clubs: Manchester United, Leeds United, West Bromwich Albion, Shamrock Rovers, Vancouver Whitecaps
Appearances: Club (League): 702
Goals: Club (League): 128
Trophies: LT 1969, 1974; FAC 1972; LC 1968; UEFAC 1968, 1971

Achievement	7.0
Skill	8.0
Teamwork	9.0
Passion	7.0
Personality	6.0
TOTAL	**37.0**

LEGEND RATING

Ginola, David

Brest, PSG, Newcastle United, Tottenham, France

29 OCTOBER 1996. Newcastle lead Ferencvaros 2-0 before a packed St James's Park in a third round UEFA Cup tie. A Newcastle corner is headed clear, but gets no further than David Ginola, lurking on the edge of the penalty area. Ginola cushions the ball on his right thigh. As a defender rushes to make a block, Ginola casually flicks the ball over his opponent's head with his right instep. With a shift of balance, and a tensing of those oh-so-perfect shoulders, he volleys the dropping ball with textbook technique. The left-foot strike finds the top corner of the net with accuracy and power. The Toon erupt.

22 December 1999. Tottenham visit Newcastle for an FA Cup third round replay after a 1-1 draw at White Hart Lane. Ginola, now a Toon hate figure but a media darling, is greeted with catcalls and abuse at every touch. Spurs are being trounced, and as half-time approaches Ginola is to be found sitting on his backside on the halfway line complaining to Graham Poll. Poll suggests, in pantomime language that maybe Ginola would like to leave the field on a stretcher to have his 'wounds' attended to. Exit a limping, gesticulating Ginola. The Toon erupt.

✍ Ginola was named PFA Footballer of the Year in 1999.

☞ Hopefully, the above text illustrates why successive French managers never deemed Ginola worth the risk of more than 17 caps – a miserable return for one so blessed.

✍ John Gregory at Aston Villa believed he was the man to handle such maverick talents as Ginola, Stan Collymore and Benito Carbone. As Mark Twain observed, (though not of Gregory!) 'He had only one vanity; he thought he could give advice better than any other person.' Like Collymore, and later, Carbone, Ginola duly flounced out of Villa Park.

☞ For such an articulate and interesting man, Ginola has maintained a low profile since his retirement. Perhaps the mockery accorded him after his foppish shampoo commercials sank home.

VITAL STATISTICS

Place of Birth:	Gasson, France		
Date of Birth:	25 January 1967	**Died:** n/a	
Caps:	17 (France)	**Goals (International):** 3	Achievement 5.0
Clubs:	Toulon, Racing Club Paris, Brest, Paris St		Skill 9.5
	Germain, Newcastle United, Tottenham Hotspur,		Teamwork 6.0
	Aston Villa, Everton		Passion 7.5
Appearances:	Club (League): 503		Personality 8.0
Goals:	Club (League): 81		
Trophies:	FLT 1994		**TOTAL 36.0**

LEGEND RATING

Glory Game

The Tottenham Hotspur Dream Team

IT REALLY WOULDN'T BE SPURS if they didn't have mesmerising attacking players and a mundane defence would it? Starting right at the back they do have an all-time great in Jennings, but fullbacks Stephen Carr (promising) and 'Nice One' Cyril Knowles (functional) might find George Best and Ryan Giggs a handful. Sol Campbell might have been an option at the back but for *that* transfer; loyalist Gary Mabbutt was a fine player, despite the handicap of diabetes. Dave Mackay is a bit of a cheat – centre half was his position at Derby after he left Spurs, but he proved he could hack it at the back.

Ossie Ardiles doing the fetching and carrying for Glenda and Danny Blanchflower: makes the mouth water. Gazza and Alan Mullery, two outstanding players, are relegated to the bench as Cliff Jones, the Welsh wizard, provides the neccessary width.

The choice of forwards was tricky. Bobby Smith, Alan Gilzean, Martin Chivers, Steve Archibald and Herr Klinsmann not even making the bench (Klinsmann on the grounds of the brevity of his tenure). Sherringham gets the nod ahead of Lineker because he would provide a better foil for the peerless Jimmy Greaves.

☞ Cyril Knowles and Joe Kinnear were Spurs' full-backs for most of the 1970s.

👍 No one from the 1901 Cup winning side makes the team – Spurs were a non-league club at the time! This victory started the 'year ends in one' tradition. Trophies followed in 1921, 1951, 1961, 1971, 1981 and 1991. In 2001 Alan Sugar relinquished control of the club, which was a triumph of sorts.

☞ Tottenham's first meeting with (Royal) Arsenal was abandoned 15 minutes from the end 'owing to darkness'.

👍 Steve Perryman made the most appearances for Tottenham, but was never more than a competent honest pro.

👌 Carr missed most of the 2000–01 season through injury, but was hoping to be back in time for the World Cup. A fine attacking fullback, he would walk into the current England side.

Manager: Bill Nicholson

4-4-2

Pat Jennings (60s/70s)

Stephen Carr (90s) Gary Mabbutt (80s/90s)
Dave Mackay (C) (60s) Cyril Knowles (60s)

Danny Blanchflower (50s/60s) Ossie Ardiles (80s)
Glenn Hoddle (80s) Cliff Jones (60s)

Jimmy Greaves (60s) Teddy Sheringham (90s)

Subs: Ted Ditchburn (G) (40s/50s) Alan Mullery (M) (60s)
John White (M) (60s) Paul Gascoigne (M) (90s) Gary Lineker (F) (90s)

Spurs' mascot shows a balance worthy of Greaves himself.

Goal!!!
Beauty and Ballet

EVERY SEASON there are special goals; curled free kicks, overhead kicks, almighty 30-yarders, ribbons of passing finished with a tap-in. But every now and then one stands out from the crowd – a goal tinged with genius. Le Tissier, Beckham, Bergkamp – all seem incapable of scoring boring goals, probably because they are the sort of players who have innate confidence in their ability to do outrageous things.

But, occasionally, players with more parochial gifts produce crackers too. Blackpool's Micky Walsh was a nondescript Division Two player who earned his place in history with a blistering strike, while Justin Fashanu secured himself a £1 m move to Nottingham Forest on the basis of a stunning turn and volley for Norwich against Liverpool in the 1980s. Perhaps the most memorable of all was the 'donkey kick' goal scored by Coventry's Ernie Hunt against Everton in the 1970s; Hunt cracked a dipping volley over the wall and into the net after his team-mate, Willie Carr, had flicked the ball up to him with his heels. Great concept, even better execution.

👍 The best goal involving Beckham was scored by Paul Scholes; an edge-of-the-box volley direct from a pinpoint Beckham corner.

👍 Dennis Bergkamp once filled the top three positions in the *MOTD* Goal of the Month competition. A special effort against Leicester eventually won goal of the season, but a sand wedge against Bayern Leverkusen in 2002 wasn't far behind.

👍 Trevor Sinclair is known for spectacular acrobatics; an overhead kick playing for QPR flew into the net from all of 25 yards. He's done it consistently enough since to prove it was no fluke.

☞ Personal favourite? Frank Worthington teeing the ball up, flicking it over his head between two defenders and volleying it in for Bolton against Ipswich in 1978.

'I went up to him afterwards, shook his hand and called him a b*****d.'

Neil Sullivan, then Wimbledon goalkeeper, after David Beckham beat him from the half-way line

Zidane's winning wonder goal against Bayer Leverkusen in the 2002 Champions League final.

Gough, Richard

Rangers, Scotland

IN THE MID-1980s, Rangers were at an all-time low. Years of watching Celtic rattle up trophies throughout the 1960s and 1970s, then to see Aberdeen supplant them in the 1980s was hard to bear for the blue half of Glasgow. It was Graeme Souness's arrival that started a run of nine consecutive league championships, the equal of Celtic's coveted record. His most important signing was one of Scotland's most cultured central defenders and a natural captain. Dundee United had already recognised his worth by refusing to sell him to an SPL rival, but following a year's sabbatical with Spurs, Rangers got their man.

Initially a right back at Ibrox, his conversion continued a Scottish central defensive pedigree that saw Gough elevated to the status of bygone defensive pillars such as Alan Hansen, Alex McLeish and Willie Miller. His departure from Glasgow at 35 appeared to be the end, but his fitness and appetite for the game made him good enough to play in the English Premier League at 38 with Everton, before he finally retired in 2001.

- ✌ The only Rangers player to win nine consecutive league winner's medals in the great teams of the 1980s and early 1990s.
- 🖑 1987. Scored the winning goal in the 1987 Cup final. Unluckily for Gough, it was a deflection at the wrong end.
- ☞ Gough attended a trial for Rangers aged 18, but was turned away. Seven years later it cost them £1.1 m to buy him back and rectify their error.
- ☞ Born in Stockholm to a Swedish mother and an English father (who played for England), Gough was brought up in South Africa. Nonetheless, he remains a true Scottish legend.
- ☞ 1997. Emotional end-of-season 'farewell' to Ibrox after announcing a move to the US, only to return in October.

VITAL STATISTICS

Place of Birth: Stockholm, Sweden

Date of Birth: 5 April 1962   **Died:** n/a

Caps: 61 (Scotland)   **Goals (International):** 6

Clubs: Dundee United, Tottenham, Rangers, Kansas City Wizz, San Jose Clash, Nottingham Forest, Everton

Appearances: Club (League): 590

Goals: Club (League): 48

Trophies: SLT 1983, 1989, 1990, 1991, 1992, 1993, 1994, 1995, 1996, 1997; SFAC 1992, 1993, 1996

LEGEND RATING	
Achievement	8.0
Skill	7.0
Teamwork	8.0
Passion	9.0
Personality	6.0
TOTAL	**38.0**

Graham, George

Arsenal, Scotland

SCOTTISH MIDFIELD PLAYMAKER, George Graham was the pivot of the 1971 Arsenal double-winning side. His performances at his next club, Manchester United, were generally considered to be a disappointment and Graham's playing career was judged past its zenith.

A four-year spell as manager of Millwall led to his appointment as manager of his old club, Arsenal, in 1986. Nine years of consistent success followed, as Graham built the formidable outfit that became known as 'boring, boring Arsenal'. A solid defence, hard-working midfield and quick strikers became legend for nicking games 1-0 after their opponents had foundered on their obduracy. Unfortunately sly victories weren't the only thing George pocketed, and he resigned as Arsenal manager in disgrace when he was found guilty of taking cash as a sweetener in two transfer deals. Banned for 12 months, Graham returned as manager of Leeds, and rapidly began rebuilding the Yorkshire club in his own image. Despite relative success he was tempted back to London by the vacant manager's job at Spurs. Graham and Tottenham never sat easily and he was sacked in 2001 to make way for Glenn Hoddle's return. Graham remains a cogent and cool analyst of the game, making frequent appearances as a TV pundit.

☞ Graham claimed the equaliser in the 1971 FA Cup final, but TV replays showed his heel did not make contact with the ball after team-mate Eddie Kelly's shot, and was denied credit for the goal.

☞ Graham's uncompromising discipline earned him the nicknames 'Ayatollah' and 'Gadaffi'. Internal discipline wasn't always mirrored on the pitch; Graham's tenure saw the start of the trend for on-field naughtiness that has dogged Arsenal in recent years.

☞ Arsenal became the first team to win both domestic cups in 1993, bizarrely playing the same team, Sheffield Wednesday, in both finals.

VITAL STATISTICS

Place of Birth:	Bargeddie, Fife
Date of Birth:	30 November 1944 **Died:** n/a
Caps:	12 (Scotland) **Goals (International):** 3
Clubs:	As Player: Aston Villa, Chelsea, Arsenal, Man United, Portsmouth, Crystal Palace; As Manager: Millwall, Arsenal, Leeds United, Tottenham Hotspur
Trophies:	LT 1989, 1991; FAC 1993; LC 1987, 1993, 1999; CWC 1994

Achievement	9
Tactical Awareness	9
Motivation	7
Team Selection/Transfers	7
Personality	6
TOTAL	**38**

LEGEND RATING

Graham's blazer was trademark but Spurs' cockerel motif never suited him.

Gray, Andy

Wolverhampton Wanderers, Aston Villa, Everton, Scotland

MEMORIES OF ANDY GRAY as a player conjure up images of a fearless battering ram throwing himself into the fray, diving in with his head amongst flailing feet. It was no wonder Gray was so often injured; few men have played the game with such scant regard for their own safety. Gray was not just a big bloke who put himself around, though. He was a prodigious header of the ball and, while not dazzling with the ball at his feet, his touch was still the equal of most of his contemporaries.

All his clubs enjoyed successful periods with him as their spearhead in attack, but it was his spell at Everton that brought him the rewards he deserved. Toffees boss Howard Kendall took a gamble purchasing Gray (at the time many regarded him to be past his best, and with dodgy knees to boot) but his partnership with his young countryman and acolyte, Graeme Sharp, provided the goals that brought the title back to Goodison. The purchase of Gary Lineker two years later saw Gray exit to Aston Villa, and retirement soon followed. Through the last decade Gray has worked as a pundit for Sky television, where his enthusiasm and entertaining use of high-tech graphics have done much to help the Rupert Murdoch-funded operation overcome initial antagonism towards their franchise.

- Gray and Sharp scored the goals that won the 1984 FA Cup final.
- He scored the winner for Wolves in the 1980 League Cup final.
- Voted PFA Player of the Year and Young Player of the Year, 1977.
- Wolves paid Villa a then British record fee of £1,469,000 for Gray in 1979.
- Gray was a surprising omission from Ally MacLeod's 1978 World Cup squad. Oh, how they missed him.

VITAL STATISTICS

Place of Birth:	Glasgow, Scotland		
Date of Birth:	30 November 1955	**Died:** n/a	
Caps:	20 (Scotland)	**Goals (International):** 6	
Clubs:	Dundee United, Aston Villa, Wolves, Everton,		
	West Bromwich Albion, Rangers, Cheltenham Town		
Appearances:	Club (All Matches): 593		
Goals:	Club (All Matches): 202		
Trophies:	LC 1980; FAC 1984; LT 1985; CWC 1985; SLT 1989		

Achievement	6.0
Skill	6.0
Teamwork	8.0
Passion	10.0
Personality	8.0
TOTAL	**38.0**

LEGEND RATING

Gray shows off the European Cup Winners' Cup for Everton in 1985.

Great Gunners

The Arsenal Dream Team

FOR ALL ARSENAL'S modern flair and expensive foreign talent, the bedrock of this team is steeped in history. Herbert Chapman's team was Arsenal's first great one, sweeping all before them in the 1930s. It's from this side that we have selected both fullbacks, Eddie Hapgood and George Male (Dixon and Winterburn have racked up the appearances but they don't possess the same pedigree).

In central defence, the newer guard holds sway. Both Adams and Campbell possess the talent and leadership, and have the happy knack of rising to the big occasion, and both were noticeably missed when injured.

The midfield combination is both a League of Nations and a Rock of Ages. Pires gives width, penetration and pace, as well as a daft beard. Vieira and Alex James provide a fascinating blend of steel and silk, and Cliff Bastin on the wing would both provide goals and score them himself. Not that the front two would be liable to dry up. Drake's direct approach and Henry's subtle skills would always boost the goal difference – the pair provide a dream combination of aerial power and blinding pace.

☞ Hardest man to leave out? Liam Brady. He with the sweetest left foot Highbury's ever seen would play a part in any squad rotation.

☞ The sight of Pat Jennings in goal will continue to stick in the throat of any Spurs fan. Blame Keith Burkinshaw for selling him.

✍ Herbert Chapman pips Arsène Wenger as manager. His Arsenal team won three successive titles, and he set new standards in tactics, professionalism and commercial awareness.

✍ No places for former record club goalscorer Ian Wright, record England cap winner Kenny Sansom or the over-rated Feddie Ljungberg.

Manager: Herbert Chapman
4-4-2

Pat Jennings (70s/80s)

George Male (30s) Tony Adams (80s/90s) Sol Campbell (00s)
Eddie Hapgood (C) (30s)

Robert Pires (00s) Patrick Vieira (90s) Alex James (30s)
Cliff Bastin (30s)

Ted Drake (30s) Thierry Henry (90s/00s)

Subs: Bob Wilson (G) (60s/70s) David O'Leary (D) (70s/80s)
Liam Brady (M) (70s) Joe Mercer (M) (40s/50s) Dennis Bergkamp (F) (90s)

Greaves, Jimmy
Tottenham Hotspur, England

ONE OF THE GREAT GOAL SCORERS, Greaves scored at a similar rate to strikers of the 1930s in the more defensive 1960s and 1970s. Although small for a forward, at only 5 ft 8 in and 10 stones wet through, he was fast and had quicksilver feet.

The sight of Greaves dancing around defenders and smacking in yet another hat-trick was one of the treats of the time. Like many natural-born goal scorers he could be selfish, when he received possession he rarely had more than one thought on his mind, and if his team were under pressure he had a tendency to go missing. Greaves maintained his scoring record in internationals, but never really fired in World Cup Finals (only one goal in seven appearances). His greatest disappointment was missing the 1966 World Cup final; he started the tournament but got injured and was unable to win back his place from Geoff Hurst.

Greaves started drinking heavily at the end of his career, but recovered well and later formed a successful TV double-act with Ian St John on ITV's *The Saint & Greavsie Show*. Greaves made an entertainingly informal pundit (St John was wooden and unfunny).

- Greaves scored on his debut for every club (including a hat-trick on his Spurs debut), and for England.
- He still holds the Spurs record for league goals in a season, 37 in 1963.
- He became the first player to score 100 goals before he was 21.
- Bill Nicholson, unwilling to saddle Greaves with the label of the first £100,000 player, paid Milan £99,999 for his services.
- Greaves once bemoaned, in his role as a pundit, the absence in the modern game of 'the old hey-diddle-diddle-down-the-middle and stick it in the net'.

VITAL STATISTICS

Place of Birth:	London, England
Date of Birth:	20 February 1940 **Died:** n/a
Caps:	57 (England) **Goals (International):** 44
Clubs:	Chelsea, AC Milan, Tottenham, West Ham
Appearances:	Club (All Matches): 528
Goals:	Club (All Matches): 366
Trophies:	FAC 1962, 1967; CWC 1963

LEGEND RATING	
Achievement	6.0
Skill	10.0
Teamwork	6.0
Passion	8.0
Personality	8.0
TOTAL	**38.0**

Greenwood, Ron
West Ham United, England

AS THE MANAGER who restored pride to the England team, Ron Greenwood's stock remains high with a press and public not noted for their kid-glove treatment of the national boss. A genial exterior belied a deep knowledge of the game, while a steely interior, honed during his centre-half playing days, was hardly ever revealed in public.

Greenwood was drifting out of the game as boss of non-league Eastbourne before West Ham resurrected his career, but his 13-year tenure continued the stylish traditions of the Upton Park 'academy'. He had already served England by nurturing the likes of Hurst and Peters for the 1966 World Cup squad, before his appointment as national manager restored respectability to a position tarnished by the sordid exit of Don Revie. Despite notable slip-ups, England qualified for the 1982 World Cup Finals (the first they had reached for 20 years) but, hampered by the loss of Kevin Keegan and Trevor Brooking, they failed to make the knockout stages despite exiting the tournament with an unbeaten record.

- 1955. Greenwood won a Championship medal with Chelsea.
- 1964 & 1965. Managed West Ham to successive Wembley victories in the FA Cup and the European Cup Winners' Cup.
- 1971. Greenwood dropped Bobby Moore at West Ham after he broke a club curfew.
- 1977. Picked seven Liverpool players for England in an early experiment, the most from one club since before the war.
- 1977. Had to overcome press hostility on his appointment as England manager (Brian Clough was the 'people's' choice).

VITAL STATISTICS

Place of Birth:	Burnley, England	
Date of Birth:	11 November 1921	**Died:** n/a
Caps:	0	**Goals (International):** 0
Clubs:	As Player: Bradford Park Avenue, Brentford, Chelsea, Fulham; As Manager: West Ham, England national side	
Trophies:	FAC 1964; CWC 1965	

Achievement	6
Tactical Awareness	9
Motivation	8
Team Selection/Transfers	7
Personality	7
TOTAL	**37**

LEGEND RATING

Greig, John
Rangers, Scotland

ONE OF AN ELITE BAND to have won the league with the same club as both player and manager, no individual contributed more to the success of the post-war Rangers team than John Greig. An inspiration at centre half after moving from right half early in his career, he became, in 1964, only the second Scot to captain a treble-winning side, but Celtic's later dominance frustrated his title ambitions for a further 11 years. His consolation was becoming the only Rangers captain to lift a European trophy, the Cup Winners' Cup in 1972.

Greig's move, during a whirlwind three weeks, from captain to the manager's desk in 1978 seemed a natural one, but in five seasons he failed to bring the title to Ibrox. It was an indication of his reputation among the fans that he kept his job for so long; an outsider with a similar record would have been dismissed without hesitation. Greig's commitment, strength and leadership, plus his telepathic understanding with playmaker Jim Baxter, served Scotland well too, never more so than in the famous 3-2 defeat of England at Wembley in 1967.

☞ His 44th and final cap against Denmark in 1976 came five years after his previous Scottish appearance.

👍 He was twice Scottish player of the year and received an MBE in 1997.

👍 He played a record 496 league games for Rangers, and scored a remarkable 120 goals from defence and right half.

☞ Greig endeared himself to the community by tirelessly leading his team to funerals and services after the Ibrox disaster in 1971.

👍 In 1999 Greig was voted 'Greatest Ever Ranger' in a fans' poll. Greig actually supported Hearts as a boy.

VITAL STATISTICS

Place of Birth: Edinburgh, Scotland
Date of Birth: 11 September 1942 **Died:** n/a
Caps: 44 (Scotland) **Goals (International):** 3
Clubs: Rangers
Appearances: Club (All Matches): 755
Goals: Club (All Matches): 120
Trophies: SLT 1963, 1964, 1975, 1976, (1978);
SFAC 1963, 1964, 1966, 1973, 1976, (1978),
(1979), (1981); CWC 1972

LEGEND RATING	
Achievement	7.0
Skill	7.0
Teamwork	8.0
Passion	9.0
Personality	6.0
TOTAL	**37.0**

Bet you're glad we used this one, Greigy!

Gullit, Ruud
Feyenoord, PSV, AC Milan, Holland

ONE OF THE GREAT PLAYERS of the modern generation, Ruud Gullit had the lot – heading, shooting, passing, and tackling all came so easily to him that he was like four players rolled into one. After starting his career as a sweeper at Feyenoord, Gullit moved on to PSV where he was quickly converted to striker, a position he also later occupied at AC Milan alongside his Dutch colleague Marco van Basten.

For his country though, Gullit turned out mostly in midfield and it was from here that he skippered the Dutch to their European Championship victory in 1988. Glenn Hoddle brought him to Chelsea in 1994, and after one season he succeeded the former Spurs midfielder as player-manager. Although he introduced some exciting overseas players to the Premiership and brought Cup success, the league championship evaded him and, after Ken Bates accused him of being a greedy playboy, he was eventually sacked in 1998. A dire spell as manager of Newcastle, where Gullit failed to adjust to the Geordie culture, left an impression that here was a man not prepared for compromise – it was his way or, er, his way. Sadly, his way didn't work.

☞ The £5.5 m Milan paid PSV for Gullit was a world record at the time.

✍ Gullit was the first overseas coach in England to win a domestic trophy (the FA Cup with Chelsea in 1997).

☞ The distinctive dreadlocks worn as a player won admirers of both sexes, and were copied by many of his younger contemporaries.

✌ He was voted European Player of the Year in 1987.

✍ He scored in Holland's win over Russia in the 1988 European Championship final, and repeated the feat for Milan in their 4-0 win over Steaua Bucharest in the European Cup final a year later.

VITAL STATISTICS

Place of Birth:	Amsterdam, Holland	
Date of Birth:	1 September 1962	**Died:** n/a
Caps:	66 (Holland)	**Goals (International):** 17
Clubs:	Haarlem, Feyenoord, PSV Eindhoven, AC Milan,	
	Sampdoria, Chelsea	
Appearances:	Club (League): 465	
Goals:	Club (League): 175	
Trophies:	EuroC 1998; DLT 1984, 1986, 1987; SA 1988,	
	1992, 1993; EC 1989, 1990; FAC (1997)	

LEGEND RATING	
Achievement	9.0
Skill	9.0
Teamwork	9.0
Passion	7.0
Personality	9.0
TOTAL	**43.0**

Hampden Park

Glasgow, Scotland

HAMPDEN PARK has been the home of the Scottish international side since 1903. Its unique bowl has been the scene of some of football's most epic encounters.

In 1960 what is regarded by many as the best match of all time took place as Real Madrid beat Eintracht Frankfurt 7-3 in front of 134,000 fans in the European Cup final. Alfredo di Stefano became the toast of Glasgow, his masterly display included a superb hat-trick.

Its many confrontations between England and Scotland include the 1937 encounter which attracted a record attendance of 149,415.

Hampden Park was rebuilt in 1998 at a cost of £65 m. The renovation of the crumbling terraces was long overdue, but the all-seater capacity of 52,000 has robbed the stadium of its imposing and intimidating qualities.

While the ground has hosted Scotland's biggest international matches in front of vast attendances, it has remained the home ground of amateur minnows Queens Park. Scotland's original club was once regarded as the best team in the world but now play their home games in front of a few hundred spectators.

☞ The stadium was designed by Archibald Leitch and remained the largest ground in the world until 1950, when Brazil's Maracana was built.

☞ The ground was so packed during big games that the terraces became known as the Nodding Gallery. Fans were unable to celebrate by any movement more animated than moving their heads, although the Hampden roar remained undiminished.

👍 Biggest club game: the 1970 European Cup semi-final epic between Celtic and Leeds. Celtic edged through the 'battle of Britain' with the only goal of the tie.

👍 Hampden Park hosted its third European Cup final in 2002. Apart from the monumental 1960 affair, the other was in 1976.

VITAL STATISTICS

Local Club:	Queens Park
Date Built:	1903
Current Capacity:	52,000
Max. Capacity:	150,000

The modern Hampden hosts another Old Firm Cup final, May 2002.

Hansen, Alan

Liverpool, Scotland

ONE OF THE MOST elegant defenders in the game's history. Hansen played over 600 matches for Liverpool without appearing to break sweat, a trait that prompted colleague Phil Neal, at the end of every game, to ask, jokingly: 'Did Hansen get dirty today?' His reading of the game was so good that he never appeared stretched but, when required, his tackling and heading were sound, and his distribution was more reminiscent of a foreign sweeper than a British stopper. Bought for £100,000 from Partick Thistle, Hansen was eased into the Liverpool side as a replacement for Emlyn Hughes. His partnerships over 13 seasons at Anfield, with Phil Thompson, Mark Lawrenson and Gary Gillespie coincided with the most successful period in the club's history.

Why successive Scottish managers chose to award Hansen only 26 caps between them remains a mystery. He would have walked into most other national teams, and Scotland were hardly blessed with high-calibre defenders. Eschewing the managerial career many predicted for him upon retirement, Hansen became a TV pundit where his scathing dismissals of Jimmy Hill's opinions on the BBC enlivened many a dull match. Ironically, as a pundit he has achieved more fame and recognition than he ever enjoyed as a player.

☞ Like his pal, Kenny Dalglish, Hansen is a top-class golfer and also played volleyball, basketball and squash to a high standard.

✍ Hansen wasn't a frequent goal scorer, but he did hit the winner against West Ham in the 1981 League Cup final replay.

☞ He memorably uttered the famous line: 'You'll never win anything with kids.' The kids in question, Man United's young side of the mid-1990s, proceeded to waltz away with the Premiership title.

☞ The Aberdeen pairing of McLeish and Miller kept Hansen out of the Scotland side – a modern coach would have played five at the back with Hansen as an attacking sweeper.

✍ Hansen won eight league titles, a record he shares with Liverpool colleague Phil Neal.

VITAL STATISTICS

Place of Birth:	Clackmannanshire, Scotland	
Date of Birth:	13 June 1955	**Died:** n/a
Caps:	26 (Scotland)	**Goals (International):** 0
Clubs:	Partick Thistle, Liverpool	
Appearances:	Club (for Liverpool): 623	
Goals:	Club (for Liverpool): 13	
Trophies:	LT 1979, 1980, 1982, 1983, 1984, 1986,	
	1988, 1990; FAC 1986, 1989; LC 1981,	
	1983, 1984; EC 1978, 1981, 1984	

LEGEND RATING	
Achievement	9.0
Skill	9.0
Teamwork	8.0
Passion	8.0
Personality	6.0
TOTAL	**40.0**

Happiest Hammers
The West Ham Dream Team

OF ALL THE DREAM TEAMS, this was the easiest to pick; West Ham legends tend to have that longevity of service that stamps them with the mark of a Hammer. Parkes was comfortably West Ham's most able goalkeeper, and was unlucky to play in an era when Clemence and Shilton traded the England number one jersey between them.

The back four played over 2,500 matches for the club, an outstanding level of passion and commitment (only Moore, in his swansong at Fulham, played for another club), but they will need to be on their mettle in this team. The ball artists ahead of them are not noted for their ability to track back.

The attacking players are so very West Ham; subtlety (Peters), touch (Brooking), pace (Devonshire), tricks (Di Canio), power (Watson) and finishing (Hurst). They might lose to some of the bigger clubs' all-time teams, but it would be glorious stuff.

A new seam has been tapped in recent years: Rio Ferdinand, Frank Lampard jnr, both now departed, have been followed by Joe Cole, Michael Carrick and Jermaine Defoe, all surely destined for England glory.

☞ Appearances: Watson (505), Moore (642), Martin (586), Lampard (665), Hurst (502), Brooking (632), Bonds (793).

☞ Jimmy Ruffell and Vic Watson played in the first FA Cup final at Wembley, the Hammers losing 2-0 to Bolton.

☞ Len Goulden played 14 times for England. It would have been more but his career was cut short by the war.

✍ Brooking, Bonds and Lampard played in both West Ham's FA Cup wins in 1975 and 1980.

☞ Rio Ferdinand ahead of Billy Bonds? On talent, yes. On being a Hammer, no thanks.

Manager: Ron Greenwood

4-3-3

Phil Parkes (80s/90s)

Billy Bonds (C) (70s/80s) Bobby Moore (60s/70s)
Alvin Martin (80s/90s) Frank Lampard (70s/80s)

Alan Devonshire (80s/90s) Trevor Brooking (60s/70s)
Martin Peters (60s/70s)

Geoff Hurst (60s/70s) Vic Watson (20s/30s)
Paolo Di Canio (90s)

Subs: David James (G) (00s) Ray Stewart (D) (80s/90s)
Len Goulden (M) (30s) Jimmy Ruffell (W) (20s/30s)
Tony Cottee (F) (80s/90s)

Billy Bonds. He spits in claret and blue.

Hard Men
The Not-So-Beautiful Game

THERE IS A DIFFERENCE between hard and dirty. A genuinely hard player can freeze an opponent out of the game purely on his reputation, whereas a dirty player who fancies himself simply gets wound up and sent off (think Dennis Wise or Alan Smith).

Higuita's conviction for kidnapping demands his inclusion; we're talking serial nutter here. Ron 'Chopper' Harris was the daddy of 1970s thuggery, and Ron Yeats easily eclipsed Tommy Smith as the hard man of Liverpool (Smith talked too much). Monti was the granddaddy, a ball-playing thug long before it was cool, and Gentile is the modern game's greatest man-marker, a man who turned wingers' bowels to water. Mackay was a legend – he would captain this side. Benetti was a vicious, cynical assassin who stood out even in a brutal Italian team. Neeskens was a great player but he wasn't afraid to leave a foot in, and Giles edges out Souness as the sly, provocative element. Up front we have Joe Jordan, all flailing elbows and tungsten head, toothless only in the literal sense. And Lineker. A decade of being hacked and harassed by the toughest defences in the world and never booked. That's hard.

☞ Mentioned in despatches: Andy Gray, Antonio Rattin, Andoni Goicochoea, Dmitri Kuznetsov, Karl-Heonz Schnellinger, Daniel Passarella.

☞ Deserved omissions: Terry Hurlock (hirsute pedestrian laughing stock), Neil Ruddock (Phil Mitchell in shorts), Robbie Savage (can't see Ron Yeats tolerating that hairstyle), Vinnie Jones (too slow to catch the good players).

☞ Lorenzo was the manager of the 1966 Argentina World Cup team, the dirtiest high-profile international side in the game's history.

☟ 'Do that again, son, and I'll break your legs,' said Tommy Smith to Gerorge Best after Best had nutmegged him. You've got to catch him first, Tommy.

Manager: Lorenzo (Argentina)

4-4-2

Rene Higuita (G)

Ron Harris (D) Ron Yeats (D) Luis Monti (D) Claudio Gentile (D)

Dave Mackay (M) Romeo Benetti (M) Johan Neeskens (M)
Johnny Giles (M)

Joe Jordan (F) Gary Lineker (F)

Clockwise from top left: Lineker, Yeats, 'Chopper' Harris, Gentile.

Haynes, Johnny
Fulham, England

IT IS RARE FOR ONE PERSON to dominate a club's history so totally, but the bar-room discussions in Fulham begin and end with a collective nod: Johnny Haynes was the greatest player ever to pull on the black and white. An inside forward of immense technique, his confidence on the ball made him a London role model for a later generation of pretenders, including Terry Venables, Rodney Marsh and Stan Bowles.

Until the return of the Cottagers to the Premier League in 2001 the era of Haynes represented Fulham's only golden age and, while today's team is good to watch, it pales compared to the one of Haynes, Hill and Jezzard. Good enough to represent England at the 1958 World Cup when still a Second Division player, Haynes remained at Fulham throughout his career. It was a measure of his importance to them that, despite modest revenues, they were always prepared to meet his salary demands following the abolition of the maximum wage (Haynes was the first £100-a-week footballer). Successive relegations in 1968 and 1969 were a sad end to his career, but even while the team around him floundered, Haynes could never do any wrong in the eyes of Fulham fans.

- 1954. Scored on his England debut in a 2-0 win over Northern Ireland in Belfast.
- 1958. Hit an international hat-trick as USSR were thrashed 5-0.
- 1961. The first player to earn £100 per week at a British club.
- 1962. Seriously injured his knee in a road accident and is never picked again for England.
- His 594 league appearances for Fulham are a club record.

VITAL STATISTICS

Place of Birth:	London, England	
Date of Birth:	17 October 1934	**Died:** n/a
Caps:	56 (England)	**Goals (International):** 18
Clubs:	Fulham, Durban City	
Appearances:	Club (League): 594	
Goals:	Club (League): 145	
Trophies:	None	

LEGEND RATING	
Achievement	4.0
Skill	9.0
Teamwork	8.0
Passion	8.0
Personality	8.0
TOTAL	**37.0**

Henry, Thierry
AS Monaco, Arsenal, France

WHEN THE TROUBLESOME and disruptive Nicolas Anelka left Arsenal in 1998, Arsène Wenger turned to another quick French attacker to replace him. Thierry Henry had emerged as a wide attacking player at Monaco under Wenger's tutelage, and won a league title there in 1997. A lucrative move to Juventus followed, but, like many others in Serie A, Henry spent more time on the bench than the pitch, and left after less than a year.

So to Arsenal, and a difficult start, when both manager and player seemed unsure as to the most satisfactory use for all that skill and speed. Only when Wenger consistently used Henry in a central striking role, an opportunity afforded by Dennis Bergkamp's injuries and loss of form, was his true potential unearthed. Henry's second and third seasons at Arsenal brought him a torrent of goals in a classy side. The discovery that he could play as an orthodox front man was of equal benefit to France, for whom the addition of a world-class striker proved to be the missing piece in their attacking jigsaw.

In 2005 he has looked fatigued and carried injuries; it has merely shown his worth in even starker relief, as Arsenal have often looked pretty but toothless without him. A wonder goal in Prague on his return in October emphasised the gap. Comparisons with Anelka are no longer relevant; as a player and a role-model, he leaves his sulky compatriot standing.

👍 Scored three goals in six games at the 1998 World Cup, but never wholly convinced, remaining on the bench for the final.

☞ He made his Monaco debut aged 17 and still looks as if he is about 17.

👍 Won the PFA's Player of the Year award for 2002–03.

👍 In October 2005, Henry broke Ian Wright's goalscoring record for Arsenal. He celebrated in the next match by sharing in the memorable penalty cock-up with Robert Pires.

VITAL STATISTICS

Place of Birth:	Paris, France		
Date of Birth:	17 August 1977	**Died:** n/a	
Caps:	73 (France)	**Goals (International):** 30	
Clubs:	Monaco, Juventus, Arsenal		
Appearances:	Club (League): 330		
Goals:	Club (League): 164		
Trophies:	WorC 1998; EuroC 2000; FLT 1997; LT 2002, 2004; FAC 2002, 2003, 2005		

Achievement	9.0
Skill	9.0
Teamwork	7.0
Passion	8.5
Personality	7.5
TOTAL	**41.0**

LEGEND RATING

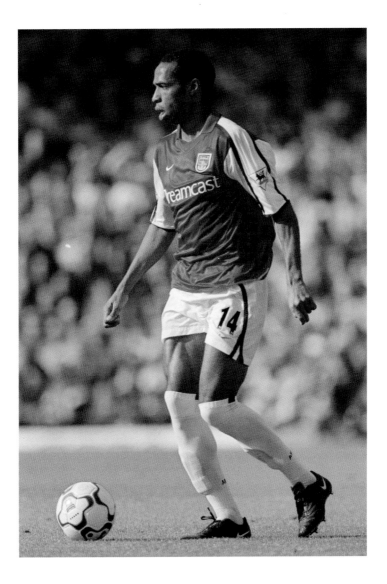

Herbert, Herbert What's the Score?
Walsall 2 Arsenal 0, 1933

AFTER MORE THAN 70 years this match is still talked about in Walsall. Like all Cup upsets it defied logic; Arsenal were in the first season of what was to be a championship winning hat-trick, while the Saddlers were muddling around in the Third Division and approached the match with little more than the hope of making some quick cash. Arsenal's line-up included the Scottish 'Wembley wizard' Alex James, Britain's costliest player David Jack and the winger who became the club's record goalscorer, Cliff Bastin. Their manager, Herbert Chapman, had already made his name by leading Huddersfield to three league title wins.

But reputations meant little to the Walsall players who were intent on proving they were the physical (if not footballing) equals of the Gunners. Two Arsenal players had already been kicked into the stand before Gilbert Alsop's header gave Walsall a second-half lead, then, illustrating that the Corinthian spirit wasn't always prevalent despite those Pathé newsreel images, a kick by Arsenal's Tommy Black on Alsop led to a mass brawl and a penalty to the home side. Bill Sheppard duly converted; a rattled Arsenal had been well and truly outgunned.

✎ Flushed with this goalscoring success, Gilbert Alsop scored 40 league goals in each of the next two seasons, a club record.

☞ Chapman, who was a strict disciplinarian, never picked Tommy Black again.

✎ Scorer Bill Sheppard had a keen sense of timing; it was his first goal for the club.

☞ Arsenal ended the season as League Champions, Walsall finished fifth in Division Three (North).

✎ Walsall's dream ended in round four, where they lost 2-0 at Manchester City.

SCORERS	**Walsall:** Alsop, Sheppard (pen)
EVENT	FA Cup Third Round, Fellows Park, 14 January 1933
WALSALL	(Man: Sid Scholey)
	1. Cunningham 2. Bennett 3. Bird 4. Reed 5. Leslie 6. Salt 7. Coward
	8. Ball 9. Alsop 10. Sheppard 11. Lee
ARSENAL	(Man: Herbert Chapman)
	1. Moss 2. Male 3. Black 4. Hill 5. Roberts 6. Sidley 7. Warnes 8. Jack
	9. Walsh 10. James 11. Bastin

Gilbert Alsop: toast of the Black Country.

Heysel Stadium
A Bleak Night In Belgium

29 MAY 1985 SHOULD HAVE BEEN a red-letter day for fans of Liverpool and Juventus. More than 60,000 of them were massed in Brussels' Heysel stadium before the European Cup final. But misguided ticket arrangements had allocated Liverpool a terrace behind one goal separated only by a thin chicken wire fence from 'neutrals' in the other half. The majority of these 'neutrals' turned out to be Juve fans who had snapped up tickets from locals when their own allocation ran dry.

How it all started will always be debatable. Some Liverpool fans claimed they reacted to missile throwing, while the Italians talk of a drunken English charge. The outcome was all too apparent. Fans fleeing from the trouble attempted to scale a wall in the now infamous sector Z, which collapsed under increasing pressure.

Thirty-nine Italians and Belgians died in the carnage and hundreds were injured, their fear and pain going out live to horrified television audiences watching across the world. Recriminations continued for years. Fingers were pointed at fans, local bar-owners, ticket allocators, Belgian police and the stadium authorities. All were a factor but the lessons were not learned, as Liverpool fans were to discover only four years later at Hillsborough.

- ☞ The stadium's age was cited as a factor but, built in 1930, it was actually seven years younger than Wembley and not unusually old for the time.
- ☞ Following the tragedy UEFA banned English clubs from Europe indefinitely. Ironically, the first club prevented from entering the European Cup were Liverpool's rivals, Everton. The ban was lifted after five years.
- ☞ Disgracefully, no memorial or plaque commemorates the disaster. The only reminder is a gate left for posterity when the stadium was razed to the ground.
- ☞ After the chaos, UEFA officials insisted the game should take place that evening, fearing further disturbances if they cancelled.

'If I had known about the fatalities I wouldn't have wanted to play. You go along to watch a game.'

Kenny Dalglish

Hill, Jimmy

Coventry City, BBC TV

JIMMY HILL CAN LAY CLAIM to being the first renaissance man of English football. Player, linesman, employment-rights activist, PFA and club chairman, media pundit … there are few areas of the modern game in which Jimmy Hill has not exerted an influence. A competent player in average sides, his most lasting achievement came in his role as PFA chairman when, leading a case on behalf of George Eastham in 1961, he brought about the abolition of football's maximum-wage system.

As a manager and then chairman, Hill transformed Third Division Coventry City, laying the foundations for a 34-year membership of the league's elite and pioneering the movement for the abolition of terracing (Highfield Road was an all-seater stadium 15 years before the Taylor Report made them compulsory).

In the media, he embraced the new culture of television coverage and became a national figure as a presenter and summariser for both ITV and the BBC. He irritates many, the Football League has never quite forgiven him for taking them on over 40 years ago, but the shadow of the most famous chin in football has cast a lasting influence.

☞ 1961. First PFA chairman to call for a players' strike over the maximum wage.

☞ 1972. Deputised for an injured linesman at Highbury. Hill was originally attending as a commentator.

☞ 1978. Key negotiator in the threatened strike over freedom of contract. This nut didn't crack until the Bosman case nearly 20 years later.

☞ 1982. Organised a rebel tour to South Africa, infuriating the FA and breaching the Gleneagles agreement not to play sport with a land still under the apartheid regime.

☞ 'Jimmy Hill is to football what King Herod is to babysitting,' Tommy Docherty once said.

VITAL STATISTICS

		LEGEND RATING	
		Achievement	7
Place of Birth:	London, England	Tactical Awareness	8
Date of Birth:	22 July 1928 **Died:** n/a	Motivation	8
Caps:	0 (England) **Goals (International):** 0	Team Selection/Transfers	7
Clubs:	As Player: Brentford, Fulham; As Manager:	Personality	8
	Coventry City		
Trophies:	None	**TOTAL**	**38**

Hillsborough
The Day It All Had To Change

PERHAPS THE MOST sickening aspect of the worst disaster in British football was that it contained so many chilling echoes of previous tragedies. Like the crowd-related disasters at Ibrox and Heysel, it unfolded in a few minutes and was the result of sudden overcrowding. What made 15 April 1989 worse, apart from the unprecedented loss of 96 lives, were the terrifying images of fans – men, women, children and even whole families – struggling for life in the chaos. Reporting of a disaster normally contains scenes of the aftermath, the venue cleared and the dead removed, but with the media already gathered for the FA Cup semi-final between Liverpool and Nottingham Forest, the camera lenses quickly turned to the Leppings Lane terrace. The central pen was filling with Liverpool fans misdirected into an area too small to contain them, while outer sections remained relatively free. The pictures of helpless fans sparked a grief that went far beyond the boundaries of football. The following days were incredibly moving: the Kop was a sea of flowers, and players mingled with fans at funerals. The legacy was the Taylor Report, resulting in all-seater stadiums and an overhaul of crowd-control measures at all British events. The tragedy is that 96 innocent lives were lost before anyone would admit there was a problem.

- Although 95 people died as an immediate result of Hillsborough, the toll was to rise several years later after one young man's failure to recover from a coma.
- *The Sun* newspaper claimed outrageously that some Liverpool fans had stolen personal items from the dead. Copies of the paper were ritually burned on Merseyside.
- A national service of remembrance was held in Liverpool's Anglican Cathedral on 29 April 1989.
- The Hillsborough Justice Campaign still fights for the bereaved and their families. The authorities have escaped punishment and compensation for victims' families has been tiny, contrasting with the large awards given to police officers affected by 'stress'.

'Football is irrelevant now.'

Kenny Dalglish

'The only safe stadium in my view is an empty one.'

South Yorkshire coroner Stefan Popper, at the inquest

Hoddle, Glenn

Tottenham Hotspur, Monaco, Chelsea, England

GLENN HODDLE WAS A continental footballer who had to overcome the misfortune of being born in Hayes, Middlesex. Not overly concerned with pace and aggression, Hoddle rose above the hurly-burly of English football. The radar-equipped right foot bent and curled some classic goals in a long career.

Hoddle spent 12 years at Tottenham before he tried his luck abroad with Monaco, where he was hugely appreciated. His performances for England were patchy – occasionally inspired, too often anonymous. To be fair to him, no one built a side around his talent, which was what he needed. He was lured back to England as player-manager of Swindon Town. His understanding of the game and tactical acumen were immediately evident as he took an ordinary side into the top flight for the first time in their history. Those instincts served him equally well at Chelsea, and the FA appointed him England manager as successor to Terry Venables. He made a decent fist of the job, and it was his strong, and sometimes quirky, personal views that saw him eased out. His abilities as a manager seem to have been confirmed by sound work at Southampton but he was a disappointment at his *alma mater*, Spurs, where his remoteness from his players was exposed.

- 👍 He scored the only goal (a penalty) in the 1982 Cup final replay against QPR.
- ☞ He started Chelsea's rush of foreign imports when he persuaded Ruud Gullit to join Chelsea. Gullit succeeded him as manager.
- 👍 Hoddle's debut for England against Bulgaria was awesome; he scored in a 2-0 win and looked a million dollars.
- 👎 A bizarre trust in Eileen Drewery, a faith healer, started the decline in Hoddle's relationship with the FA and the media whilst England manager.

VITAL STATISTICS

Place of Birth: Hayes, Middlesex, England

Date of Birth: 27 October 1957   **Died:** n/a

Caps: 53 (England)

Goals (International): 8

Clubs: As Player: Tottenham, Monaco, Swindon Town, Chelsea (player-manager); As Manager: England, Southampton, Tottenham, Wolverhampton Wanderers

Appearances: Club (League for Tottenham): 377

Goals: Club (League): 88

Trophies: FAC 1981, 1982; UEFAC 1984; FLT 1988

MANAGER		PLAYER	
Achievement	8.0	Achievement	7.0
Tactical Awareness	8.0	Skill	9.0
Motivation	6.5	Teamwork	6.5
Team Selection/Transfers	8.5	Passion	8.5
Personality	7.5	Personality	7.0
TOTAL 38.5		**TOTAL 38.0**	

LEGEND RATING

Holy Trinity

Holland, 1988

THEIR FAILURE TO QUALIFY for the Finals of the 1982 and 1986 World Cups prompted Holland to call once again for the services of their greatest coach, Rinus Michels. Michels' 'Total Football' philosophy, born at Ajax in the late 1960s, was to serve Holland well yet again. The core of the team was Koeman, the captain, along with the Holy Trinity of Gullit, Rijkaard and Van Basten. Koeman was a decent defender who also happened to be a terrific attacking playmaker, and almost every Dutch move seemed to start with his precision passing from the back. Be it a short ball to the ever-willing Rijkaard or a longer pass to meet the run of an attacker, Koeman rarely missed his target. Gullit could attack or defend with equal aplomb, and Van Basten was a brutally efficient finisher. And for once a Dutch team delivered what it promised. At Euro 88 they produced the fluent, attacking football for which they were famous, and a first victory for 32 years over hosts West Germany won them a place in the final. A terrific game saw them wear down a skilful USSR team – a trophy had come home at last.

- Van Breukelen saved a penalty that would have brought Russia back into the game in the final – he was a superior keeper to any of the 1970s custodians.
- The second goal in the final was a masterpiece, Van Basten volleying a deep cross with stunning power past Rinat Dasaev.
- Even this squad had its internal ructions. There were rumours of a racial divide in the camp.
- The Dutch performance at the 1990 World Cup Finals was a sad coda to these heroics. With virtually the same team, they managed three dreary draws and were eliminated by Germany.

Manager: Rinus Michels

Key Players

Hans van Breukelen (G) Jan Wouters (D) Ronald Koeman (D)
Frank Rijkaard (M) Ruud Gullit (M/F) Marco van Basten (F)

Trophies
EuroC 1988

Van Basten shows off the European Championship trophy after Holland's victory in 1988.

Home Internationals
We Want Them Back!

BY 1884 ENGLAND, Scotland, Wales and Ireland were all playing international football. So the idea that they should all play each other in an annual league was a logical step, and thus the Home Internationals were born. Scotland quickly gained the upper hand, winning three and sharing one of the first four tournaments, but it wasn't long before England rose to the challenge and, bar the occasional triumph for Wales and N. Ireland, it was the auld enemies that grew to dominate the event. For fans north of the border a visit to Wembley was always a trip to savour. Indeed, such was their enthusiasm for the fixture they were even known to outnumber the home fans on occasion. But after nearly a century, the Home Internationals began to fall apart. England and Wales refused to play in Belfast, wary of the political situation, and when Scotland and England cancelled games against the other home nations after 1984, the tournament was effectively over. Although the England/Scotland fixture continued for another five years, the extended season and the importance of other tournaments had finally taken its toll.

- Best English game? A 9-3 drubbing of Scotland in 1961. Jimmy Greaves helped himself to a hat-trick. Scottish keeper Frank Haffey never played for his country again.
- Best Scottish game? The 3-2 win at Wembley in 1967, England's first defeat since winning the World Cup.
- Best Welsh game? A 4-1 drubbing of England at Wrexham in 1980. Leighton James and Mickey Thomas put paid to Larry Lloyd's England career.
- Best Irish game? A 1-0 win against Wales in 1980 earned them their first outright championship victory for 66 years.
- The final tally of outright wins reads: England 34, Scotland 24, Wales 7, Northern Ireland 3.

'It meant more for the Scots to beat the English than it did for the English to beat the Scots.'

Bobby Charlton makes a dubious claim after the Scots win at Wembley in 1967

Coppell and Hansen attempt a pas de deux in 1982.

Hooligans
Mobs And Monsters

FOOTBALL HOOLIGANISM: a disease cultivated by the game itself or merely the reflection of a violent society? Your opinion on this subject tends to depend on whether you love or despise the game. One undeniable truth is that football violence is nothing new.

Rivalry, large crowds and a contact sport have provided a violent cocktail as long as the game has been played. In 1909, a major riot took place in Glasgow after officials unwisely refused to play extra-time to settle an Old Firm derby. The result was a burned stand, a ruined pitch and widespread damage to local property.

Even in the golden age of the 1940s, Millwall fans pelted the referee and linesmen during a routine match against Exeter. The late 1960s saw the dawn of organised gangs, with premeditated 'taking' of away ends and railway stations setting an unwelcome trend. As police tactics grew more sophisticated in the 1980s, so did the hooligans. Sharply dressed casuals with Stanley knives replaced the skinheads and their Dr Martens. Today the problem is controlled at league games with more season tickets and all-seater stadiums but away from the stadiums, in city centres, car parks and even on cross-channel ferries, the threat of hooliganism still lingers.

- 1972. Chelsea became the first British club to erect a perimeter fence. Although Hillsborough brought their eventual removal, they are still a common sight in grounds throughout the world.
- The scourge of racism against black players, particularly in Italy and Eastern Europe, is still a persistent stain that UEFA have been slow in erasing.
- In 1985 televised rioting at a match between Luton and Millwall led to the introduction of an ill-fated identity card scheme.
- February 2002. A reconciliatory football match in Kabul following the Afghan War sparked a riot. The stadium had a more grisly recent history as a Taliban execution venue.

'These people are society's problems and we don't want your hooligans at our sport.'

FA Secretary Ted Croker bites back at Prime Minister Thatcher, 1985

A Liverpool fan gets some far too literal stick.

Hoop Heroes
The Celtic Dream Team

WITH A CLUB LIKE CELTIC, who have been winning domestic trophies hand over fist ever since their formation, the list of potential Dream Team candidates is far too long. One could easily select a squad that would require a convoy of team coaches to get to away games.

Inevitably, the Lisbon Lions feature heavily: McNeill, Gemmell, Johnstone, Murdoch and Lennox are all represented. The most devastating combination is up front. Henrik Larsson has proved himself one of the most consistent and prolific finishers in the history of the game in Scotland, while his striking partner, Kenny Dalglish, is one of the most complete forwards Britain has produced since the war. The midfield is as perfect as they come, a unit capable of turning from intricate ball-juggling to biting tackles at the flick of a tactical switch.

As manager, only Martin O'Neill as Celtic boss can touch Jock Stein's hem. Not only did Stein win nine championships in a row and win the 1967 European Cup, he also tilted the balance of power that had been weighted in Rangers' favour for a decade.

- John Thomson may well have become Celtic's greatest-ever keeper. Sadly, aged just 22, he died from injuries sustained in an Old Firm game.
- Tom Boyd deserves a place on the bench for loyalty during the 1990s, a decade dominated by Rangers.
- Frank McAvennie wins the cheeky chappie award ahead of Charlie Nicholas: he could drain a mini-bar quicker.
- Unluckiest omissions: Collins and Auld. Celtic's midfield is so strong that even these club legends from the 1950s and 1960s fail to be included.
- Apart from Larsson the only modern 'mercenary' to make this 16 is Stilian Petrov; the Bulgarian signed as a 20 year-old in 1999, and is a consistent creative influence and scorer from midfield. Like Larsson, he is treated as an 'honorary Scot' and talks in marvellously inflected Glaswegian.

Manager: Jock Stein

4-4-2

Pat Bonner (80s/90s)

Danny McGrain (70s) Billy McNeill (60s/70s)
John Clark (60s) Tommy Gemmell (60s)

Jimmy Johnstone (60s/70s) Paul McStay (80s/90s)
Bobby Murdoch (60s) Bobby Lennox (60s)

Kenny Dalglish (70s) Henrik Larsson (90s/00s)

Subs: John Thomson (G) (20s/30s) Tom Boyd (D) (90s) Stilian Petrov (M) (00s) Jimmy McGrory (F) (20s/30s) Frank McAvennie (F) (80s)

Howlers

How High Do You Want The Goal?

WE'VE ALL DONE IT. Fortunately for the rest of us, the repercussions of shanking an open goal or letting a tiddler through the legs are restricted to the banter of team-mates in the pub after the game.

Imagine if you can the misery of making the same error in front of a 30,000 crowd and a sniggering armchair audience of millions. How Villa's Peter Enckelman must look forward to visiting St Andrew's again. In 2002, during the first Birmingham derby for 16 seasons, he let a throw-in from one of his own players gently caress his studs as a near air-shot trickled past him and into the net.

Goalkeepers are in a unique position regarding howlers but strikers too have their own hall of infamy. Ryan Giggs can point to a groaning, personal trophy cabinet as proof of his talent but his pass into the Stretford End, when an open-goal beckoned during an FA Cup tie against Arsenal in 2003, will be replayed on out-take compilations for years to come. The bigger they are….

The blooper of the 2003–04 Premiership season is reserved for Ian Walker, whose mishandling of a gently trundling effort from Kevin Davies handed Bolton an equaliser. And so the first physical requirement for a keeper was demonstrated: a thick skin.

- David Seaman. Being beaten by Nayim from the halfway line in 1995 had finally become a distant memory. Then Ronaldinho approached an innocuous-looking free kick in Shizuoka seven years later…
- Paul Gascoigne. Fame and fortune in Italy should have awaited Gascoigne after the 1991 FA Cup final, his last appearance for Tottenham. The worst tackle of the decade left him the poorer by one cruciate ligament and with a career that never recovered.
- Gary Sprake. But for the ex-Leeds and Wales keeper, Elland Road would have bulged with trophies in the 1960s and 1970s. The jewel in his tarnished crown was an own goal caused by his throwing the ball backwards.

'David James. Superstar. Drops more
b******s than Grobbelaar'

**Manchester United fans at Anfield point
out 'Calamity' James' propensity for
dropping the occasional clanger**

Seaman misses Ronaldinho's free kick. England v Brazil, 2002 World Cup quarter-final.

Hughes, Emlyn
Liverpool, England

WHEN BILL SHANKLY was looking around for a passionate, call-to-arms leader for his Liverpool side, he spotted a young wing half at Blackpool. The player in question, Emlyn Hughes, went on to play over 650 games for the Anfield club, reinforcing Shankly's reputation as one of the game's shrewdest judges.

'Crazy Horse', as he became known, missed only three games through injury in his first nine seasons at Liverpool, and in 12 years at Anfield he was never asked to play in the reserves.

Although not remarkably gifted, Hughes showed great understanding, was difficult to knock off the ball, and possessed almost boundless reserves of energy and heart. He was also an immensely disciplined player, and his commitment never crossed the line into nastiness. Even after leaving Liverpool with arthritic knees, Hughes gave unstinting service to a variety of clubs lower down the leagues. There are many who feel his 62 caps flatter him but, like cricket captain Mike Brearley, Hughes' value to a side as a leader more than compensated for his shortcomings as a player.

☞ On retirement, Hughes made a career as a motivational speaker, and was a popular team captain on TV's *A Question Of Sport*.

👍 He was Football Writers' Player of the Year in 1977.

👍 Hughes scored both goals in a Merseyside derby victory at Goodison Park in the 1973 title-winning campaign. And duly celebrated both goals by running around like a madman.

☞ 1972. Hughes scored his only international goal against Wales in a 3-0 win.

👍 1977–78. Scored the winning goal in a European Cup tie in Lisbon that ended Benfica's 46-match unbeaten run.

VITAL STATISTICS

Place of Birth:	Barrow-in-Furness, England
Date of Birth:	28 August 1947 **Died:** n/a
Caps:	62 (England) **Goals (International):** 1
Clubs:	Blackpool, Liverpool, Wolverhampton, Rotherham United, Hull City, Mansfield Town
Appearances:	Club (for Liverpool): 665
Goals:	Club (for Liverpool): 48
Trophies:	LT 1973, 1976, 1977, 1979; FAC 1974; EC 1977, 1978; UEFAC 1973, 1976

LEGEND RATING	
Achievement	9.0
Skill	5.0
Teamwork	8.0
Passion	10.0
Personality	8.0
TOTAL	**40.0**

Rome, 1977. Hughes brandishes Liverpool's first European Cup.

Hughes, Mark

Wales, Manchester United, Chelsea

WITH HIS FEARLESS, lion-hearted approach to striking, Mark Hughes could have easily made his mark in the eras of Dean or Lawton. A powerful forward with legs like tree trunks, he was less than 6 ft tall but huge in stature. To judge him by his goalscoring record alone is a mistake, as his phenomenal work rate made him a favourite of fans and colleagues alike wherever he has played. His shielding of the ball brings grateful tributes from fellow strikers, while his waist-high volleys and control of a bouncing ball have produced countless goals from half-chances.

Despite his frequent later moves, he remains a son of Manchester United, who performed canny business by buying him back from Barcelona for a profit. His combative nature has inevitably brought dismissals, but he was never a dirty player. It is unlikely that anyone else would have been appointed Welsh national boss with no previous managerial experience, his inspiration as Red Dragon as well as Red Devil made him a popular choice. A promising start to the qualification campaign for Euro 2004 petered out, and it was no surprise when Hughes accepted the lure of the Premiership at Blackburn Rovers, who he has moulded to reflect his own spiky style.

☞ Hughes' physique inspired the epithets 'Sparky' (the battery boy) in England and 'El Toro' (the bull) at Barcelona.

👆 1990. Scores twice in the FA Cup final against Crystal Palace.

👆 1994. Scores another Cup final goal against Chelsea, whom he joins and leads to another Cup victory in 1997, his fifth winner's medal.

👆 1998. Awarded an MBE for services to football.

👆 1999. Appointed manager of Wales whilst still a player at Southampton.

VITAL STATISTICS

Place of Birth:	Wrexham, Wales
Date of Birth:	1 November 1963 **Died:** n/a
Caps:	72 (Wales) **Goals (International):** 16
Clubs:	Manchester United, Barcelona, Bayern Munich, Chelsea, Southampton, Everton, Blackburn
Appearances:	Club (League): 646
Goals:	Club (League): 164
Trophies:	FAC 1985, 1990, 1994, 1996, 1997; CWC 1991; LC 1992; LT 1993, 1994

LEGEND RATING	
Achievement	7.0
Skill	7.5
Teamwork	10.0
Passion	8.0
Personality	6.5
TOTAL	**39.0**

Hunt, Roger
Liverpool, England

AS THE LIVERPOOL TEAM was re-built in the early 1960s, Roger Hunt emerged as a key player in Shankly's new order. At only 5 ft 9 in Hunt wasn't the tallest striker, but his pace and the timing of his runs made him a difficult player for defenders to keep track of while his fierce shot ensured that he rarely needed a second invitation to find the target.

His strike-rate for Liverpool was stunning, better than a goal every two matches, and the club struggled to replace him before raiding Scunthorpe for a long-haired prospect called Kevin Keegan. A year after he left Liverpool for a spell at Bolton, 'Sir' Roger, as the Kop dubbed him, returned to Anfield for a testimonial attended by a capacity 55,000 fans. Hunt was a member of England's World Cup winning side of 1966, although he was resented by many fans for keeping Jimmy Greaves out of the side in the latter stages of the competition. Actually, Hunt played in every game during the tournament; it was hat-trick hero Geoff Hurst who was preferred ahead of Greaves.

- Hunt scored 41 goals in Liverpool's 1962 promotion campaign, a club record.
- His 245 league goals remains a club record, although Ian Rush scored more overall.
- He was awarded the MBE in 1999, along with the other 'forgotten' members of the World Cup-winning side.
- He scored one of the goals in extra-time as Liverpool beat Leeds 2-1 to win the FA Cup for the first time in 1965.
- Hunt on his manager, Bill Shankly: 'He was dynamic. If you lost a game you lost to rubbish. If you won, you had beaten a great team.'

VITAL STATISTICS

Place of Birth:	Golborne, Lancashire, England	
Date of Birth:	20 July 1938	**Died:** n/a
Caps:	34 (England)	**Goals (International):** 18
Clubs:	Liverpool, Bolton Wanderers	
Appearances:	Club (for Liverpool): 492	
Goals:	Club (for Liverpool): 245	
Trophies:	LT 1964, 1966; FAC 1965; WorC 1966	

		LEGEND RATING
Achievement	8.0	
Skill	8.0	
Teamwork	7.0	
Passion	7.0	
Personality	6.0	
TOTAL	**36.0**	

Hurst, Geoff
West Ham United, England

THE SIGHT OF an airborne Geoff Hurst smashing his hat-trick to seal England's World Cup final victory is one of the country's indelible post-war images. Inevitably, it dwarfed the rest of his career, but at the beginning of the tournament Hurst was a squad player, drafted in by Sir Alf Ramsey merely as cover for the more experienced Roger Hunt and Jimmy Greaves (Hurst had only made his debut for England earlier that year). But an injury to Greaves in the group stage provided Hurst with his opportunity. It was one he seized, scoring the only goal against Argentina in the quarter-finals.

Hurst was groomed as a striker by Ron Greenwood at West Ham; along with England team-mates Martin Peters and skipper Bobby Moore, he was a graduate of the Upton Park academy. After tasting the ultimate success at 24, Hurst's career rather stagnated and by the time he left the Hammers for Stoke at the age of 30 it was all but over. Like nearly all the 1966 England team, he was a managerial failure and excused himself from football for 15 years before returning as a promotional figurehead for England's successful Euro 96 bid. More recently he was part of the team that fought Germany for the right to host the 2006 World Cup Finals. On this occasion he lost.

👍 Hurst is still the only man to score a hat-trick in a World Cup final. It was Hurst's third different winner's medal at Wembley in successive seasons, having earlier won the FA Cup and European Cup Winners' Cup with West Ham.

☞ In the 1964 FA Cup final Hurst scored via the underside of the crossbar, a Wembley precursor to his more famous effort two years later in the World Cup final.

👍 1998. Hurst was made a Knight of the Realm.

☞ In 2001 Hurst finally published his long-awaited autobiography, *1966 And All That*.

☞ A talented all-round sportsman, Hurst considered becoming a professional cricketer.

VITAL STATISTICS

Place of Birth:	Ashton, England	
Date of Birth:	8 December 1941	**Died:** n/a
Caps:	49 (England)	**Goals (International):** 24
Clubs:	West Ham, Stoke, West Bromwich	
Appearances:	Club (League for West Ham): 410	
Goals:	Club (League for West Ham): 180	
Trophies:	FAC 1964; CWC 1965; WorC 1966	

LEGEND RATING	
Achievement	8.0
Skill	8.0
Teamwork	7.0
Passion	7.0
Personality	6.0
TOTAL	**36.0**

Impossible!
P38 W26 D12 L0

ARSÈNE WENGER SUGGESTED in November 2002 that his team were strong enough to go a season unbeaten. They were, but not that year. Some uncharacteristically brittle defending and a late surge by Manchester United cost them the title.

In 2003–04 the weaknesses of the previous campaign had been erased. Young Kolo Toure's strength and assurance had replaced the indecision of Pascal Cygan, and Ashley Cole's defending had tightened. Sol Campbell was a colossus. In midfield the slightly muted displays of Ljungberg were compensated by the surprising improvement in the form of Edu; Pires and Vieira remained outstanding influences. Ahead of them Bergkamp's divine touch and vision allowed him to defy advancing years, and the purchase of Jose-Antonio Reyes left the disappointing Wiltord looking for a new club. Oh, and there was Henry, the best player in the world.

After the pivotal encounter at Old Trafford, Arsenal looked a team with a mission, but also a team at peace. The anger and sense of injustice seemed to vanish, replaced by a firmness of purpose and self-belief. There were ordinary performances (at home to Birmingham and Fulham) and tough encounters (at Bolton and Liverpool), but the last few games were negotiated with a certainty and inexorability that their rivals reflected on over the summer. With some justification as it turned out – the Gunners roared into the 2004–05 season with a similar run of success.

☞ The Old Trafford game was a key. Van Nistelrooy's penalty miss meant the Gunners had negotiated their hardest game of the season with a point.

☞ The suspensions as a result of the shenanigans during that game were lighter than the club may have feared, and the replacements performed admirably to maintain the team's momentum.

☜ The identical fixture the following season saw Arsenal's run end. In their 50th game since defeat at Leeds in 2003, they went down 2-0 in another fractious and unedifying encounter.

☝ Perhaps the team's finest performance came in Europe against Inter in their Champions League group. A 5-1 thrashing of a team which had beaten them 3-0 at Highbury was a monumental result.

Manager: Arsène Wenger

Best XI:

Jens Lehmann (G)

Lauren (D) Kolo Toure (D) Sol Campbell (D) Ashley Cole (D)

Edu (M) Patrick Vieira (M) Robert Pires (M) Freddie Ljungberg (M)

Dennis Bergkamp (F) Thierry Henry (F)

Indiscipline

Cards And Chaos

THERE ARE FAR MORE RED CARDS these days, so football must be a dirtier game, right? Nothing could be further from the truth.

Yes, we know that neither Stanley Matthews or Bobby Charlton were cautioned during their careers, but in those days the referee sharpened his pencil just about once every 10 years. In the days of black-and-white TV, a player had to clock up two falls and a submission to warrant a red card. Nowadays, a dozen red cards is a standard haul on any given Saturday. And yet there are still players with unblemished records. In a recent season at Spurs Sol Campbell managed to complete an entire campaign without collecting a single booking, while Gary Lineker, like Matthews and Charlton, kept his nose clean throughout his career.

Of course there are players whose middle names might as well be Trouble. In the modern era Mark Dennis, Vinnie Jones and Alan Smith have all periodically forgotten what it feels like to shower with the rest of the team. But do footballers behave any worse today than they did 40 years ago? Not in our view.

- Take a bow Vinnie Jones. His booking for Chelsea after three seconds remains the quickest ever in the game's history.
- It was 96 years before a player was sent off while playing for England. Alan Mullery achieved this distinction against Yugoslavia in 1968.
- Red and yellow cards were invented by an ex-referee, Ken Aston. He must have got the idea after taking charge of Brazil versus Chile in the 1962 World Cup. The 'Battle of Santiago' was one of the dirtiest games ever played.
- 2003. Sheffield United's First Division league game with West Brom was abandoned after a combination of red cards and injuries reduced them to six players. Rules state that a team must number at least seven.

'The lad was sent off for foul and abusive language, but he swears blind he didn't say a word.'

Oldham manager Joe Royle tries unsuccessfully to explain his player's dismissal

Injuries

Ow!

INJURY IS A PROFESSIONAL footballer's greatest dread, even worse than being a fullback and discovering that Ryan Giggs has passed a fitness test. At their worst, they can make even spectators wince. Coventry's David Busst, sandwiched in a tackle at Old Trafford, snapped a leg at such a hideous angle that it made Peter Schmeichel physically sick and moved him to attend a post-match counselling session. But not all injuries are career threatening. Dave Beasant once missed several games after dropping a bottle of salad cream on his foot. (Sadly for Chelsea, his handling didn't improve noticeably on his return to the first team.)

It is one of the quirks of the game that some players can tackle their way through seasons of campaigning without collecting a scratch, while others can limp off after a pre-match kickabout with the club mascot. For his frequent absences from the first team during his spell at Aston Villa, Dalian Atkinson acquired the unenviable nickname of 'Sick Note' from sections of the Holte End. This tag has recently been inherited by Tottenham's Darren Anderton. Any career can be ended at a stroke by a mistimed tackle or an awkward landing. Despite the money, adulation and glamour, job security is not one of the benefits offered by professional football.

- Injuries can cost a team in more ways than one. In 1996 Middlesbrough were deducted three points after cancelling a fixture against Blackburn. Boro claimed most of their players were injured or had flu.
- Wembley acquired a hoodoo after players were badly injured in Cup finals during the 1950s and 1960s. In these pre-substitute times, they often changed the course of the match.
- 1980. Proving that danger lurks round many corners, Charlie George lost one finger and mangled two more after a run-in with a lawn mower.
- An injury crisis once forced Man City to name Tony Book and Glyn Pardoe as 'A' team substitutes. Their combined age was 92.

'He'll probably injure himself getting off the bus.'

TV summariser Brian Clough has harsh words for Stuart Pearson before the 1977 FA Cup final

An innocuous but sickening clash shatters David Busst's leg.

Jack, David

Bolton Wanderers, Arsenal, England

LIKE ALF COMMON (the first £1,000 player) and Trevor Francis (the first £1 m player), David Jack's name is a favourite point of reference for pub quizmasters up and down the country. A star of Bolton's 1923 and 1926 FA Cup-winning sides, Jack was a primary target for Herbert Chapman, manager of Arsenal. Legend has it that during the lengthy negotiations, Chapman plied the Bolton board with strong gin while he sipped enthusiastically from a glass of tonic water. True or not, Chapman was successful in persuading a reluctant Bolton board to part with Jack. But it would cost him an unprecedented £10,750, a landmark first-ever five-figure transfer fee. Actually, it could have been more; initially Bolton had demanded £13,000. The money proved well spent. Jack was to return to Wembley twice with the Gunners, once as a winner, and was a vital component of the side that won three league championships in the early 1930s. A clever inside forward with a good shot, Jack was part of the legendary Arsenal forward line of Hulme, Jack, Lambert, James and Bastin. Like many of his team-mates, Jack was shocked by Chapman's premature death in 1934, and was one of the pallbearers at the great man's funeral.

☞ Jack won his first two caps in 1924, but had to wait four years to be given another.

👆 Jack scored the opening goal in the first Wembley FA Cup final, as Bolton beat West Ham 2-0.

👆 Three years later he repeated the feat, this time scoring the only goal of the game against Manchester City.

☞ Jack's brother Rollo also played professional football, following David from Plymouth to Bolton.

☞ 'No player in the world is worth £10,000.' Sir Charles Clegg, FA President.

VITAL STATISTICS

Place of Birth:	Bolton, England		
Date of Birth:	3 April 1899		**Died:** 1958
Caps:	9 (England)	**Goals (International):** 0	
Clubs:	Plymouth Argyle, Bolton, Arsenal		
Appearances:	Club (League for Arsenal): 181		
Goals:	Club (League for Arsenal): 113		
Trophies:	FAC 1923, 1926, 1930; LT 1931, 1933, 1934		

LEGEND RATING	
Achievement	7.0
Skill	7.0
Teamwork	8.0
Passion	6.0
Personality	7.0
TOTAL	**35.0**

James, Alex

Arsenal, Scotland

THE ARSENAL SIDE of the 1930s was brimming with fantastic players, but Alex James was probably its most gifted. James was short and wiry and the baggy shorts of the day made him look almost Chaplinesque, but there was nothing slapstick about his football. Like his manager, the legendary Herbert Chapman, James was ahead of his time and, as a natural reader of the game, he adapted well to Chapman's innovative tactics. Arsenal fought off fierce competition to sign him from Preston, beating Liverpool, Aston Villa, Birmingham and Manchester City, although initially they may have wondered if it had been worth the trouble; James struggled to settle and was even dropped for a spell. Then one day, in a typically unconventional move, Chapman turned up at James's house and hauled him out of bed to play in an FA Cup replay at Birmingham. From thereon James never looked back, forming a successful partnership with the prolific Cliff Bastin on the left side of Arsenal's 3-4-3 formation. Both were consistently inspirational as Arsenal walked away with trophy after trophy. Eight caps for Scotland was a scandalous waste of his talent, especially as he was one of the architects of their finest pre-war hour: the 5-1 thrashing of England by the 'Wembley Wizards' in 1928.

☞ Arsenal paid Preston £8,750 for James in 1929 – a huge fee at the time.

☞ Preston were frequently referred to as 'Alex James and 10 others'.

👆 James's eight Scotland caps were spread over seven years, and included four goals, two of them in the annihilation of England in 1928.

☞ James's obituary appeared in *The Times*, a rare accolade for a footballer in 1953.

👆 James scored a cracking goal in the 1930 FA Cup final. Taking a free kick quickly, he played a one-two with Bastin and smashed the ball into the roof of the net.

VITAL STATISTICS

Place of Birth:	Mossend, Scotland	
Date of Birth:	14 September 1901	**Died:** 1 June 1953
Caps:	8 (Scotland)	**Goals (International):** 4
Clubs:	Raith Rovers, Preston North End, Arsenal	
Appearances:	Club (League for Arsenal): 231	
Goals:	Club (League for Arsenal): 26	
Trophies:	FAC 1930, 1936; LT 1931, 1933, 1934, 1935	

Achievement	8.0
Skill	9.0
Teamwork	8.0
Passion	7.0
Personality	7.0
TOTAL	**39.0**

LEGEND RATING

Jargon And Gibberish
Thoughts From The Box

FOOTBALL IS NOT UNIQUE in having its own 'trade' vocabulary. All professions like to shroud themselves with an air of mystery by inventing a language that confuses and belittles outsiders. Computer programmers, financiers, doctors – all rely on our fear of their superior knowledge to protect their interests. Football is unique in having a language that is lacking in poetry and invention, but what it lacks in these departments it makes up for in sheer and utter nonsense. Without further ado, here are some favourites:

'*Well we got nine … and you can't score more than that.*' Bobby Robson.

'*When a player gets to 30, so does his body.*' Glenn Hoddle

'*I think we just ran out of legs.*' David Pleat

'*You half fancied that to go in as it was dipping and rising at the same time.*' Ron Atkinson

'*Hagi could open a tin of beans with his left foot.*' Ray Clemence

All masterpieces of verbal effluvium, but these individuals are only competing for the best-supporting role. Not even Atkinson's bizarre pronouncements threaten the pre-eminence of Keggy Keegle (as he was once dubbed by Brian Moore). Always ready with a cliché or banality, Our Kev is the nonpareil of football jargon-merchants.

The Very Best of Kev:

- 'Shaun Wright-Phillips has got a big heart. It's as big as him, which isn't very big, but it's bigger.'
- 'In some ways, cramp is worse than having a broken leg.'
- 'You get bunches of players like you do bananas, though that is a bad comparison.'
- 'It's like a toaster, the ref's shirt pocket. Every time there's a tackle, up pops a yellow card.'
- 'I know what is round the corner, I just don't know where the corner is. But the onus is on us to perform and we must control the bandwagon.'

'We must have had 99 per cent of the game. It was the other three per cent that cost us the match.'

The normally coherent Ruud Gullit forgets his calculator

Keggy Keegle, espousing words of wisdom on the pitch.

Jennings, Pat

Tottenham Hotspur, Arsenal, Northern Ireland

WHEN TOTTENHAM sold the 32-year-old Pat Jennings for a paltry £40,000 in 1977 their fans were deeply unhappy. So imagine how they felt when, shortly after, it was revealed that the team who had bought him were Arsenal. On second thoughts, don't even go there….

Jennings played for a further seven seasons at Arsenal, and continued playing for Northern Ireland for a couple of years after that, before returning to Spurs in 1993 as goalkeeping coach.

In an era when British football was littered with great goalkeepers (except Scotland, of course), Jennings was up there with the best of them. A big man, with almost comically large hands, he exuded a comforting presence behind the defence not unlike Peter Schmeichel, although he was less inclined to fits of apoplectic rage than the excitable Dane. 'Big Pat' was perhaps marginally less acrobatic than one or two of his contemporaries, but his handling was impeccable. Jennings was a fixture in the Northern Ireland team in an international career spanning an amazing 22 years. He played in two World Cup Finals, making his final appearance in the 1986 Finals against Brazil in Mexico – on his 41st birthday.

- Probably his finest moment was a brilliant performance in Northern Ireland's 1-0 win over hosts Spain at the 1982 World Cup Finals.
- Jennings scored a freak goal in the 1967 Charity Shield, a huge punt bouncing over Alex Stepney into the Manchester United goal.
- He was Football Writers' Player of the Year, 1973 and PFA Player of the Year in 1976.
- Undoubtedly, Jennings' most embarrassing moment was being dressed as a car battery in a ludicrous 1970s TV advertisement.
- He received an MBE in 1976 and an OBE in 1987.

VITAL STATISTICS

Place of Birth:	County Down, Northern Ireland	
Date of Birth:	12 June 1945	**Died:** n/a
Caps:	119 (N. Ireland)	**Goals (International):** 0
Clubs:	Watford, Tottenham, Arsenal	
Appearances:	Club (League): 757	
Goals:	Club (League): 0	
Trophies:	FAC 1967, 1979; LC 1971, 1973; UEFAC 1973	

LEGEND RATING	
Achievement	7.0
Skill	9.0
Teamwork	8.0
Passion	9.0
Personality	7.0
TOTAL	**40.0**

Jock's Delight
Celtic 2 Internazionale 1, 1967

IN THE TUNNEL it looked like a mismatch. Favourites Internazionale stood tall, tanned and experienced, and numbered Facchetti, Mazzola and Domenghini amongst their team of European all-stars. Celtic, in comparison, appeared pale, undersized and more used to scrapping in a frost-bound Glasgow than the Portuguese sunshine, and when Mazzola converted a penalty on six minutes after Craig had fouled Cappellini, few gave the Scots an earthly chance against Inter's famous catenaccio ('doorbolt') defence. Led by the peerless Facchetti, the Milan side were pioneers of the cagey game, defending in numbers and countering with speed.

But the turning-point came on the hour; making amends for his earlier indiscretion, Craig combined with Murdoch to create a chance that Gemmell converted with aplomb. A rattled Inter had been hustled into altering their game plan, but couldn't raise the pace. The match was heading for extra-time when a speculative cross-shot from the edge of the box was swept in by Chalmers with six minutes to go. Lucky perhaps, but no more than the Bhoys' performance merited. Inter had been sunk by Glaswegian passion, the Cup belonged to Celtic.

- Celtic were the first British team ever to win the European Cup, beating Manchester United to it by a year.
- Tommy Gemmell also scored in the 1970 final, but Celtic lost 2-1 to Feyenoord.
- The match proved to be third time unlucky for Inter (they had won the trophy in 1964 and 1965).
- A genuine triumph for the city: all of Celtic's team were born within 15 miles of Glasgow.
- For Celtic the match completed a clean sweep; they had already won a domestic treble.

SCORERS	**Celtic:** Gemmell, Chalmers
	Internazionale: Mazzola (pen)
EVENT	European Cup final, Lisbon, 25 May 1967
CELTIC	(Man: Jock Stein)
	1. Simpson 2. Craig 3. Gemmell 4. Murdoch 5. McNeill 6. Clark
	7. Johnstone 8. Wallace 9. Chalmers 10. Auld 11. Lennox
INTER	(Man: Helenio Herrera)
	1. Sarti 2. Burgnich 3. Facchetti 4. Bedin 5. Guarneri 6. Picchi
	7. Bicicli 8. Mazzola 9. Cappellini 10. Corso 11. Domenghini

Johnstone, Jimmy
Celtic, Scotland

IF JOCK STEIN was the architect of Celtic's greatest-ever team and Billy McNeill its keystone, then Jimmy 'Jinky' Johnstone was its magician-in-chief. A small, mercurial winger from a rich Scottish tradition of natural ball-players, Johnstone could win a game in a moment and was dubbed the 'flying flea' by a laudatory French press after a European tie against Nantes.

Although a member of the 1967 European Cup-winning team, his most memorable games were Celtic's most infamous, namely the two ties against Racing Club in the 1967 World Club Championship. Johnstone's reputation saw him cynically hacked and abused in the first-drawn game (he had to wash opponents' spittle from his hair at half-time) and, determined to give as good as he got in the replay, he eventually received a red card for elbowing an opponent.

His greatest game came in 1970 when, against Leeds in a European Cup semi-final, he teased and tormented the English team's defence in a famous victory. He was ineffective in the final though, well shackled by an impressive Feyenoord rearguard. Despite his success, the game failed to make him his fortune and he was later forced to take jobs as a lorry driver and construction worker.

- Johnstone would have won more than 23 Scottish caps but for a lifelong fear of flying.
- His debut in 1963 was also his heaviest defeat as a player; a 6-0 trouncing by Kilmarnock.
- Johnstone once scored twice in a 5-1 drubbing of Red Star Belgrade. Before the match Jock Stein had promised him he would not have to fly to the return leg if Celtic won easily.
- Johnstone wasn't the only player sent off against Racing Club – three Celtic players were dismissed along with two opponents.

VITAL STATISTICS

Place of Birth:	Viewpark, Lanarkshire, Scotland	
Date of Birth:	30 September 1944	**Died:** n/a
Caps:	23 (Scotland)	**Goals (International):** 4
Clubs:	Celtic, San Jose Earthquakes, Sheffield United,	
	Dundee	
Appearances:	Club (League): 332	
Goals:	Club (League): 84	
Trophies:	SLT 1966–1974; SFAC 1965, 1967, 1969,	
	1971, 1972, 1974, 1975; EC 1967	

Achievement	7.0
Skill	9.0
Teamwork	6.0
Passion	8.0
Personality	7.0
TOTAL	**37.0**

LEGEND RATING

Jones, Vinnie

Wimbledon

VINNIE JONES does not appear in this volume for his ability with a ball (just as well, we hear you shout), but rather for his status as a footballing personality. There are myriad examples of footballers being exploited by the media, but Jones was one of the first to manipulate the media to further his own non-footballing career.

After making his mark as a player in the Wimbledon 'crazy gang' (he was a member of their famous 1988 FA Cup-winning side), Jones built up a deserved reputation as a hard man, collecting red and yellow cards with a rare enthusiasm. That said, he was probably a better player than people would care to admit; he hit a mean long ball and was a threat in the air at set-pieces. As the famous Wimbledon team broke up, Jones began his wanderings around the league, including spells at Chelsea and Leeds and even a brief flirtation with international football after he discovered some ancient Welsh blood in his family tree. Now firmly established in green-belt Hertfordshire, country squire Jones made his movie debut in 1998 in Guy Ritchie's landmark Brit-gangster movie *Lock, Stock and Two Smoking Barrels*. Hollywood beckoned, and Vinnie was a made man.

- Jones holds the record for the fastest booking in British football. Playing for Chelsea against Sheffield United he received a yellow card after only three seconds, breaking his own record of five seconds playing for Sheffield United the year before.
- 'He wouldn't have lasted five minutes in my day,' said Tommy Smith, still the macho braggart years after his retirement.
- 'I'm 27 years old and the referee tells me I'm not allowed to swear.' Vinnie never really got to grips with the rules.
- 2002. Jones turns recording artist and sings on BBC's *Later with Jools Holland*.

VITAL STATISTICS

Place of Birth:	Watford, England		
Date of Birth:	5 January 1965	**Died:** n/a	
Caps:	9 (Wales)	**Goals (International):** 0	
Clubs:	Wimbledon, Leeds, Sheffield United, Chelsea,		
	Queens Park Rangers		
Appearances:	Club (League): 393		
Goals:	Club (League): 33		
Trophies:	FAC 1988		

LEGEND RATING	
Achievement	5.0
Skill	5.0
Teamwork	7.0
Passion	9.0
Personality	9.0
TOTAL	**35.0**

It's been emotional....

Keane, Roy

Manchester United, Republic Of Ireland

ROY KEANE WAS PLAYING for Cobh Ramblers when he was spotted by a Nottingham Forest scout and brought to England by Brian Clough in 1990. Three years later Forest turned their £10,000 investment into £3.75 m from Manchester United. What seemed an extraordinary fee in 1993 now looks a snip, as Keane has been the driving force behind the Old Trafford club's recent run of success.

In the 2000–01 season Keane was vociferous in his criticism of his team-mates, accusing them of failing to maintain their hunger for success after the treble-winning season. Keane could lay claim to being the most complete midfielder in British football in recent times – only Patrick Vieira runs him close and, like Vieira, Keane has a dark side to his game. Fans will remember sendings-off for vicious tackles and violent outbursts alongside the dominant, driving performances. Keane's influence is keenly felt at international level as well. In a team big on passion but short on world-class players, it is Keane who is frequently asked to stand tall in crucial games. His outburst before the 2002 World Cup did him little credit, and seemed to have ended his international career, before a surprise recall in 2004.

☞ A new United contract in 2000 worth £52,000 per week made him – for a brief spell – the highest paid player in the Premiership, and destroyed Old Trafford's established wage structure.

👍 He was the 2000 PFA and Football Writers' Player of the Year.

☞ 1996–2001. United won the league title every year, except the one Keane spent sidelined with cruciate ligament damage.

☞ Keane has been critical of United's passionless corporate fans, once famously dismissing them as the 'prawn sandwich brigade'.

👍 2004. He set a modern-era record, playing in six FA Cup finals; Lord Arthur Kinnaird played in nine between 1873 and 1883.

☞ Failure to qualify for the 2006 World Cup finally brought the curtain down on Keane's time with Ireland. There are hints 2006 may see him leave Old Trafford as well.

VITAL STATISTICS

Place of Birth:	Cork, Ireland		Achievement	9.0
Date of Birth:	10 August 1971	**Died:** n/a	Skill	8.0
Caps:	67 (R. Ireland)	**Goals (International):** 9	Teamwork	9.0
Clubs:	Nottingham Forest, Manchester United		Passion	9.5
Appearances:	Club (League): 440		Personality	7.0
Goals:	Club (League): 55			
Trophies:	EC 1999; LT 1994, 1996, 1997, 1999, 2000, 2001, 2003; FAC 1994, 1996, 1999, 2004		**TOTAL 42.5**	

LEGEND RATING

Keegan, Kevin

Liverpool, Hamburg, Southampton, Newcastle United, England

HUGELY COMMITTED, deeply passionate – and, at times, comically naive – Kevin Keegan is one of the great characters of the modern game. Plucked from obscurity at Scunthorpe by Bill Shankly, Keegan became the focal point of Liverpool's attack, and his almost telepathic understanding with John Toshack proved to be one of the club's most successful striking partnerships. Never afraid of a new challenge, Keegan later moved to Hamburg, where his enthusiasm won colleagues and fans over after a shaky start. Back to England and another successful spell at Southampton under Lawrie McMenemy, and a final flourish at Newcastle.

Twenty-one goals in 63 internationals was a decent return for a striker, but Keegan rarely got the opportunity to shine in major tournaments – a 20-minute stint as a substitute against Spain in 1982 was his only appearance at a World Cup Finals. As a club manager Keegan has always sent out teams with one objective in mind: to attack. This approach has made his teams popular but has not seen him collect any major silverware. He was an absurd choice as England manager, clearly lacking the tactical wherewithal for international football. He does deserve credit for reviving the fortunes of Newcastle, Fulham and Manchester City, but he was unable to lead any of them to a trophy.

- He was Footballer of the Year, 1976 and European Footballer of the Year, 1978 and 1979.
- He retired from international football when he was left out of Bobby Robson's first squad in 1982.
- His song, 'Head Over Heels', was a minor hit in both England and Germany.
- He resigned as England manager after a home defeat by Germany in 2000, and was honest enough to admit to his tactical shortcomings.

VITAL STATISTICS

		MANAGER		PLAYER	
Place of Birth:	Armthorpe, Yorkshire, England				
Date of Birth:	14 February 1951 **Died:** n/a				
Caps:	63 (England) **Goals (International):** 21				
Clubs:	Scunthorpe United, Liverpool, Hamburg,	Achievement	5	Achievement	9
	Southampton, Newcastle	Tactical Awareness	5	Skill	7
Appearances:	Club (for Liverpool): 323	Motivation	9	Teamwork	9
Goals:	Club (for Liverpool): 100	Team Selection/Transfers	9	Passion	9
Trophies:	LT 1973, 1976, 1977; FAC 1974;	Personality	8	Personality	8
	UEFAC 1976; EC 1977; BLG 1979;				
	European Player of the Year 1978, 1979	**TOTAL**	**36**	**TOTAL**	**42**

LEGEND RATING

Klinsmann, Jurgen
Tottenham Hotspur, Germany

WHEN JURGEN KLINSMANN returned to Tottenham Hotspur for a second spell in December 1997 he faced one of his biggest challenges. Under the inept management of Christian Gross, an unpopular appointment by an unpopular chairman, Alan Sugar, the club were facing relegation. That the club stayed up confirmed Klinsmann's status as a Spurs legend, after his prolific season in 1994–95.

Klinsmann's appetite for new adventures is evidenced by his willingness to play in Italy, France and England, as well as his native Germany. He was a consistent scorer in all leagues, even the notoriously defensive Serie A. Quick and incisive in the box, as well as good in the air, Klinsmann was a natural predator. He was also an intelligent player – more articulate in English than most of his Spurs colleagues.

Klinsmann played in three World Cups, scoring 11 goals in 17 games, a fabulous record. It was a foul on him that won the penalty from which Breheme scored to win the 1990 World Cup final. His appointment as coach of the national team was generally popular. With no qualifiers as a yardstick it remains to be seen whether the hosts, short of class players, give a decent account of themselves at the World Cup.

☞ The much-travelled Klinsmann spent 15 years in search of a league title before he finally won one – the Bundesliga with Bayern Munich in 1997.

☞ He arrived at Spurs in 1994 amidst media furore about his penchant for diving. A headlong plunge towards the corner flag on scoring his first goal for the club revealed a sense of humour.

👍 His 15 goals in Bayern's successful 1996 UEFA Cup campaign remains a record for European competition.

👍 In the 1990 World Cup Klinsmann gave one of the great individual performances, seeming to beat Holland almost single-handed after the early dismissal of his strike partner Voller.

VITAL STATISTICS

Place of Birth:	Goppingen, Germany	
Date of Birth:	30 July 1964	**Died:** n/a
Caps:	108 (Germany)	**Goals (International):** 47
Clubs:	Stuttgart Kickers, VfB Stuttgart, Inter Milan,	
	Monaco, Tottenham, Bayern Munich, Sampdoria	
Appearances:	Club (League): 491	
Goals:	Club (League): 194	
Trophies:	SA 1989; WorC 1990; BLG 1997; EuroC 1996;	
	UEFAC 1996	

LEGEND RATING	
Achievement	9.0
Skill	8.0
Teamwork	9.0
Passion	8.0
Personality	7.0
TOTAL	**41.0**

Lampard, Frank

West Ham United, Chelsea, England

CHELSEA ARE UNDOUBTEDLY a team of stars. Although their financial muscle has borne a squad packed with international talent, Frank Lampard is one of only two who have earned the tag 'irreplaceable'.

It wasn't always so. Lampard arrived at Stamford Bridge in 2001 for what seemed a hefty £11 m with a reputation as a solid performer in the centre of midfield. Once he hit form, that fee began to look a snip. Lampard's contribution was consistency itself, and the arrival of Jose Mourinho saw his game develop at a rapid pace. In the competitive environments of the Premiership and Champions League, no player has matched Lampard's industry, fitness and achievement. Squad rotation is an anathema, Lampard's *raison d'etre* is to be the pivot of every match, and an ability to link with attack has brought him a goals-to-game ratio that is the envy of many strikers.

At international level, Lampard took some time to reproduce his club form, but he has now made himself indispensable, scoring winners in England's last two qualifying matches and easing their progress to Germany 06. For a midfielder who can lay claim to be Europe's most consistent, it is a fitting stage.

☞ Lampard forms one half of a rare father-and-son international partnership. Frank senior, also a West Ham player, won two caps for England.

👍 In a recent game against Portsmouth Lampard set a new record of 160 consecutive Premiership appearances, beating previous record holder David James.

👍 Named as Footballer of the Year in 2005, Lampard's intelligent and touching acceptance speech drew a prolonged ovation. Not all footballers are avaricious idiots.

☞ Did you know? Lampard has also played, and scored, for Swansea City. He was loaned to the Welsh club in 1995 by West Ham.

VITAL STATISTICS

Place of Birth:	Romford, England	
Date of Birth:	21 June 1978	**Died:** n/a
Caps:	37 (England)	**Goals (International):** 10
Clubs:	West Ham United, Chelsea	
Appearances:	Club (League): 317	
Goals:	Club (League): 65	
Trophies:	LT 2005; LC 2005	

Achievement	6.0
Skill	7.5
Teamwork	10.0
Passion	8.5
Personality	8.0
TOTAL	**40.0**

LEGEND RATING

Larsson, Henrik

Celtic, Sweden

SWEDEN'S FINEST EXPORT since Abba got a boyhood taste for football watching English league matches live on television, but it is north of the border where Henrik Larsson has made his name, becoming the biggest Celtic icon of the past 10 years.

Eye-catching both for his striking ability and fashionable dreadlocks, his 16 goals were a major factor in the title coming home to Parkhead after nine years of Rangers domination. It nearly ended there. After breaking his leg during a UEFA Cup match against Lyon in October 1999, there were fears that Larsson would never play again. Larsson's response when he finally made it back ended any doubts. Under new manager Martin O'Neill, a 42-goal season helped Celtic sweep all before them in 2001, and he followed that with near-identical campaigns in the following three seasons.

A seasoned international, he was one of the scorers in Sweden's quarter-final defeat of Romania in USA 94, and did his reputation no harm in the Far East in 2002, before announcing his retirement from internationals. It was a short-lived retirement – he was still scoring for his country in World Cup qualifiers in 2005. At the end of his Celtic contract he bade an emotional farewell to Parkhead in 2004, and left for a final flourish at Barcelona, where injuries seriously hampered his first season.

- His 2001 European Golden Boot award was the first made to a Scottish-based player since Ally McCoist in 1993.
- He scored on his international debut as Sweden qualified for USA 94.
- Larsson was signed twice by Wim Jansen, for Feyenoord and Celtic.
- His son Jordan is named after his hero, basketball star Michael Jordan.
- Scores twice for Celtic in the 2003 UEFA Cup final, only for the Bhoys to succumb 3-2 to Porto.

VITAL STATISTICS

Place of Birth:	Helsingborg, Sweden			
Date of Birth:	20 September 1971	**Died:** n/a		
Caps:	87 (Sweden)	**Goals (International):** 34	Achievement	7.0
Clubs:	Hogabog BK, Helsingborgs BK, Feyenoord, Celtic,		Skill	8.5
	Barcelona		Teamwork	8.0
Appearances:	Club (League): 455		Passion	7.0
Goals:	Club (League): 276		Personality	6.5
Trophies:	SLT 1998, 2001, 2002, 2004, 2005; SFAC 2001,			
	2002, 2004		**TOTAL**	**37.0**

LEGEND RATING

Last Gasp Title

Liverpool 0 Arsenal 2, 1989

IT REMAINS THE MOST dramatic finish to a championship race in history. A rearranged fixture had inadvertently brought the top two together for the season's final game. Liverpool held all the aces; only a two-goal Arsenal victory would bring the title to Highbury.

A goalless first-half suited Liverpool, but the home crowd's celebrations were put on ice at 52 minutes, when Alan Smith, applying the faintest of touches to a Nigel Winterburn free kick, gave Arsenal the lead. The goal made Liverpool edgy, and as the final whistle drew closer they retreated towards their own goal, inviting pressure from the Gunners.

Deep into injury time the score remained 1-0 and the Kop's volume was increasing. Steve McMahon rallied the Liverpool ranks, gesturing frantically to his team-mates that there was just one minute to go. But a minute was all Arsenal needed. Dixon pumped a hopeful last effort to Smith, who spotted the desperate gallop of Michael Thomas. The pass was precise, the flick over Grobbelaar ice-cool. On 91 minutes and 22 seconds, Arsenal had won it.

- Ray Kennedy's goal at White Hart Lane to clinch the 1971 title and Alan Sunderland's winner in the FA Cup final eight years later had brought Arsenal fans to the brink. This result reduced them to gibbering wrecks.
- Both teams finished with virtually identical records: W22 D10 L6 GD +37. Arsenal won by scoring 73 goals to Liverpool's 65.
- Arsenal's task had looked impossible after Liverpool beat West Ham 5-1 in their previous home game to create a two-goal cushion. The *Daily Mirror* headline the following day was typical: 'You Haven't Got A Prayer, Arsenal'.
- Brian Moore's commentary is familiar to Arsenal fans: 'Thomas … it's up for grabs now … Thomasss!'

Michael Thomas (yellow shirt) lifts the ball over a prone Grobbelaar for Arsenal's clincher.

SCORERS	Smith, Thomas
EVENT	Division One, Anfield, 26 May 1989
LIVERPOOL	(Man: Kenny Dalglish)
	1. Grobbelaar 2. Ablett 3. Staunton 4. Nicol 5. Whelan 6. Hansen
	7. Houghton 8. Aldridge 9. Rush 10. Barnes 11. McMahon
ARSENAL	(Man: George Graham)
	1. Lukic 2. Dixon 3. Winterburn 4. Thomas 5. O'Leary 6. Adams
	7. Rocastle 8. Richardson 9. Smith 10. Bould 11. Merson

Laudrup, Brian & Michael
Denmark

DENMARK'S EMERGENCE as a major force in European football is a relatively recent phenomenon, roughly starting around 25 years ago with the arrival of Allan Simonsen. Since then they have produced a string of talented players, not least the brothers Michael and Brian Laudrup. Michael, the elder by nearly five years, was the bright young thing in the side that helped illuminate Mexico 86 before their disappointing capitulation to Spain in the second round. A modern attacking midfielder with pace and touch, Michael's list of clubs (Juventus, Barcelona, Real Madrid, Ajax) bears witness to his quality. And yet, ironically, he was to miss his country's finest hour; a dispute with coach Richard Moller Nielsen led to him being left out of Denmark's stunning victory at Euro 92.

His brother, Brian, did win a medal at that tournament and went on to follow in his brother's footsteps, enjoying spells at several of Europe's finest club teams. His best days were probably at Ibrox where, after a spellbinding first season, he won over a sceptical Rangers crowd. It was often said that the brothers rarely played well together but on Michael's international finale, a memorable quarter-final at France 98 that Denmark narrowly lost 3-2 to Brazil, they made a mockery of this theory. Both played out of their proverbial skins.

☞ Between them the Laudrup brothers have turned out for most of the great European clubs.

☜ Brian is the first foreign player to be voted Scottish Footballer of the Year.

☞ Unlike the Rangers faithful, Chelsea fans do not have fond memories of Brian Laudrup. He left the club in bizarre circumstances to return to Denmark after only a few games.

☞ After the quarter-final with Brazil at France 98 Michael threw his boots into the crowd to signal his retirement. Brian's retirement from internationals followed soon after.

VITAL STATISTICS
BRIAN LAUDRUP

Place of Birth:	Vienna, Austria		
Date of Birth:	22 February 1969	**Died:** n/a	
Caps:	82 (Denmark)	**Goals (International):** 21	
Clubs:	Brondby, Bayer Uerdingen, Fiorentina, AC Milan,		
	Rangers, Chelsea, Copenhagen, Bayern Munich		
Appearances:	Club (League): 342		
Goals:	Club (League): 84		
Trophies:	SLT 1995, 1996, 1997; SFAC 1996; DLT 1987,		
	1988; SA 1994; EuroC 1992; ESC 1998		

Achievement	8.0
Skill	9.0
Teamwork	8.0
Passion	6.0
Personality	7.0
TOTAL	**38.0**

LEGEND RATING

Brian (left) holds the 1992 European Championship trophy.

VITAL STATISTICS
MICHAEL LAUDRUP

Place of Birth:	Copenhagen, Denmark
Date of Birth:	15 June 1964 **Died:** n/a
Caps:	104 (Denmark) **Goals (International):** 37
Clubs:	KB Copenhagen, Brondby, Juventus, Lazio, Barcelona, Real Madrid, Vissel Kobe, Ajax
Appearances:	Club (League): 464
Goals:	Club (League): 117
Trophies:	EC 1992; PLA 1991, 1992, 1993, 1994, 1995; SA 1986; DLT 1998

LEGEND RATING	
Achievement	8.0
Skill	9.0
Teamwork	8.0
Passion	6.0
Personality	7.0
TOTAL	**38.0**

Law, Denis
Manchester United, Scotland

HE SQUINTED, was scrawny and his unkempt, spiky hair gave him the appearance of a toilet brush. Yet, all this appeared little hindrance to Denis Law, who emerged as one of Manchester United's and Scotland's finest-ever strikers. The 'flying Scot' was as quick as a greyhound and with an aerial game few have surpassed.

He owes a huge debt to Bill Shankly, his first manager at Huddersfield, who moulded a novice schoolboy into an 18-year-old international. Like Jimmy Greaves, he failed to settle in Italy and it was only his return to Manchester, swapping a blue shirt for a red one, that revived his career. His forward combination with George Best and Bobby Charlton was the finest in English club football. Law left Old Trafford after being kicked out of the club by Tommy Docherty who, keen to assert his authority on his arrival in 1972, made an example of him. Law joined Man City and came back to haunt Docherty the following season when his back-heeled goal for City in the Manchester derby contributed to United's relegation to Division Two. Famously, Law did not celebrate the goal. Head bowed, he simply turned round and walked solemnly back to the centre circle. Since his retirement, his partnership with former team-mate Paddy Crerand, has made him one of the circuit's most popular after-dinner speakers.

☞ Law broke three transfer records: £35,000 to Man City (UK); £100,000 to Torino (world); £115,000 to Man United (world).

✄ He was voted European Footballer of the Year, 1964.

☝ 1968. Missed United's European Cup final victory through injury.

☟ His 30 goals for Scotland set a national record, now jointly held with Kenny Dalglish.

☞ Law retired with over 300 goals in club football.

VITAL STATISTICS

Place of Birth:	Aberdeen, Scotland		
Date of Birth:	24 February 1940	**Died:** n/a	
Caps:	55 (Scotland)	**Goals (International):** 30	
Clubs:	Huddersfield Town, Manchester City, Torino,		
	Manchester United		
Appearances:	Club (All Matches): 566		
Goals:	Club (All Matches): 301		
Trophies:	FAC 1963; LT 1965, 1967		

Achievement	7.0
Skill	9.0
Teamwork	8.0
Passion	8.0
Personality	9.0
TOTAL	**41.0**

LEGEND RATING

Lawton, Tommy
Everton, England

ASK THE OLD BOY in the pub, the one who always sits at the bar with a pint of mild and a copy of the *Sporting Life* (there's always one), why he thinks players in the old days were superior to their modern counterparts, and the name of Tommy Lawton is guaranteed to crop up within five seconds. Brave, strong, supreme in the air and with a cannonball shot, Lawton was the archetypal English centre forward. Bought to replace the immortal Dixie Dean at Everton, he took on and achieved the daunting task of filling the great man's shoes. In the days of five forwards, goalscoring comparisons with today are unwise, but a career record of nearly two goals every three games, plus 22 goals from 23 England caps are a reliable indicator of his quality. Strangely, for a man whose prime years were taken by the war, he opted to play most of his career in the lower divisions, even dropping into the Third Division with Notts County before Second Division Brentford offered him a player-manager role. Due to wage restrictions Lawton made little money from the game, and spent his later years living close to poverty until his death in 1996.

☞ He managed Notts County and Brentford but was never a success in this role.

👌 He scored a hat-trick on his debut, aged 16.

👌 His 28 goals in the 1946–47 season was a Chelsea club record.

☞ John Arlott on Tommy Lawton: 'I have faith in genius'.

☞ 1948. His £20,000 move to Notts County set a British record; Third Division County saw gates rocket.

VITAL STATISTICS

Place of Birth:	Bolton, England		
Date of Birth:	6 October 1919	**Died:** 6 November 1996	
Caps:	23 (England)	**Goals (International):** 22	
Clubs:	Burnley, Everton, Chelsea, Notts County,		
	Brentford, Arsenal, Kettering Town		
Appearances:	Club (League): 390		
Goals:	Club (League): 231		
Trophies:	LT 1939		

Achievement	5.0
Skill	8.0
Teamwork	8.0
Passion	9.0
Personality	5.0
TOTAL	**35.0**

LEGEND RATING

Griffin Park, Brentford. Lawton rounds the keeper to score for the Bees.

Le Tissier, Matthew
Southampton

PERHAPS THE GREATEST ENIGMA of the modern English game, Matt Le Tissier's achievements do not merit him an entry into the hall of fame, but in many ways it is his lack of success that marks him out. His touch, and his use of the ball were reminiscent of Glenn Hoddle, his free kicks were Beckhamesque, and his dribbling was worthy of any of the 1970s mavericks with whom he is often compared.

Le Tissier's natural diffidence off the field may explain why he stayed with Southampton, then an unfashionable and struggling club, throughout his career, although many have argued that fear of failure was his prime motivation in not seeking a move to a bigger one. There may be an element of truth in this, but it would be churlish not to give Le Tissier credit for his loyalty. There have been numerous campaigns for his inclusion in the England side, but on the rare occasions he appeared he seemed to lack the confidence to express himself. Maybe, in a parallel universe, Le Tissier did move to Chelsea, win the Cup and captain England. But if he did, that means that out there somewhere is another Ken Bates. And that's not something we should even joke about.

☞ Glenn Hoddle had the excellent idea of holding a couple of B internationals to check out some fringe players. Le Tissier scored a hat-trick, but was still left out of the World Cup squad. Go figure….

👍 He scored 24 goals in 1989–90 and was voted PFA Young Player of the Year.

👍 He has only missed one penalty in over 50 attempts.

👍 He scored some astonishing goals, including one against Blackburn where he waltzed through the defence playing keepy-uppy and stroked the ball into the net.

☞ Appropriately, as their greatest contemporary player, Le Tissier scored the last-ever goal at The Dell in a 3-2 win over Arsenal.

VITAL STATISTICS

Place of Birth:	Guernsey		
Date of Birth:	14 October 1968	**Died:** n/a	
Caps:	10 (England)	**Goals (International):** 0	
Clubs:	Southampton		
Appearances:	Club (League): 443		
Goals:	Club (League): 163		
Trophies:	None		

Achievement	5.0
Skill	10.0
Teamwork	6.0
Passion	8.0
Personality	6.0
TOTAL	**35.0**

LEGEND RATING

League Cup
It Seemed A Good Idea At The Time

IT TOOK AN AGE to get going, and but for the persistence of league secretary Alan Hardaker it would never have got off the ground. The idea of a Cup purely for the top four divisions had been mooted for years but it didn't exactly arrive with a fanfare.

Most top clubs viewed 'Hardaker's folly' as an irrelevance and refused to enter, and Rochdale's appearance in the second final was indicative of its lack of cachet.

It was not until the final was switched to Wembley in 1967 that the tournament acquired the respect it so desperately needed, and QPR and Swindon provided further interest by winning it as Third Division sides, both beating First Division opposition in their respective finals against West Brom and Arsenal. The award of a UEFA Cup place for the winners has helped maintain its importance over the years, but the recent growth of the Champions League has eroded its importance to the big clubs who now regularly field weakened teams in the competition.

In 2003–04 the competition, with its new sponsors Carling, received a shot in the arm thanks to a keenly-contested final. Bolton and Middlesbrough provided a welcome change, the latter's 2-1 victory earning them their first major silverware in over a century of trying.

☞ The League Cup has been through several incarnations. Bizarrely known as the Milk Cup for a while, it has also lent its name to sponsors Rumbelows, Coca-Cola, Littlewoods and Worthington's.

✍ The 1967 and 1969 finals were the making of Rodney Marsh and Don Rogers. Both scored winners and moved to bigger clubs.

✍ Liverpool fans were particularly scathing about the League Cup, mainly because it took them 20 years to win it. After four straight wins (1981–84) the 'tea kettle' jibes disappeared.

☞ The Aston Villa v Everton final went to a third game in 1977. After two dull encounters, Villa won 3-2 after extra time.

☞ Oxford and Luton won the trophy in the late 1980s. Both subsequently played in the bottom division.

Q: What is taken to Wembley every year and never used?

A: Malcolm McDonald

Sunderland quip after the 1976 League Cup final; it was his second Wembley disappointment in three seasons

Middlesbrough madness after defeating Bolton 2-1 in the 2004 League Cup.

Leeds United – The Revie Years
Leeds, 1968–75

THE WORD PROFESSIONAL has several shades of meaning, and Don Revie's Leeds knew them all. Fit, organised and skilful they were the epitome of mechanical excellence but, at Revie's behest, they were also hard, ruthless and prone to bending the rules when it suited them. None of this should disguise their ability, though. Leeds lost only twice in winning the league in 1969, the lowest total in a 42-game season, and when they won the league again five years later it was with essentially the same team – togetherness was undoubtedly a factor in their success. Yet, at times, they could be their own worst enemy, and often failed at the final hurdle. They were league runners-up five times and blew two FA Cup finals, notably against Second Division Sunderland in 1973. They weren't always the prettiest or most popular team, but few sides got the better of them.

- Harvey's emergence as a replacement for the error-prone Gary Sprake was a major improvement to the side.
- The downside of the close-knit team was that they aged together; Leeds fell into sharp decline after this team broke up, and only re-emerged as a force in the early 1990s.
- Cooper was a great attacking fullback who ought to have won more than his 20 caps. He scored the goal that won the 1968 League Cup, bringing the squad their first trophy.
- Even in their title winning seasons Leeds weren't prolific scorers; Jones top scored in both campaigns with just 14.

Manager: Don Revie

Key Players

David Harvey (G) Jack Charlton (D) Norman Hunter (D)
Paul Reaney (FB) Terry Cooper (FB) Billy Bremner (M)
Johnny Giles (M) Peter Lorimer (F) Eddie Gray (W)
Allan Clarke (F) Mick Jones (F)

Trophies
LT 1969, 1974; FAC 1972; LC 1968; UEFA 1968, 1971

Leeds United
The Dream Team

A TEAM THAT TAKES no prisoners. The defence is entirely from the great Revie team of the 1960s and 1970s, one of the meanest in domestic history, and two players from that era, Bremner and Giles, also occupy the central midfield positions. The sixth and final member of the Revie side to make this Dream Team starting XI is Alan 'Sniffer' Clarke, a striker who rarely failed to live up to his nickname.

Lest these players are not considered combative enough, Gordon Strachan adds more bite in midfield, leaving Harry Kewell free to link with the front two. The sole representative of Corinthian sportsmanship is provided by the Gentle Giant himself at centre forward, John Charles. One shudders to think what he would have made of Revie's team talks, the shin-high tackles or the incessant baiting of the officials, but if his sensibilities were too offended, he could always be replaced by toothless assassin Joe Jordan. Make no mistake, this team will autograph a few shins. The referee will need an A4 notebook.

☞ If Revie's team had enjoyed the benefit of Nigel Martyn in goal rather than the accident-prone Gary Sprake, they may have finished runners-up less often.

☞ Despite less than two full seasons, Rio Ferdinand deserves his place on the bench for his improvement and increased maturity. It also means we don't have to pick Gordon McQueen.

☞ The dependence on the modern era is entirely justified. Leeds won nothing prior to the Revie years.

☞ Two great flair players are not included: Eric Cantona and Tony Currie both enjoyed better spells with other clubs.

Manager: Don Revie
4-4-2

Nigel Martyn (90s/00s)

Paul Madeley (60s) Jack Charlton (60s/70s)
Norman Hunter (60s/70s) Terry Cooper (60s/70s)

Gordon Strachan (80s) Billy Bremner (C) (60s/70s)
Johnny Giles (60s/70s) Harry Kewell (00s)

John Charles (50s) Alan Clarke (70s)

Subs: David Harvey (G) (70s) Rio Ferdinand (D) (00s)
David Batty (M) (90s) Eddie Gray (W) (60s/70s) Joe Jordan (F) (70s)

The last decent Leeds side, prior its unravelling during the 2002–03 season following disastrous financial results.

Liddell, Billy

Liverpool, Scotland

THERE HAVE ARGUABLY been better Liverpool players, and there have certainly been players who won far more at Anfield, particularly in the glory days of the 1970s and 1980s, but the more decorated names of Neal, McDermott or Souness are not the ones that Liverpool fans are currently campaigning to have inscribed on the Shankly Gates. That honour is reserved for one man: Billy Liddell. A hugely versatile player, his favourite role was as a marauding striker with a wicked shot in either foot. He signed for Liverpool as an amateur in 1938, but his name was made as a winner of the first post-war league title nine years later. Ironically, this lone league medal came courtesy of Manchester United, whose 2-1 defeat of Stoke on the final day handed Liverpool the championship. Older Kopites still maintain that Liddell's injury in the 1950 FA Cup final robbed them of victory against Arsenal, and he remained their only hope during the wilderness years that saw them relegated in 1954. Despite his efforts, he never played again in the First Division. His death, at 79 in July 2001, prompted grief on a scale not witnessed since the passing of Shankly.

☞ The club was dubbed 'Liddellpool' due to his huge influence.
☞ The archetypal 'Boys Own' hero had an unlikely beginning, training as an accountant.
☞ Liddell played in every outfield position for Liverpool.
☞ Liddell and Stanley Matthews are the only players to have twice appeared in a United Kingdom XI.
✎ A true Corinthian, Liddell was never booked despite his tenacious attitude.

VITAL STATISTICS

Place of Birth:	Dunfermline, Scotland		Achievement 5.0
Date of Birth:	10 January 1921	**Died:** 3 July 2001	Skill 8.0
Caps:	28 (Scotland)	**Goals (International):** 6	Teamwork 8.0
Clubs:	Liverpool		Passion 9.0
Appearances:	Club (League): 537		Personality 6.0
Goals:	Club (League): 229		
Trophies:	LT 1947		**TOTAL 36.0**

LEGEND RATING

Lineker, Gary
Leicester City, Everton, Tottenham Hotspur, England

THE GOLDEN BOY. Lineker is a man it is hard to dislike, even if you find his personality a little anodyne. A model professional with all his clubs, not a season went by without Lineker delivering his quota of goals; he was top scorer in England three times, each time with different clubs. Despite recent gags regarding a longstanding toe problem, Lineker was rarely injured until moving to Japan and, incredibly for a player who regularly suffered intense provocation, went through his entire career without receiving a yellow card.

Lineker's game was based around pace and a true poacher's instinct for knowing where the ball would arrive; a huge number of tap-ins from inside six yards is testimony to intelligence, not luck.

Having been successful in England, Lineker moved to Barcelona, and soon proved he could adapt to European life and football just as easily. He only left because Johann Cruyff, bizarrely chose to play him on the wing. Lineker returned to play in Terry Venables' strong Spurs side with Gazza, winning his first domestic trophy, the FA Cup, at the age of 30.

Since retiring Lineker has had a successful media career, eventually succeeding Des Lynam as the face of *Match Of The Day*. His light sparring with Alan Hansen sets the tone for the programme in the twenty-first century.

- He scored 10 goals in two World Cup Finals, winning the Golden Boot at Mexico 86 with six goals.
- He scored after four minutes of the first all-Merseyside FA Cup final in 1986, but Everton lost.
- He scored all four goals for Barcelona against Real Madrid in 1987.
- Lineker was controversially substituted by Graham Taylor during England's defeat to Sweden at the 1992 European Championships. It was to be his last appearance for his country.
- He was voted PFA Player of the Year, 1986 and 1992.

VITAL STATISTICS

Place of Birth:	Leicester, England	
Date of Birth:	30 November 1960	**Died:** n/a
Caps:	80 (England)	**Goals (International):** 48
Clubs:	Leicester City, Everton, Barcelona, Tottenham,	
	Nagoya Grampus	
Appearances:	Club (All Matches): 447	
Goals:	Club (All Matches): 236	
Trophies:	CWC 1989; FAC 1991	

LEGEND RATING	
Achievement	8.0
Skill	9.0
Teamwork	8.0
Passion	9.0
Personality	7.0
TOTAL	**41.0**

Loadsabentmoney

Corruption

IN A PROFESSIONAL GAME where millions, and now billions, change hands in transfer fees and sponsorship deals, it was always hoping against hope to assume that a sporting spirit would prevail.

The maximum wage system has got a lot to answer for. During its existence players would routinely supplement their income with under-the-counter cash payments, often surreptitiously placed in a pocket or shoe after the game. And old habits die hard. Even in the modern era, several clubs and individuals have been relegated, fined or expelled for conducting their financial business in a less than honest fashion.

Betting has brought the most severe problems. In 1964 tabloid revelations exposed three Sheffield Wednesday players in a match-fixing scandal. This proved to be the tip of a decidedly sleazy iceberg. The spiralling transfer fees and use of third-party agents in recent times have also led to some high-profile cases of skulduggery, the most notorious example being that of George Graham and agent Rune Hauge. For every one found guilty, you can be almost certain there are at least a dozen getting away with it.

- Match officials are not whiter than white. In 1979, a Scottish referee and both linesmen were banned for three years after accepting gifts from Milan before taking charge of their UEFA Cup tie against Levski Spartak. More recently a number of top-level German referees were struck off for rigging games.
- 1982. A major Italian betting scandal claimed several high-profile casualties, including Paolo Rossi.
- In a 1990s match-fixing scandal, Bruce Grobbelaar and Hans Segers faced court action after they were alleged to have accepted cash for conceding goals. Grobbelaar's case started a legal storm as his acquittal was quashed by an appeal court.
- Corruption isn't a modern preserve. In 1919 Leeds City were expelled from the league for making irregular payments.

'What I know most surely about morality and the duty of man I owe to sport.'

Albert Camus, novelist and philosopher (1913–60). Camus briefly played professional football as a goalkeeper

If you've just been convicted of a crime, why not look like a criminal for good measure? Bruce Grobbelaar leaves court.

Loadsamoney
Celebrity Chairmen

CHAIRMEN TEND TO FALL into two categories. The first are the local businessmen who, made wealthy by their acumen in scrap metal or toilet paper, wish to realise a childhood dream, while the second are a disparate bunch of entertainers and media puppies who have nothing better to do with their money.

That said, many are genuine fans whose input is far more than financial; Elton John racks up enormous international phone bills and charters private jets in his desire to follow Watford, while Jasper Carrott stood on the St Andrews terraces for years before his fame brought him greater influence in the affairs of Birmingham City. Delia Smith, although a director rather than chairwoman, brings more than a decent half-time pie to Norwich City. Some of them are in it simply for the dough, though. Take Stan Flashman, whose principal interest at Barnet was never anything other than to turn a fast buck. 'Why sleep when you can make money,' reflected an attitude that many of his peers share but dare not utter in public.

☞ 'He's fat, he's round, he's never in the ground, Cap'n Bob.' Like their fanzine's editors, Derby fans fail to join the Robert Maxwell fan club.

☞ Elton John has always retained a philosophical attitude to some unacceptable homophobic chanting from opposing fans.

☜ Uri Geller's 'positive energy' had the opposite effect on Reading, who finished bottom of Division One in 1998. If he'd bent the goalposts instead of spoons they might have scored more often.

☞ Visiting fans at Craven Cottage collectively wave British passports at Mohamed al Fayed. It takes more than ownership of Fulham to obtain one, apparently.

'Maxwell Chairman? We may as well have Max Wall.'

Derby County fanzine the *Sheep* gets justifiably splenetic

Elton John laments on what Watford have done with his cash.

Lofthouse, Nat
Bolton Wanderers, England

'LA BANDIERA' is an Italian expression used to describe a player whose career is so intertwined with the fortunes of his club he becomes a symbol of its very soul. Nat Lofthouse is the 'Il Bandiera' of Bolton Wanderers. By far their most famous and successful player, he was the inspiration behind their most recent success, and as president still retains close ties with the Trotters.

Bolton were a robust Division One club in the 1950s and Lofthouse's battering-ram style suited them; powerful and dominant in the air he was the sort of player that coaches and pundits like to describe as 'a real handful'. In the 1958 FA Cup final against Manchester United, who were fielding a team weakened by the Munich air crash, he was able to put sentiment aside and scored both goals in a 2-0 win.

In a fine England career Lofthouse's greatest moment came in a 3-2 win against an Austrian team who were one of the best in Europe. A scratch England team had done well to stay level and, with just 10 minutes left, Lofthouse broke from inside his own half and finished in style. From that day forward he was universally referred to as 'The Lion of Vienna'.

- 👍 Lofthouse scored the opening goal in the 1953 'Matthews Final'.
- ☞ The second goal in the 1958 FA Cup final was highly controversial; Lofthouse barged United keeper Harry Gregg into the net with the ball.
- 👍 Lofthouse was the First Division's top scorer with 33 goals in 1956.
- 👍 He scored twice in a 2-2 draw on his England debut against Yugoslavia in 1950.
- ☞ Lofthouse displaced Jackie Milburn in the England team, and his impressive scoring rate saw him retain his place until the emergence of Tommy Taylor.

VITAL STATISTICS

Place of Birth:	Bolton, England		
Date of Birth:	27 August 1925	**Died:** n/a	
Caps:	33 (England)	**Goals (International):** 30	
Clubs:	Bolton Wanderers		
Appearances:	Club (for Bolton): 485		
Goals:	Club (for Bolton): 285		
Trophies:	FAC 1958		

LEGEND RATING	
Achievement	6.0
Skill	8.0
Teamwork	9.0
Passion	9.0
Personality	6.0
TOTAL	**38.0**

Losing It In Leon
England 2 West Germany 3, 1970

HARD DONE BY after the 1966 World Cup final when, but for the intervention of that famous Russian linesman, they would have almost certainly taken home the trophy, Germany were eager for revenge against England. And, in the sweltering heat of Leon in 1970, they extracted it with great relish.

England approached the game confidently. They were, after all, defending champions and had progressed through a group in which they were only narrowly defeated by the brilliant Brazilians. With 21 minutes left they were comfortably holding a 2-0 lead and their progress to the semi-finals looked assured but, proving that a chain is only as strong as its weakest link, stand-in keeper Peter Bonetti dived over a speculative effort from Beckenbauer and the match was suddenly back in the balance. Then, with the hapless Chelsea keeper a stranded spectator, Uwe Seeler's bizarre back-header looped agonisingly into the net with eight minutes remaining to send the match into extra-time. The German swagger had returned, while England looked exhausted. Gerd Müller had had a quiet game thus far, so quiet that it's doubtful if he had even broken sweat, but, great striker that he was, 'Der Bomber' took his only chance and England were out.

- With England 2-0 up, Alan Mullery missed a sitter and the chance to put the game beyond Germany's reach.
- For the substituted Bobby Charlton, it was to be a sad end to his 106th and final England game.
- Peter Bonetti was also never to play for England again.
- It has been claimed that England's loss altered the mood of the nation and contributed to Labour's defeat in the British General Election that took place a few weeks later.
- This match helped set up an Italy versus West Germany classic in the semi-final that the Germans lost.

SCORERS   **England:** Mullery, Peters
                West Germany: Beckenbauer, Seeler, Müller
EVENT   World Cup quarter-final, Leon, Mexico, 14 June 1970

ENGLAND   (Man: Sir Alf Ramsey)
             1. Bonetti 2. Newton, K 3. Cooper 4. Mullery 5. Labone 6. Moore 7. Lee, F
             8. Ball 9. Charlton, R 10. Hurst 11. Peters
W. GERMANY (Man: Helmut Schoen)
             1. Maier 2. Schnellinger 3. Vogts 4. Fichtel 5. Höttges 6. Beckenbauer
             7. Overath 8. Seeler 9. Libuda 10. Müller 11. Löhr

Gerd Müller fires the killer third past Bonetti.

Mackay, Dave

Tottenham Hotspur, Derby County, Scotland

EVERY TEAM NEEDS a hard man and Dave Mackay filled that role with distinction for his various clubs, and for Scotland. Indeed, the image of Mackay taking exception to a tackle by a young Billy Bremner is one of the most enduring football photographs.

Mackay shot to fame in the midfield of the Hearts side that won the Scottish League in 1958, before moving to Spurs, where he became the cornerstone of the side that won the double in 1961.

After nearly a decade at White Hart Lane, Brian Clough persuaded Mackay to move to Derby County, where he captained the side that won promotion to the First Division. He then enjoyed spells as a manager at Swindon and Nottingham Forest, before returning to the Baseball Ground to help his old side through the aftermath of Clough's sudden departure to Leeds. With Mackay at the helm Derby won a second league title in 1975, but the suspicion that he was merely enjoying the fruits of Clough's earlier groundwork were borne out by his inability to start rebuilding the team effectively, and he was dismissed in 1976.

- 👍 He was joint (with Tony Book) Football Writers' Player of the Year in 1969.
- 👎 He had a reputation as a fearsome drinker, matched only by Alan Gilzean at Spurs.
- 👍 Battled back from two broken legs in 1963–64 (not so easy then, no micro-surgery).
- 👎 Missed the European Cup Winners' Cup final in 1963 with a stomach upset.
- ✍ Mackay played in the Hearts team that won the title with 132 league goals (a Scottish record), and a Spurs side that won the title with 115 goals (a joint English record).

VITAL STATISTICS

Place of Birth:	Edinburgh, Scotland
Date of Birth:	14 November 1934 **Died:** n/a
Caps:	22 (Scotland) **Goals (International):** 4
Clubs:	As Player: Heart of Midlothian, Tottenham Hotspur, Derby County, Swindon Town; As Manager: Swindon Town, Nottingham Forest, Derby County, Walsall, Birmingham City
Appearances:	Club (All Matches): 669
Goals:	Club (All Matches): 88
Trophies:	SFAC 1956, 1957; SLT 1958, 1959; LT 1961, (1975); FAC 1961, 1962, 1967

Achievement	8.0
Skill	6.0
Teamwork	8.0
Passion	10.0
Personality	7.0
TOTAL	**39.0**

LEGEND RATING

Magyar Magic
Hungary, 1950s

GOING INTO the 1954 World Cup, Hungary had the footballing world at its feet. They were unbeaten since 1950 and had left a trail of strong sides in their wake, many of whom were still coming to terms with the humiliating nature of their defeats.

Like most great teams, the key to their success lay in the quality of their personnel. They had the best goalkeeper in the world in Grosics, a decent defence, a good prompter in half back Bozsik and the best forwards the planet had ever seen. Kocsis, the bull-headed bomber, Hidegkuti, a subtle and deep-lying centre forward, and Czibor their flying winger were all outrageous technicians. And then there was Puskas, the dumpy maestro, tormenting defenders with his trademark drag-backs, and scoring goals for fun.

They were the best side in the tournament in 1954, surviving a 22-man battle in the quarter-final against Brazil and a classic semi-final against Uruguay, to reach their first and only major final. They blew it, throwing away a 2-0 lead to hand a workaday West German team the trophy. Two years later the Soviets invaded Hungary and within a year Puskas, Kocsis and Czibor had all fled to Spain, never to be reunited in the colours of their country.

☞ Having hammered South Korea 12-0 in the 1952 Olympics, Hungary restricted themselves to nine goals in the 1954 World Cup. One of the Korean players, suffering from cramp, was given a massage by the Hungarian fullback, Buzansky.

🖐 Puskas went on to European Cup fame with Real Madrid as a member of their all-conquering side, and Kocsis played in a European Cup final for Barcelona.

🖐 The World Cup final against Germany was painful; Hungary were 2-0 up, but Morlock and Rahn got Germany back level, then Rahn settled the game with a late breakaway.

🖐 Puskas missed most of the 1954 World Cup Finals. He was injured in the first game against Germany.

Manager: Gustav Szebes

Key Players
Gyula Grosics (G) Jozef Bozsik (HB) Sandor Kocsis (F)
Ferenc Puskas (F) Nandor Hidegkuti (F) Zoltan Czibor (F)

Trophies
They did not win a professional trophy (surprisingly they were beaten in the 1954 World Cup final by West Germany), but they did win the 1952 Olympic title in Helsinki and were also the first overseas country to beat England at home (they won 6-3 at Wembley on 25 November 1953). To prove that was not a one-off, they beat England 7-1 in Budapest on 23 May 1954.

Max Morlock of West Germany scores the first for his country to get them back in the game during the 1954 World Cup final against Hungary.

Mannion, Wilf

Middlesbrough, England

DESPITE MIDDLESBROUGH'S RELIANCE on expensive, overseas imports in recent years, it is the homeboy who made his debut in 1937 who is considered to be their best-ever player. A wonderful dribbling forward, he never won the acclaim of his contemporary Stanley Matthews, but to Teessiders there was no finer sight than Wilf Mannion in full flow. Like Matthews, his prime years were interrupted by the Second World War, during which Mannion was one of thousands dramatically evacuated from Dunkirk.

The absence of top-flight football during the war meant that an England cap didn't materialise until he was nearly 29, but he quickly made up for lost time. His 26 caps included a hat-trick against the Republic of Ireland, and a trip to Brazil as a member of England's first World Cup Finals' squad in 1950. In 1954, his last season at Middlesbrough brought the anti-climax of relegation, and effectively signalled the end of his career. A brief flurry with Hull followed but his heart was never truly in it, and he soon returned to Middlesbrough, where he remained until his death in April 2000.

- Mannion is still Middlesbrough's most-capped player.
- He scored Boro's first post-war goal in 1946.
- He was once suspended by the Football League for a controversial newspaper article.
- 'Can't we play them again tomorrow?' Mannion after England's 1-0 defeat by the USA in the 1950 World Cup.
- 'Hello. I'm Wilf Mannion.' Made occasional appearances on Baddiel and Skinner's *Fantasy Football League* TV show.

VITAL STATISTICS

Place of Birth:	Middlesbrough, England	
Date of Birth:	16 May 1918	**Died:** 14 April 2000
Caps:	26 (England)	**Goals (International):** 11
Clubs:	Middlesbrough, Hull City	
Appearances:	Club (for Middlesbrough): 368	
Goals:	Club (for Middlesbrough): 110	
Trophies:	None	

LEGEND RATING	
Achievement	5.0
Skill	9.0
Teamwork	8.0
Passion	8.0
Personality	7.0
TOTAL	**37.0**

Maradona, Diego
Napoli, Argentina

THE MOST NATURALLY GIFTED PLAYER football has ever seen, or a despicable drug-ridden cheat? Whatever your opinion, Maradona's talent was undeniable. After emerging in his native Argentina with Argentinos Juniors, for whom he made his league debut aged only 15, Maradona quickly attracted the attention of European scouts.

A move to Spain for £4.2 m should, in theory at least, have made him the jewel in Barcelona's star-studded crown, but the young and immature Diego failed to settle and, in 1984, joined Napoli in Italy's Serie A for £6.9 m. Maradona brought unprecedented success to Naples, single-handedly shifting the powerbase of Italian football from north to south, but he also fell in with the wrong crowd. Throughout his time at the club he was repeatedly seen in the company of local mobsters, and rumours of his cocaine addiction were rife.

The 1986 World Cup quarter-final versus England provided an insight to his personality: a flagrant punch past Peter Shilton for Argentina's first goal was followed by a 60-yard run and wonder-goal minutes later. Maradona's personal flaws make him an unattractive figure, but should not obscure his vast talents as a footballer. His poor origins and volatility made him susceptible to bad advice off the pitch and provocation on it, compounded by his failure to ignore either.

- Maradona was the subject of three world-record transfer fees, and was the first £1 m teenager.
- Maradona inspired Napoli to their first Scudetto. When he left, their fortunes immediately declined.
- Maradona was banned twice for drug use and is still battling against cocaine addiction.
- He was South American Player of the Year in 1979 and 1980 and was voted FIFA's Player of the Twentieth Century.
- A tackle, by the 'Butcher of Bilbao' Andoni Goicochea, that ruled Maradona out for four months, sparked an attempted storming of Bilbao's team hotel by enraged Catalans.

VITAL STATISTICS

Place of Birth:	Lanus, Argentina		
Date of Birth:	30 October 1960	**Died:** n/a	
Caps:	91 (Argentina)	**Goals (International):** 34	
Clubs:	Argentinos Juniors, Boca Juniors, Barcelona, Napoli, Seville, Newell's Old Boys		
Appearances:	Club (All Matches): 749		
Goals:	Club (All Matches): 311		
Trophies:	WorC 1986; SA 1987; UEFAC 1988		

LEGEND RATING

Achievement	9.0
Skill	10.0
Teamwork	8.0
Passion	10.0
Personality	6.0
TOTAL	**43.0**

Maradona snakecharms the Belgians during the 1982 World Cup in Spain.

Matthews' Final
Blackpool 4 Bolton Wanderers 3, 1953

ONE OF WEMBLEY'S most sentimental occasions, the 'Matthews Final', saw the nation's favourite balding winger with baggy shorts finally win an FA Cup final at 38.

The drama was perfectly scripted. Blackpool, 3-1 down after an hour, were heading for their third final defeat in six seasons when, as if on cue, Stanley Matthews embarked on a trail of destruction down the right wing, setting up Stan Mortensen to score. With only three minutes left, it still looked like mere consolation, but a Mortensen free kick to complete his hat-trick set up the FA Cup's most memorable finale. Again, it was a dribble from Matthews, who seemed to lose his footing before squaring for Bill Perry to smash the winner.

For the nation it was all part of the 1953 pageantry that inspires images of the Coronation, Everest and Compton's Ashes. For Bolton, it could have been so different had an injury not reduced England left back Banks to the role of passenger for the last, vital half an hour. But the enduring image is that of Matthews standing proud, finally holding the FA Cup.

- This was Matthews' third FA Cup final; he was a loser in 1948 and 1951.
- Blackpool nearly didn't make it to Wembley. Outplayed by Spurs, they won their semi-final in the last minute.
- Hat-trick hero Stan Mortensen scored in every round.
- Mortensen later managed the club, from 1967–69.
- Like many north-west clubs, both Blackpool and Bolton faded in the 1960s.

SCORERS **Blackpool:** Mortensen 3, Perry
Bolton Wanderers: Lofthouse, Moir, Bell
EVENT FA Cup final, Wembley, 2 May 1953

BLACKPOOL (Man: Joe Smith)
1. Farm 2. Shimwell 3. Garrett 4. Fenton 5. Johnston 6. Robinson 7. Matthews
8. Taylor 9. Mortensen 10. Mudie 11. Perry
BOLTON (Man: Bill Ridding)
1. Hanson 2. Ball 3. Banks 4. Wheeler 5. Barrass 6. Bell 7. Holden 8. Moir
9. Lofthouse 10. Hassall 11. Langton

Matthews (left) on England duty.

Matthews, Stanley
Blackpool, Stoke City, England

ASK ANY LEFT BACK between 1930 and 1965 who was the opponent they most feared and the answer would have been instant: Stanley Matthews. One of the quickest players ever over 10 yards, Matthews defined modern wing play and pioneered standards of fitness that enabled him to play beyond his 50th birthday. Pointless arguments still rage about how he would have fared in the modern game, but there have been few bigger draws. Stoke's attendance leapt from 8,000 to 35,000 when he re-signed in 1961, returning to his hometown club after 13 years away. His defining match was with Blackpool, whom he joined after a clash with management at Stoke in 1947. The sight of Matthews transforming the 1953 FA Cup final by laying on three late goals for a 4-3 win is now as much a part of Wembley folklore as the twin towers and Billy the white horse. Yet, for all his ability, that game produced his only major trophy. Still, trophies and medals were not what made Matthews popular. He won his acclaim as the people's champion for his innate modesty and sportsmanship. His death, in February 2000, solicited immaculate one-minute's silences at grounds throughout the country.

- Matthews was the inaugural European Footballer of the Year in 1956 and Football Writers' Player of the Year in 1948 and 1963.
- 1965. He became the first footballer to be knighted.
- He was the oldest ever First Division player at 50 years, 5 days.
- He never earned fortunes, taking home a basic £50 per week on his retirement.
- The ultimate gentleman, Matthews was never booked in a 35-year career.

VITAL STATISTICS

Place of Birth:	Stoke-on-Trent, England	
Date of Birth:	1 February 1915	**Died:** 23 February 2000
Caps:	54 (England)	**Goals (International):** 11
Clubs:	Stoke City, Blackpool	
Appearances:	Club (League): 698	
Goals:	Club (League): 71	
Trophies:	FAC 1953	

Achievement	6.0
Skill	10.0
Teamwork	8.0
Passion	9.0
Personality	7.0
TOTAL	**40.0**

LEGEND RATING

Maximum Wage
No One's Worth That Much!

ROY KEANE IS REPORTED to earn £200,000 every month. Yet, just over 40 years ago, players nearly came out on strike over the less than princely sum of £20 per week. The argument had been rumbling for years. The legendary Billy Meredith had led a players' revolt as early as 1907 over a £4 per week ceiling and a contract that tied players to a club effectively for an entire career. He succeeded in establishing a players' union, but the maximum wage remained. It was not until 1961 that the next instalment of this saga erupted. PFA Chairman Jimmy Hill had successfully managed to get the maximum wage abolished when he took up the case of George Eastham. Eastham's contract had expired at Newcastle and though Arsenal were keen to sign him the Magpies refused to release him. The case went to the Ministry of Labour, who ruled in Eastham's favour. The days of the tied contract were over. Today's complaint that all players earn too much misses an important point. For every Keane, there are 10 YTS lads at Halifax scraping a living.

☞ The first beneficiary of the maximum wage's demise was Johnny Haynes. Fulham made him the country's first £100 per week player.

☞ 1950. Following the post-war boom in attendances, players threatened to strike unless their pay was increased. They won a rise but the maximum wage was to remain for another 11 years.

☞ The rise of agents has helped inflate players' pay packets. Some, like Eric Hall, admit only a passing interest in football.

☞ Most former players are philosophical about the riches they missed out on. As Stanley Matthews remarked in 1987: 'People say the wages are too high, but it's a short career.'

☞ For top players today, merchandising rights are as important as salary. 'Image rights' is the latest phrase in contract negotiations.

'A slave contract.'

Jimmy Hill defines the maximum wage system

George Eastham.

McCoist, Ally

Rangers, Scotland

PERHAPS MORE THAN ANY other player, Ally McCoist was responsible for the transformation of Rangers from football Cinderellas into Scotland's dominant force of the 1980s and 1990s. In that period the Gers collected nine league titles on the bounce, equalling the record held by their Glasgow neighbours, Celtic.

McCoist, Rangers' highest-ever goalscorer, was the attacking spearhead of the team, a man whose confidence in front of goal seemed to invest his colleagues with added belief in their own abilities. But success was not immediate for McCoist. Three inauspicious years at St Johnstone saw him offloaded to Sunderland in 1981, where two indifferent seasons followed before his life-changing move to Rangers.

McCoist introduced himself to the Ibrox faithful by scoring within one minute of his debut in an Old Firm derby and went on, in his 15-year association with the club, to become the most decorated player of his generation. An easy-going nature and confidence on camera saw him recruited to BBC's *A Question of Sport* as a team captain, and this has led to further TV roles, his latest being as a wisecracking analyst on ITV's *The Premiership*.

☞ Despite a Rangers record of 355 goals, McCoist's first league strike was in England against no less a keeper than Peter Shilton.

👆 He was the first Scottish player to win Europe's golden boot for most league goals in a season.

☞ In his last years as a player McCoist became known as 'The Judge', due to the amount of time he spent on the bench.

👆 He scored the crucial goal against Norway that gave Scotland entry to the 1990 World Cup Finals.

👇 At the 1990 Finals he was left on the bench for most of the defeat by Costa Rica.

VITAL STATISTICS

Place of Birth:	Glasgow, Scotland	
Date of Birth:	24 September 1962	**Died:** n/a
Caps:	61 (Scotland)	**Goals (International):** 19
Clubs:	St Johnstone, Sunderland, Rangers, Kilmarnock	
Appearances:	Club (All Matches): 637	
Goals:	Club (All Matches): 363	
Trophies:	SLT 1987, 1989, 1990, 1991, 1992, 1993, 1994, 1995, 1996, 1997; SFAC 1992, 1993, 1996	

LEGEND RATING	
Achievement	8.0
Skill	8.0
Teamwork	6.0
Passion	7.0
Personality	9.0
TOTAL	**38.0**

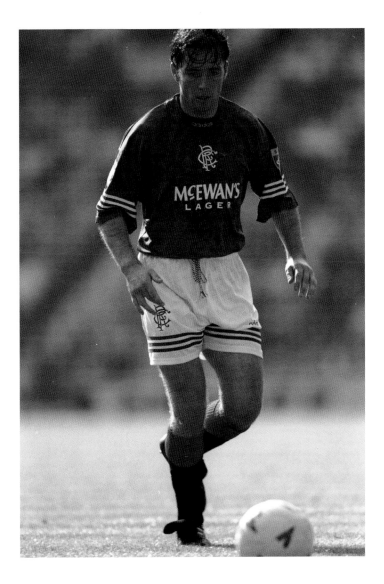

McGrath, Paul

Aston Villa, Manchester United, Republic of Ireland

AS ONE OF THE FIRST black players to emerge from Ireland, Paul McGrath knows a thing or two about defying the odds. His ability to fight a battling rearguard was evident on a football pitch too. McGrath was one of the bravest players of the last 20 years, and a defiant example to those who maintain that all contemporary players burst into tears at the first sign of a blister. McGrath's bravery brought a catalogue of injuries that would have forced lesser men into retirement but, defying the pain and the doctors, he continued to play at a high level well into his thirties. Later in his career, at Aston Villa, he was scarcely able to train due to the strain on his battered knees, but his level of performance rarely deviated beyond the exceptional.

Having signed for Man United in 1982 after schoolboy and club football in Ireland, his seven years at Old Trafford made him a terrace hero. In 1985, that status was cemented when, following the sending off of Kevin Moran, McGrath single-handedly kept out Everton to set up United's unlikely FA Cup final victory. Throughout his career he was the backbone of the Republic of Ireland side, underpinning their charge to the World Cup quarter-finals in 1990, and is a player for whom the Republic have yet to discover a worthy replacement.

👍 Hugely respected by colleagues, McGrath was PFA Player of the Year in 1983.

☞ Surprisingly, he gained only one FA Cup medal and no championship medals despite seven years at Old Trafford.

☞ Always a transfer bargain, McGrath cost Manchester United only £30,000 and Villa £400,000.

☞ McGrath has re-emerged recently as an occasional TV pundit, making engaging contributions with a wry grin and soft accent.

👍 He is Villa's most capped player with 51 full internationals.

VITAL STATISTICS

Place of Birth:	Greenford, England	
Date of Birth:	4 December 1959	**Died:** n/a
Caps:	83 (R. Ireland)	**Goals (International):** 8
Clubs:	Manchester United, Aston Villa, Derby County	
Appearances:	Club (All Matches): 519	
Goals:	Club (All Matches): 25	
Trophies:	FAC 1985; LC 1994, 1996	

LEGEND RATING	
Achievement	5.0
Skill	7.0
Teamwork	8.0
Passion	10.0
Personality	7.0
TOTAL	**37.0**

McLeish, Alex & Miller, Willie

Aberdeen, Scotland

NEITHER ALEX MCLEISH nor Willie Miller was ever short-listed for the European Footballer of the Year award, but together they formed a central defensive partnership that was the equal of any in Europe. McLeish was the dour one, an unflappable stopper and tackler, while Miller was the more elegant playmaker, sometimes fancying his chances with Beckenbauer-style forays into opposition territory. Their 10 years at Pittodrie spanned the entire decade of the 1980s, and coincided with the most successful period in Aberdeen's history.

Both have tried their hand in management, with McLeish proving to be the more successful. Miller was an ordinary boss of the club where he played with such distinction, and was eventually sacked in 1995 after three seasons. McLeish wisely chose to make a clean break from Aberdeen, and performed impressively at Motherwell and Hibs before taking the hot seat at Ibrox in December 2001.

☞ Miller was signed by Aberdeen as a striker in 1971, and was not converted into a centre back for several years.

✍ McLeish is Aberdeen's most capped player with 77, while Miller holds the club record for league appearances (556).

☞ Both have played under Alex Ferguson for club and country. All three represented Scotland at the 1986 World Cup Finals.

✍ Miller was Scottish Player of the Year in 1984, and McLeish won the same award six years later.

☞ McLeish's managerial career had a stuttering start. Motherwell were relegated in his first season, but bounced straight back with the First Division title in 1999.

VITAL STATISTICS

ALEX MCLEISH

Place of Birth:	Glasgow, Scotland		Achievement	8.0
Date of Birth:	21 January 1959	**Died:** n/a	Skill	6.0
Caps:	77 (Scotland)	**Goals (International):** 1	Teamwork	8.0
Clubs:	Aberdeen		Passion	9.0
Appearances:	Club (League): 492		Personality	6.0
Goals:	Club (League): 25			
Trophies:	SLT 1980, 1984, 1985; SFAC 1982, 1983, 1984, 1986, 1990, (2002); CWC 1983		**TOTAL**	**37.0**

LEGEND RATING

Miller keeps his eye on the ball (left). McLeish holds up the Scottish League Championship trophy.

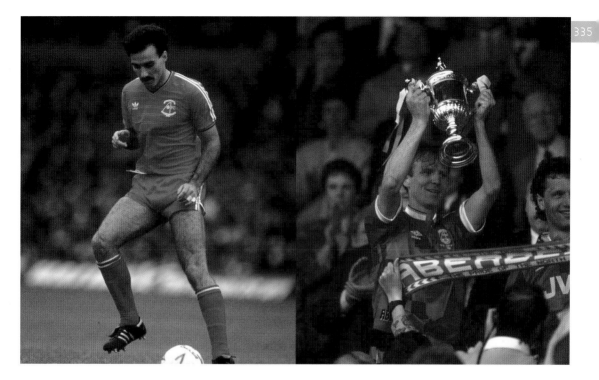

VITAL STATISTICS

WILLIE MILLER

Place of Birth:	Glasgow, Scotland
Date of Birth:	2 May 1955 **Died:** n/a
Caps:	65 (Scotland) **Goals (International):** 1
Clubs:	Aberdeen
Appearances:	Club (League): 556
Goals:	Club (League): 21
Trophies:	SLT 1980 1984, 1985; SFAC 1982, 1983, 1984, 1986; CWC 1983

LEGEND RATING	
Achievement	7.0
Skill	7.0
Teamwork	8.0
Passion	9.0
Personality	6.0
TOTAL	**37.0**

McNeill, Billy

Celtic, Scotland

ON HIS 17TH BIRTHDAY in 1957, Billy McNeill began a 34-year association with Celtic that eventually made him the club's most decorated captain and one of its most popular figures. McNeill was the centre-half keystone around which Jock Stein built Celtic's famous 'Lisbon Lions', the European Cup winners of 1967. He won his first league title with Celtic in 1966, and went on to win it a further eight years in a row, setting a record that remained in tact until Rangers enjoyed an identical period of domination in the 1980s and 1990s.

Like his mentor Jock Stein, he won the double with Celtic both as player and manager. Unlike Stein, however, he lasted longer in English management, although his four years with Aston Villa and Manchester City were undistinguished. Rejoining his *alma mater*, he was fired unsentimentally in 1991 after two trophy-less seasons. A triple heart bypass has since curtailed his public appearances, but the family-run McNeill's bar in the city centre stands both as a testament to his Glasgow roots and a museum to his achievements.

- On McNeill's international debut Scotland lost 9-3 to England.
- McNeill's 486 league appearances are a Celtic record.
- He scored the opening goal in a 4-0 thrashing of Rangers in the 1969 Scottish Cup final.
- McNeill also scored the winner in the 1965 Scottish Cup final.
- He earned the nickname 'Caesar' (presumably due to his commanding leadership rather than fondness for wearing a toga).

VITAL STATISTICS

Place of Birth:	Blantyre, Scotland			
Date of Birth:	2 March 1940	**Died:** n/a	Achievement	8.0
Caps:	29 (Scotland)	**Goals (International):** 3	Skill	7.0
Clubs:	Celtic		Teamwork	9.0
Appearances:	Club (League): 486		Passion	9.0
Goals:	Club (League): 22		Personality	7.0
Trophies:	EC 1967; SLT 1966–74; SFAC 1965, 1967, 1969, 1971, 1972, 1974, 1975		**TOTAL**	**40.0**

LEGEND RATING

1967. McNeill poses with the European Cup.

Mercer, Joe
Everton, Arsenal, Manchester City, England

AS A PLAYER Joe Mercer was the heartbeat of two formidable sides. He played left half in the Everton team that won the last pre-war championship and, at the end of the war when Arsenal were looking to shore up their ranks with some experience and know-how, he added to his medal collection as the Gunners claimed league titles in 1948 and 1953. Mercer had been expected to stay at Arsenal for no more than a couple of seasons, but eventually stayed eight years, only retiring in 1953 when, after skippering them to the title, he received a rousing final ovation from the Highbury faithful.

Managerial spells with Sheffield United and Aston Villa were followed by a successful period at Manchester City, where he teamed up with Malcolm Allison. Mercer's genial man-management and Allison's tactical inventiveness proved to be a potent combination, and they duly delivered the FA Cup and the club's first and only league title. When England sacked Alf Ramsey after he failed to take England to the 1974 World Cup Finals, Mercer was appointed caretaker boss. But he had no desire to inherit the job permanently, and his brief tenure served as little more than light relief before the appointment of Don Revie.

- City axed Mercer in 1972. Allison stayed, amid rumours of political dirty tricks.
- England lost only one of Mercer's seven games in charge, despite his apparently carefree approach.
- He was voted PFA Player of the Year in 1950.
- Joe Mercer to newly-appointed Stoke boss, Tony Waddington: 'My advice is never to trust anyone in the game, and when I put down this phone, don't trust me either.'

VITAL STATISTICS

		MANAGER		PLAYER	
Place of Birth:	Ellesmere Port, Cheshire, England				
Date of Birth:	9 August 1914 **Died:** 9 August 1990				
Caps:	5 (England)	Achievement	7	Achievement	8
Goals (International): 0		Skill		Skill	6
Clubs:	As Player: Everton, Arsenal;	Tactical Awareness	8	Skill	6
	As Manager: Sheffield United,	Motivation	8	Teamwork	8
	Aston Villa, Manchester City,	Team Selection/Transfers	6	Passion	9
	Coventry City	Personality	8	Personality	7
Trophies:	LT 1948, 1953, (1968); FAC 1950,				
	(1969); LC (1970)	**TOTAL**	**37**	**TOTAL**	**38**

LEGEND RATING

Meredith, Billy

Manchester United, Wales

ONE OF WALES' greatest internationals, the original 'wizard of the wing' dazzled crowds in an amazing career lasting 30 years. An adopted son of Manchester, his two spells with City and one for United made him the forerunner of Ryan Giggs, Peter Barnes and co. Not surprisingly, since he played until he was nudging 50, most of Meredith's records surround his incredible longevity, although his own claim to have played in over 1,500 games and scored 470 goals has never been convincingly validated.

However, the stocky ex-miner's legacy was more enduring than his mighty playing career. As a feisty chairman of the maverick player's union, Meredith and his United sidekick, Charlie Roberts, eventually persuaded the FA to recognise them as an official body in 1908 and, though their fledgling union collapsed following a revolt a year later, their work is now acknowledged to have been a significant step in the advancement of player's rights.

- His 48 caps for Wales was an astonishing total for a team playing scarcely more than home internationals.
- 1920. He became the oldest man to play international football at 45 years and 229 days.
- 1924. Became the oldest player to play in the FA Cup aged 49.
- Meredith's maximum wage was £4 per week in 1907. Roy Keane earns the same today in just over 46 seconds.
- He captained Wales to their first Home International title in 1907.

VITAL STATISTICS

Place of Birth:	Black Park, Chirk, Wales		
Date of Birth:	30 July 1875	**Died:** 19 April 1958	
Caps:	48 (Wales)	**Goals (International):** 11	
Clubs:	Northwich Victoria, Manchester City,		
	Manchester United		
Appearances:	Club (League for Man Utd): 303		
Goals:	Club (League for Man Utd): 35		
Trophies:	LT 1908, 1911; FAC 1904, 1909		

Achievement	7.0
Skill	8.0
Teamwork	7.0
Passion	8.0
Personality	9.0
TOTAL	**39.0**

LEGEND RATING

Suits you sir. Style guru Meredith (left) sports a new neckwear range.

Mighty Maccams
The Sunderland Dream Team

SUNDERLAND'S GREATEST DAYS were long ago, when they won four championships between 1891 and 1902. Jimmy Millar, an inside forward, played in all of them, alongside another Scot, Johnny Campbell. Sunderland's next title came in 1913, when the opposition was a bit stiffer. Their playmaker was the great Charlie Buchan, and it was his right-sided partnership with half back Cuggy and winger Jackie Mordue that was regarded as the key to their success.

Perhaps the club's greatest achievement was wrestling the title from Herbert Chapman's Arsenal in 1936, after the Gunners had won the previous three. Sunderland scored a marvellous 109 goals that season, with 31 each for Raich Carter and Bobby Gurney. The same squad won the FA Cup the following season, but it was 36 years before the club won another major trophy. In 1973, Sunderland, by now a Division Two side, pulled off a shock FA Cup win, beating Don Revie's Leeds 1-0 in the final with a goal from Ian Porterfield. An unsuccessful return to Wembley in 1992 was the closest they have come since. Peter Reid's modern team flirted with success without quite delivering. In 2002, he paid the price and was sacked. Sunderland's spectacular fall from grace in 2002–03 means that it could be some time yet before the good times return.

- Goalkeepers Jimmy Montgomery and John Doig totted up over 1,000 first-team appearances between them. Montgomery is the club's longest-serving player. His finest moment was the 1973 Cup final, where he made one breathtaking double save.
- Bobby Kerr, the lively moustachioed Scottish winger, is the only other representative of the Cup-winning team here.
- Charlie Hurley won the most caps while at the club; 38 of his 40 caps for the Republic of Ireland were as a Sunderland player.
- The consistent Gary Rowell is the only representative of the modest 1980s teams. A frequent scorer from midfield, Rowell was a much underrated performer.

Manager: Johnny Cochrane

4-4-2

Jimmy Montgomery (70s)

Charlie Gladwin (10s) Dave Watson (C) (70s)
Charlie Hurley (50s/60s) Michael Gray (90s)

Jackie Mordue (10s) Charlie Buchan (10s/20s)
Raich Carter (30s) Gary Rowell (80s/90s)

Len Shackleton (50s) Kevin Phillips (90s)

Subs: John Doig (G) (1890s) Frank Cuggy (D/M) (10s)
Bobby Kerr (M) (70s) Bobby Gurney (F) (30s) Jimmy Millar (F) (1890s)

Milburn, Jackie

Newcastle United, England

JOHN EDWARD THOMPSON MILBURN, or 'Wor Jackie', was the son of Alec Milburn. Alec's brother Tanner had four sons, all of whom played league soccer, while Tanner's daughter, Cissie, had two more sons, Jackie and Bobby Charlton. On these grounds, it is probably safe to say that Jackie Milburn came from decent footballing stock.

In his long career at St James's Park, Milburn's name became synonymous with Newcastle United. On his death, thousands poured on to the streets to pay their respects, and a statue has been erected in his memory in the city centre. Milburn started his professional career late due to the war, and played initially as an inside forward, then on the wing before moving to centre forward in 1947. He wasn't tall, but he terrorised defences with his speed and quick feet, and his 13 England caps were a meagre reflection of his ability. Had he been a little more selfish, his goals tally may have been even more impressive than the 177 league goals he notched for the Magpies.

Upon his retirement Milburn briefly tried his hand as a manager, notably taking over an ageing Ipswich team from Alf Ramsey. They were relegated two years after winning the title, and Milburn moved back to the north-east to work in the local media.

☞ 46,000 turned out for Milburn's testimonial – 10 years after he left Newcastle.

👍 His tally of 177 league goals for Newcastle remains a record.

👍 He scored both goals in a 2-0 FA Cup final defeat of Blackpool in 1951, and after 45 seconds in the 1955 final against Manchester City.

👍 He scored on his debut for England and got one hat-trick, against Wales.

☞ Milburn left Newcastle for a successful spell as player-manager at Linfield in Northern Ireland. He even appeared in the European Cup for the club.

VITAL STATISTICS

Place of Birth:	Ashington, England		
Date of Birth:	11 May 1924	**Died:** 9 October 1988	
Caps:	13 (England)	**Goals (International):** 10	
Clubs:	Newcastle United		
Appearances:	Club (League): 354		
Goals:	Club (League): 177		
Trophies:	FAC 1951, 1952, 1955		

LEGEND RATING	
Achievement	6.0
Skill	9.0
Teamwork	7.0
Passion	9.0
Personality	7.0
TOTAL	**38.0**

Mine's A Treble!
Manchester United 2 Bayern Munich 1, 1999

IT WAS FAR FROM the greatest European Cup final, and a much inferior game to Man United's previous final appearance in 1968. But for late, jaw-dropping drama there will probably never be another game like it. Bayern scored after six minutes and after 90 minutes United were still 1-0 down. The referee's assistant held up a board showing three minutes of injury time. Up in the stand the ribbons of Bayern Munich were being attached to the giant trophy. Then, a minute later, United won a corner. Maybe Bayern were distracted by the sight of Peter Schmeichel haring into the penalty area. If so the great Dane proved to be an ideal decoy, leaving Sheringham to sweep the ball past Oliver Kahn for the equaliser. It was more than United had dared hoped for, and a minute later their wildest dreams had been realised. Beckham curled in another corner, Sheringham flicked on and supersub Ole Gunnar Solskjaer volleyed past a disbelieving Kahn. The Bayern team sank to their knees as United capered back to the half-way line.

☞ The game was won on the 90th anniversary of Matt Busby's birth.

☜ United played poorly. To cover the loss of Keane and Scholes (both suspended) Beckham was forced inside and Giggs played on the right, where he failed to offer his customary threat.

☞ The referee was Pierluigi Collina, who would witness another English triumph over German opposition in Munich in 2001.

☞ There was sympathy for most of the German team, but not for Mario Basler, whose triumphal exit as he was substituted in the last minute was premature and presumptuous.

� Consolation came two years later for Bayern, as they beat Valencia on penalties to win the Cup, having beaten Man United home and away in the quarter-finals.

SCORERS	**Manchester United:** Sheringham, Solskjaer
	Bayern Munich: Basler
EVENT	European Champions League final, Nou Camp, Barcelona, 26 May 1999
MAN UTD	(Man: Alex Ferguson)
	1. Schmeichel 2. Neville, G 3. Irwin 4. Butt 5. Johnsen 6. Stam 7. Beckham
	8. Blomqvist (Sheringham) 9. Cole (Solskjaer) 10. Yorke 11. Giggs
BAYERN	(Man: Ottmar Hitzfeld)
	1. Kahn 2. Babbel 3. Tarnat 4. Linke 5. Matthaus 6. Kuffour 7. Jermies
	8. Effenberg 9. Jancker 10. Basler 11. Zickler

Supersub Solskjaer basks after his late, late winner.

Moore, Bobby
West Ham United, England

'WORDS CANNOT SUM UP the grief I feel for my great friend. He was one of the world's finest defenders and a great sportsman.' So said Pelé after the sudden death, from cancer, of Bobby Moore in 1993.

Moore was the ultimate example of mind over body. He appeared to possess few of the physical attributes required in a great defender, but made up for his lack of muscle with an ability to read the game that bordered on the psychic. Moore took the ball by stealth rather than power and, though he rarely needed to resort to tackling, when he did so it was always surgical and clean. Rattling bones wasn't his style. He was loyal too; with the exception of a swansong alongside George Best and Rodney Marsh at Fulham, Moore spent his entire career at West Ham. Upton Park now has a stand named after him, and the ground is home to a bust and plaque honouring his achievements.

His England career started in 1962, and continued almost unbroken until his retirement from internationals in 1973. He competed in three World Cups, winning the Player of the Tournament award in 1966 when he captained England to a 4-2 victory over Germany in the final.

☞ Moore was outstanding in the 1970 World Cup Finals, despite having spent four days in a Colombian jail after a woman falsely accused him of stealing a bracelet.

☞ Moore nearly missed the 1966 World Cup as he was in contractual dispute with West Ham. Under FA rules this made him ineligible for England, so a temporary contract was arranged to see him through the tournament.

☜ Moore was not the saint he is often made out to be. He was twice reprimanded for breaking pre-match curfews for West Ham and England.

☝ He was PFA Player of the Year in 1964, and received an OBE in 1967.

VITAL STATISTICS

Place of Birth:	Barking, Essex, England	
Date of Birth:	12 April 1941	**Died:** 24 February 1993
Caps:	108 (England)	**Goals (International):** 2
Clubs:	West Ham United, Fulham, Seattle Sounders,	
	San Antonio Thunder	
Appearances:	Club (All Matches): 823	
Goals:	Club (All Matches): 29	
Trophies:	WorC 1966; FAC 1964; CWC 1965	

LEGEND RATING	
Achievement	9.0
Skill	10.0
Teamwork	9.0
Passion	9.0
Personality	6.0
TOTAL	**43.0**

Mortensen, Stanley

Blackpool, England

THE NORTH-EAST has been a fertile breeding ground for traditional English centre forwards, but one who slipped through the local net was Stan Mortensen. Initially, timing was not on his side. He signed as a professional for Blackpool in May 1939, but the Second World War ensured that his league career didn't start until he was past 25. Mind you, once he got going, there was no stopping him. Mortensen's height and strength made him a natural target man. Unlike some tall players, he was a natural jumper and deadly in the air. The combination of Stanley Matthews' accurate crosses and Mortensen's aerial strength was fully exploited. The result was three FA Cup finals in six seasons, though Mortensen's efforts rank amongst the most ignored in Wembley history; despite scoring a hat-trick in 1953 the match became universally celebrated as 'The Matthews Final'. Shabbily treated by Blackpool, he left under a cloud for Hull City in 1955. He continued playing until the age of 40, dropping into non-league football before returning to Blackpool as manager where, after two competent seasons, he was sacked. Blackpool did not deserve him.

- Mortensen's career almost never saw the light of day. He cheated death in a practice parachute jump in 1943 and, as an RAF pilot, was seriously injured in active service.
- He scored four times on his international debut as England trounced Portugal 10-0 in 1947. His 25 caps produced 23 goals, a record to compare with the best.
- Mortensen's first season as manager saw Blackpool finish third, missing out on promotion to Division One on the final day of season 1967–68.
- Wag on Mortensen's death: 'I suppose they'll call it the Matthews funeral.'

VITAL STATISTICS

Place of Birth:	South Shields, England	
Date of Birth:	26 May 1921	**Died:** 7 May 1991
Caps:	25 (England)	**Goals (International):** 23
Clubs:	Blackpool, Hull City, Southport	
Appearances:	Club (League for Blackpool): 316	
Goals:	Club (League for Blackpool): 197	
Trophies:	FAC 1953	

LEGEND RATING	
Achievement	6.0
Skill	8.0
Teamwork	8.0
Passion	7.0
Personality	6.0
TOTAL	**35.0**

Mourinho, Jose

FC Porto, Chelsea

WHATEVER QUALITIES Jose Mourinho may lack, self-belief is not one of them. Like Brian Clough, here is a manager who revels in the added pressure that his outspoken comments inevitably attract. Irksome at times, he never descends into the platitudes used by most colleagues.

Mourinho's command of star-studded dressing rooms is made all the more remarkable by his lack of achievements as a player. His break came as a 29-year-old translator for Bobby Robson on the veteran manager's appointment as Sporting Lisbon's coach. He followed him, this time as assistant coach, to Barcelona, and continued in the role under Louis van Gaal after Robson's exit. He learned well, and in 2000 made the step up to Benfica.

After a false start, Mourinho's career regained its momentum at Porto. League titles, including a Portuguese treble in 2004, followed. It was consecutive triumphs in the UEFA Cup and Champions League, the latter with 66-1 outsiders, which made a lucrative offer inevitable. Enter the giant Abramovich chequebook.

In his first season at Chelsea, he returned the league title to Stamford Bridge after a 50-year absence, thus ensuring a sanctified position in the club's history. He has yet to learn Clough's humour, but his achievements may well surpass him.

☞ Jose is the son of Felix Mourinho, a former Portuguese international goalkeeper.

☞ Mourinho resigned from Benfica after only nine matches of the 2000–01 season, after falling out with the board.

☞ The innate self-belief doesn't stop Mourinho learning from others. Sam Allardyce's tactics in a league game at Stamford Bridge prompted Mourinho to believe (rightly) that Bolton's 4-5-1 cum 4-3-3 could be effective against Bayern Munich in the Champions League.

☞ June 2005. Mourinho was fined £200,000 by the FA for his part in the 'tapping-up' of Ashley Cole. The authorities ruled that Mourinho's approach to a player still under contract at Arsenal was illegal. The fine was halved on appeal, but was indicative of the tightrope that Mourinho has often walked when dealing with officialdom.

VITAL STATISTICS

Place of Birth:	Setubal, Portugal		Achievement	9
Date of Birth:	26 January 1963	**Died:** n/a	Tactical Awareness	9
Clubs:	Benfica, FC Porto, Chelsea		Motivation	9
Trophies:	UEFAC 2003; EC 2004; PLT 2003, 2004;		Team Selection/Transfers	7
	LT 2005; LC 2004		Personality	8

LEGEND RATING

TOTAL 42

Munich Air Disaster
End Of An Era

6 FEBRUARY 1958 is a date that will remain a black-letter day in the world of football. A plane crash with fatalities was a tragic event in itself, but that the airliner involved should also include most of English football's finest post-war club side was headline news that numbed fans across the globe. In the freezing conditions at Munich airport the plane had already made one abortive attempt at a take-off but, undeterred, the pilot made the decision to try again. On the second attempt the plane left the ground but could not climb high enough to avoid hitting a fence and airport building, whereupon it broke in two and burst into flames.

Although eight players died, some miraculously managed to escape the wreckage alive. They included manager Sir Matt Busby and a young Bobby Charlton, who was to continue playing for another 15 years after the crash. Charlton's long career served as a poignant reminder of what may have lain ahead for his less fortunate colleagues. The names of the dead are a roll-call of unfulfilled talent:

Geoff Bent; Roger Byrne; Eddie Colman; Duncan Edwards; Mark Jones; David Pegg; Tommy Taylor; Bill Whelan.

☞ Duncan Edwards was not killed in the crash, but died from his injuries on 21 February 1958.

☞ Seven of the dead were 25 or younger; Busby's famous Babes had been almost totally wiped out.

☞ Three members of United's staff also died, plus the journalist Frank Swift, an ex-Manchester City and England goalkeeper.

☞ A memorial clock was erected at Old Trafford. It contains the date of the crash and is a popular meeting point for fans.

☞ The programme for United's next league match contained 11 blank spaces where the players' names would normally have been inserted.

'People still haven't forgotten. Strangers come up and tell me: "He were a good 'un."'

Anne Edwards, mother of Duncan, 1993

Matt Busby lies critically ill. Amazingly, he made a complete recovery.

New Theories
England 3 Hungary 6, 1953

A PACKED HOUSE arrived at Wembley confidently expecting an easy England victory. A bullish press had led the nation to believe that England were unbeatable, largely on the basis that no overseas team had won at Wembley before. The England team, ageing and complacent in their heavy boots, scoffed at the men wearing 'carpet slippers,' especially the 'little fat chap' leading them out. It is unthinkable that a modern coach would be so badly prepared (England's opponents were a highly dangerous outfit, unbeaten for 20 games). Hungary scored in the first minute, a precise angled strike from Nandor Hidegkuti. An England equaliser offered false hope before Hidegkuti scored again and 'the little fat chap,' Ferenc Puskas, added two more.

The rest of the detail is irrelevant. Hungary went into cruise mode, giving the impression they could score at will. Their passing triangles and sudden sprints forward into space completely flummoxed an unimaginative England defence. Puskas had breezed past Billy Wright, England's best defender, on numerous occasions, and the use of the deep-lying centre forward Hidegkuti had given prosaic England untold problems.

☞ The headlines the next day compared Hungary to the Scottish 'Wembley Wizards' of 1928, who had embarrassed England at Wembley in much the same fashion.

☞ The England side featured Matthews and Mortensen fresh from their heroics at the FA Cup final. Mortensen got a consolation but Matthews hardly saw the ball.

☞ The sides played again six months later as a last warm-up for Hungary's World Cup campaign. England made seven changes in an effort to counter the Hungarian tactics. The plan failed dismally as Hungary won 7-1. Back to the drawing board, chaps.

SCORERS	**England:** Sewell, Mortensen, Ramsey (pen)
	Hungary: Hidegkuti (3), Puskas (2), Bozsik
EVENT	Friendly International, Wembley, 25 November 1953
ENGLAND	(Man: Walter Winterbottom)
	1. Merrick 2. Ramsey 3. Eckersley 4. Wright 5. Johnston 6. Dickinson
	7. Matthews 8. Taylor 9. Mortensen 10. Sewell 11. Robb
HUNGARY	(Man: Jimmy Hogan)
	1. Grosics 2. Buzansky 3. Lantos 4. Bozsik 5. Lorant 6. Zakarias 7. Budai
	8. Kocsis 9. Hidegkuti 10. Puskas 11. Czibor

Puskas (No. 10) celebrates another Hungary goal.

Nicholson, Bill
Tottenham Hotspur, England

WHEN BILL NICHOLSON RESIGNED as manager of Spurs in 1974, it brought a 36-year love affair to an end. With Bill Shankly retiring the same year it also marked the passing of the last remaining manager from the old school. 'I am abused by players, there is no longer respect,' lamented Nicholson, announcing his decision to step down.

If anyone deserved respect it was Nicholson. As a player he had served the club well in the post-war years; starting at fullback, he later switched inside to centre half, then moved again, this time to half back, in the 1951 league title-winning side. As manager he brought success and consistency to the club, while always remaining mindful of his obligation to play exciting football. The 1961 double-winning team scored over 100 goals, playing scintillating football at odds with Nicholson's dour, uncompromising demeanour.

Under his tutelage, after a difficult first season, Spurs only once finished in the bottom half of the First Division. They were a notable cup team, too, becoming the first British side to win a European trophy. Nicholson was incensed when the club appointed an Arsenal man, Terry Neill, to replace him, arguing that Danny Blanchflower would have been a better choice. His instincts proved right. Neill took Spurs into Division Two within three years.

- In Nicholson's first game as a manager, Tottenham was a 10-4 winner against Everton.
- Nicholson scored after 19 seconds of his England debut, but was never picked again.
- He won a PFA merit award in 1984 for his services to the game.
- In 1961, the Spurs double-winning team had just one player booked all season.
- Nicholson was a contributor to *Soccer – The Fight For Survival, A Blueprint For The Future*, a 1980–81 review of a game in crisis.

VITAL STATISTICS

Place of Birth:	Scarborough, England	
Date of Birth:	26 January 1919	**Died:** 23 October 2004
Caps:	1 (England)	**Goals (International):** 1
Clubs:	As Player: Tottenham Hotspur; As Manager: Tottenham Hotspur	
Trophies:	LT (1951), 1961; FAC 1961, 1962, 1967; LC 1971, 1973; CWC 1963; UEFAC 1972	

LEGEND RATING	
Achievement	9
Tactical Awareness	8
Motivation	8
Team Selection/Transfers	9
Personality	8
TOTAL	**42**

Nicknames
The Poetic And The Preposterous

TEAM NICKNAMES are a proud tradition in football, with most teams having an official alternative to their full title. Some are derivations of the name of the team, like The O's (Orient) or The Gills (Gillingham), while some reflect the team's traditional colours, such as The Canaries (Norwich) or The Clarets (Burnley). Others take their inspiration from the local community, reflecting the working traditions of a town or city; The Cobblers (Northampton – a traditional shoe-making town), The Hatters (Luton – a millinery centre) or The Mariners (Grimsby – a fishing port). Some of the names become indistinguishable from the team, like Wolves or Spurs, and others are used just as frequently as the team's real name. For instance, a match between The Saints and Pompey means a local derby in Southampton or Portsmouth.

Players have nicknames too, although these tend to be less official and often uncomplimentary. In Brazil players rarely go by their real names, preferring to abbreviate their long-winded Portuguese surnames to a single, lyrical word. Zico would never have seemed as cool if commentators had referred to him by his real name: Arthur just doesn't have the same ring to it.

☞ The most literal use of a colour-derived name must be the team from Essen. They play in red and white and their name is Rot Weiss Essen.

☞ Chelsea used to be known as The Pensioners, but dropped it as it seemed a little inappropriate to a football team. Seats for the uniformed veterans are still reserved at Stamford Bridge.

☞ Players occasionally adopt self-styled nicknames. Paul Ince adopted the absurd moniker 'The Guv'nor' because he thought it made him sound hard. He was wrong.

👍 Some nicknames are derived from players' names, (Gordon 'Jukebox' Durie), 'Lambchop' (Paolo Wanchope); or their playing style ('The Lawnmower' – Stig Tofting: he covers so much grass!).

'Ronaldo' trips off the tongue easier than Ronaldo Luis Nazario de Lima, doesn't it?

'A nickname is the heaviest stone that the devil can throw at a man.'

William Hazlitt, *Sketches And Essays*, 1839

Nistelrooy, Ruud Van

Manchester United, Holland

WHEN MANCHESTER UNITED unveiled £19 m Ruud van Nistelrooy from PSV Eindhoven in April 2000, only for him to fail a medical, the snigger from their rivals was almost audible. When the same player ruptured cruciate ligaments a few weeks later during routine training in Holland, they could hardly contain themselves. To paraphrase the chant, they're not laughing anymore.

Since recovering from injury the Dutchman has become one of Europe's most complete and feared strikers. Strong, skilful, with acute positional sense and a deadly finish; his only demerit is a propensity for the occasional theatrical tumble.

His impact was immediate. A goal on his debut in the 2001 Charity Shield was followed by two more on his first Premiership appearance. So began a season that was to finish with 36 goals, an incredible total in these days of squad rotation. Even though his fee was a British record, albeit a short-lived one, it already looks judicious compared to the £58 m lavished by United on Veron and Ferdinand.

Holland's failure to qualify for the 2002 World Cup Finals robbed the world stage of his talents, and Euro 2004 again saw the Dutch underachieve. They qualified impressively for the 2006 World Cup, and, after an injury-hit 12 months, van Nistelrooy seems to be approaching that tournament at something near his peak.

2001–02. Voted PFA Player of the Year. Van Nistelrooy also won the Dutch equivalent whilst at PSV.

Biggest disappointment – knee injury not only scuppers his United transfer but robs him of the entire Euro 2000 tournament.

2002–03. Van Nistelrooy breaks the Premiership record by scoring in nine consecutive League games.

In February 2004 he scored his 100th United goal in only his 131st game. Only Denis Law reached his United century quicker.

In November 2004, just before his four-month injury lay-off, Van Nistelrooy destroyed Sparta Prague, scoring all four goals in a 4-1 Champions League victory.

VITAL STATISTICS

Place of Birth:	Oss, Holland	
Date of Birth:	1 July 1976	**Died:** n/a
Caps:	49 (Holland)	**Goals (International):** 25
Clubs:	Den Bosch, SC Heerenveen, PSV Eindhoven,	
	Manchester United	
Appearances:	Club (League): 291	
Goals:	Club (League): 174	
Trophies:	DLT 2000; LT 2003; FAC 2004	

Achievement	6.0	
Skill	9.0	
Teamwork	8.0	
Passion	8.0	
Personality	7.0	
TOTAL	**38.0**	

LEGEND RATING

Offside

Oi, linesman, get that flag up!

FOOTBALL IN THE 1920s was becoming defensive and stale, with as many as 40 offside decisions per game, so the authorities introduced a simple but effective antidote. They decided, from that point on, that an attacker needed just two (rather than three) players between him and the goal to be called onside. Teams immediately had to rethink their tactics, with many sides introducing a withdrawn centre half as a third defender to combat the new ruling. Recently the offside law was once again changed in favour of the attacking side; where previously an attacking player who was level with the opposition's last defender was considered offside, he is now free to continue (in other words he's onside). This makes defending against players with the pace of Ronaldo, Thierry Henry or Michael Owen very difficult.

Less satisfactory is the 'not interfering with play' rule affecting players in 'secondary' and 'non-active' areas. This is blurred and confusing, and leads to the sort of inconsistency that gives managers premature heart attacks.

☞ Combined with the back-pass rule, the 'level' ruling has spawned a generation of goalkeepers adept at coming off their line and playing the ball with foot or head. Shay Given and David James, for example, are adept at operating as sweeper when required.

☞ The ability to stay onside is a good measure of a striker's awareness and timing, and a handy guide to the intelligence of a footballer. Alan Shearer hardly ever gets caught offside. Craig Bellamy does. We rest our case.

✍ Arsenal are the masters of the offside trap. Their 'fab five' of Seaman, Dixon, Winterburn, Adams and Bould were great defenders, and played the tactic to near-perfection.

☞ Pet hate #1: braying buffoons in the stand who berate the linesman for an offside decision when they are 100 yards away behind the goal.

☞ Pet hate #2: said buffoon who howls at the linesman for not raising the same flag when the opposition striker reaches the ball beyond the centre half, ignoring the fact that said striker was five yards behind the pedestrian stopper when the ball was played.

'There's a big misconception. We never actually played offside. You'll see countless pictures of us standing in a line with our hands up appealing, but we were not actually going out to get sides offside.'

Lee Dixon talking crap

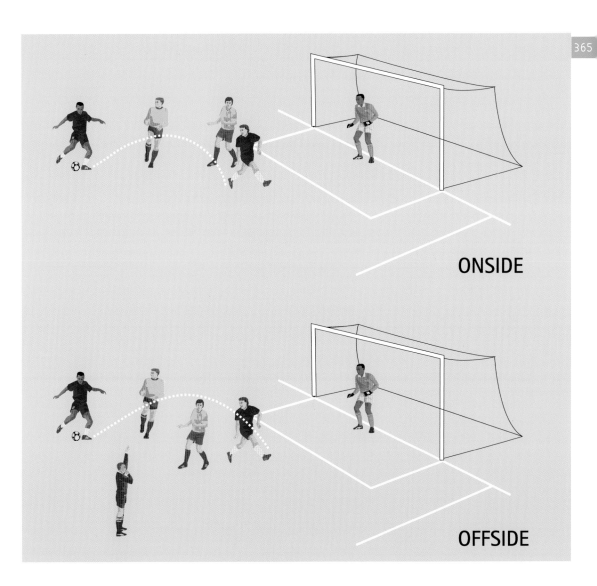

ONSIDE

OFFSIDE

Okocha, Augustin 'Jay-Jay'
PSG, Bolton Wanderers, Nigeria

JAY-JAY. So good they named him twice. So say supporters of Bolton Wanderers; a homage to the enormous talent of their Nigerian captain. Nigerian supporters wouldn't disagree. Okocha rethought his retirement from international football to lead his country in the 2004 African Nations Cup; despite elimination in the semi-finals Jay-Jay was voted the tournament's most valuable player. Victory in that competition in 1994, in the Olympics in 1996 and appearances in three World Cup Finals tournaments add up to a significant international career. Failure to qualify for the 2006 World Cup Finals was a disappointing end.

Okocha came to prominence as a precocious teenager with Eintracht Frankfurt. A couple of good years at Fenerbahce followed, and prefaced a high-profile transfer to Paris Saint-Germain. When the PSG contract expired, Sam Allardyce spent hours persuading the Nigerian captain that the Reebok Stadium should be his next destination. After a slow start Okocha's joyful skills and powerful shooting were instrumental in keeping Wanderers in the Premiership. A brace of goals in a 5-2 win over Aston Villa secured Bolton's place in the 2004 Carling Cup final; the second, a free kick, personified Okocha. Faced with a wall and an acute angle, he bent the ball with power around the 'wrong' side of the wall.

☞ Okocha played in Fenerbahce's 1996–97 win at Old Trafford in the Champions League; probably the club's finest moment in Europe.

☞ Okocha hit the bar three times in a Premiership match at Spurs in 2003 – at least Wanderers won.

✍ Okocha scored in the 2000 African Nations Cup final, but Nigeria lost to Cameroon on penalties. Jay-Jay's revenge came in 2004 when his curling free kick saw Nigeria defeat their rivals in the quarter-final.

☞ Okocha is an engaging interviewee, but he likes his privacy. There was a much-publicised incident whilst at Fenerbahce when he lashed out at an intrusive cameraman.

VITAL STATISTICS

Place of Birth:	Enugu, Nigeria	
Date of Birth:	14 August 1973	**Died:** n/a
Caps:	59 (Nigeria)	**Goals (International):** 8
Clubs:	Eintracht Frankfurt, Fenerbahce, Paris St	
	Germain, Bolton Wanderers	
Appearances:	Club (League): 313	
Goals:	Club (League): 74	
Trophies:	None	

LEGEND RATING	
Achievement	7.0
Skill	9.0
Teamwork	6.0
Passion	8.0
Personality	7.0
TOTAL	**37.0**

O'Leary, David
Arsenal, Leeds United, Republic Of Ireland

WHEN HE FIRST APPEARED in Arsenal's first team as a skinny, gangling teenager, David O'Leary looked too fragile to last 90 minutes. But in a distinguished career at Highbury he eventually managed over 600 appearances for Arsenal, including 558 in the league. O'Leary became one of the best defenders in Europe during his 20-year career. An excellent reader of the game, he was the rock at the heart of the Arsenal team, much as Tony Adams has been in the last decade.

O'Leary picked up 67 caps for the Republic of Ireland, and would surely have played many more internationals but for a long spell in the wilderness following a row with Jack Charlton. But the two did patch up their differences sufficiently for O'Leary to be picked in the squad for the 1990 World Cup Finals in Italy.

O'Leary served his management apprenticeship under George Graham at Leeds, stepping into Graham's job after he left for Tottenham. Under him, Leeds quickly made progress. Despite building a strong side with a series of expensive purchases in the transfer market, O'Leary left the club, seemingly unsure what do when the team started to decline. Another chance at Aston Villa has seen the club make little progress, and O'Leary's excuses and constant *non mea culpa* have become wearisome.

☞ David's brother Pierce was capped seven times by Ireland. He once came on for David in a Wembley international.

☞ His gangling appearance earned him the nickname 'Spider' at Arsenal.

👍 Leeds came through tough groups to reach the semi-final of the 2001 Champions League. They beat Milan, Lazio and Deportivo La Coruna, and eliminated Barcelona in the initial group stages.

👍 O'Leary scored the winning penalty in a play-off against Romania to qualify for the 1990 World Cup Finals.

👎 He irritated many football followers with his avowal that his team are merely boys, and his Wenger-like defence of their indiscipline.

👎 His departure from Leeds in 2002 was followed by months of dispute over his severence pay.

VITAL STATISTICS

Place of Birth:	Dublin, Ireland		
Date of Birth:	2 May 1958	**Died:** n/a	
Caps:	67 (R. Ireland)	**Goals (International):** 1	
Clubs:	As Player: Arsenal; As Manager: Leeds United,		
	Aston Villa		
Appearances:	Club (League): 558		
Goals:	Club (League): 10		
Trophies:	LT 1989, 1991; FAC 1979; LC 1987		

Achievement	7.5
Skill	6.5
Teamwork	8.0
Passion	8.5
Personality	7.5
TOTAL	**38.0**

LEGEND RATING

O'Neill, Martin

Nottingham Forest, Leicester City, Celtic, Northern Ireland

ONE OF THE MORE ENTERTAINING features of Leicester City and Celtic matches in recent years has been the sight of a slender, curly-haired man hopping up and down maniacally on the touchline. Martin O'Neill wears his heart on his sleeve; if a referee or player has incurred his wrath, there's no need to wait for the press conference.

O'Neill was a fine player, winning trophies at home and in Europe under Brian Clough at Nottingham Forest. The width provided by O'Neill and John Robertson were crucial to that side's success. Playing for Northern Ireland his chances of winning international trophies were limited, but he captained the side in one of their proudest moments when they defeated hosts Spain in the 1982 World Cup. O'Neill as manager was able to combine the spirit of that Irish side with the tactical wiles and subtle motivation of Brian Clough. An excellent record in the lower divisions with Wycombe took him eventually to Leicester, where he made the club competitive in the Premier League. Then the big one, Celtic, and the restoration of pride for the green half of Glasgow. O'Neill has built a reputation that allows his name to be spoken in the same sentence as Jock Stein.

- O'Neill has earned respect for the honourable way he has approached moves in his career; he turned down a huge job at Leeds in respect of his commitments at Leicester.
- O'Neill took Wycombe Wanderers into the league for the first time in their history, overcoming huge local apathy in commuter-belt Buckinghamshire.
- May 2005. O'Neill earned tremendous respect from both within and outside the game for his decision to leave Celtic to care for his sick wife. Not all football people are unable to recognise that some things are more important than the game.

VITAL STATISTICS

Place of Birth:	Kilrea, County Derry, N. Ireland					
Date of Birth:	1 March 1952	**Died:** n/a				
Caps:	64 (N. Ireland)	**Goals (International):** 8	MANAGER		PLAYER	
Clubs:	As Player: Distillery, Nottingham Forest,		Achievement	8	Achievement	9
	Norwich City, Manchester City, Notts		Tactical Awareness	7	Skill	7
	County; As Manager: Wycombe		Motivation	9	Teamwork	8
	Wanderers, Norwich City, Leicester		Team Selection/Transfers	8	Passion	7
	City, Celtic		Personality	9	Personality	8
Trophies:	EC 1979–80; LT 1978; LC 1978–79, (1997,					
	2000); SLT (2001–02, 2004); SFAC (2001)		**TOTAL**	**41**	**TOTAL**	**39**

LEGEND RATING

Over The (Blue) Moon
The Manchester City Dream Team

ALTHOUGH OFTEN IN THE SHADOW of their neighbours, this team would give the current Manchester United side a run for its money.

Few teams in the history of the game can boast a stronger goalkeeping duo; Frank Swift was the finest keeper of his generation and relegates Joe Corrigan to the familiar role of understudy, a position he filled so often for England, covering for Shilton and Clemence in the 1970s.

In defence, Book and Doyle are obvious candidates from the side that won the Championship, FA Cup and Cup Winners' Cup in the 1960s, while Dave Watson was England's finest centre half of the 1970s. In midfield, Kinkladze and Summerbee would stretch opponents wide, leaving Bell and Revie to surge forward into the gaps. Up front, Lee justifies his place on the grounds that City, and later Derby, enjoyed their most successful spells with him leading the line. Tilson fired the bullets in City's other championship-winning side in 1937. The bench is conspicuous by its lack of defenders, so in the event of a back-four injury this team would have to revert to 3-5-2. This shouldn't pose a problem; attack has always been City's preferred form of defence.

- Frank Swift became a distinguished football journalist after retiring. Tragically, he died in the 1958 Munich air crash.
- Dennis Tueart would be encouraged to attempt as many overhead kicks as possible. His effort won the 1976 League Cup and remains one of Wembley's most eye-catching goals.
- Colin Bell could stake a claim for inclusion in a post-war England side. His pace over short distances earned him the nickname 'Nijinsky'.
- Steve Daley or Michael Robinson are not selected; despite their expensive price tags, neither justifies inclusion.
- Mercer and Allison formed a potent manager/coach team in the 1960s. Can Mercer forgive Allison for ruining his legacy?

> **Managers: Joe Mercer and Malcolm Allison**
>
> 4-4-2
>
> **Frank Swift (30s/40s)**
>
> **Tony Book (C) (60s/70s) Mike Doyle (60s/70s) Dave Watson (70s)**
> **Willie Donachie (70s)**
>
> **Georgiou Kinkladze (90s) Don Revie (50s)**
> **Colin Bell (70s) Mike Summerbee (70s)**
>
> **Francis Lee (70s) Fred Tilson (30s)**
>
> **Subs:** Joe Corrigan (G) (70s) Asa Hartford (M) (70s) Peter Doherty (M/F) (30s)
> Rodney Marsh (W) (70s) Dennis Tueart (F) (70s)

1968: Joe Mercer presents the League Championship at Maine Road.

Owen, Michael
Liverpool, Real Madrid, England

FEW FOOTBALLERS ACHIEVE in a lifetime what Michael Owen had by the time he was 22. He became the youngest Liverpool player ever at the age of 17 years, 144 days. He became the youngest England player in the twentieth century, and he scored a sensational solo goal against Argentina, still aged only 18.

After a wobbly spell, when doubts emerged, Owen hit back late in the 2000–01 season, leading the Liverpool line as they won a unique treble of cups, and scoring two late goals to steal the FA Cup from Arsenal. Early the following season he scored a quite brilliant hat-trick as England slaughtered Germany 5-1.

The injuries resurfaced in 2003, and a shocking record from the penalty spot allowed the doubters to find their voices again. Owen approached the end of the 2003–04 season at a crossroads. After an ordinary Euro 2004, he was used as a liquid asset by Liverpool, and sold to Real Madrid.

Owen's principal asset is his blistering pace, but to dismiss him as simply quick would be to take him lightly. He is able to use either foot, has a good first touch, good balance, and takes a high percentage of his chances. Despite a creditable goals-to-game ratio, Owen was an infrequent starter and he became unhappy with the 'supersub' tag. When a desperate Newcastle offered a club-record £16 m, the lure of first-team football proved too great.

- Voted PFA Young Player of the Year in 1998.
- Voted BBC Sports Personality of the Year in 1998, and third in the same poll in 2001.
- Owen scored his 100th goal for Liverpool early in 2002, still aged only 22.
- In May 2005 Owen scored a hat-trick against Colombia in a friendly in the USA, and moved into fourth place on England's all-time scoring list with a total of 32.
- Real Madrid emerged with a tidy profit after only one season of Owen's services. They had signed him for £9 m.

VITAL STATISTICS

Place of Birth:	Chester, England		
Date of Birth:	14 December 1979	**Died:** n/a	
Caps:	74 (England)	**Goals (International):** 34	
Clubs:	Liverpool, Real Madrid, Newcastle United		
Appearances:	Club (League): 257		
Goals:	Club (League): 135		
Trophies:	FAC 2001; LC 2001, 2003; UEFAC 2001		

LEGEND RATING	
Achievement	7.5
Skill	9.0
Teamwork	7.5
Passion	8.5
Personality	7.5
TOTAL	**40.0**

Munich, 2001. Owen celebrates one-third of his hat-trick in England's famous 5–1 triumph.

Own Goal

Oops!

SOME OWN GOALS are just down to plain bad luck. A defence can hardly legislate for a cruel deflection or unavoidable ricochet. Gary Mabbutt could hardly be blamed for the goal that won the FA Cup for Coventry in 1987, as his outstretched leg diverted a cross over Ray Clemence.

Other instances are simply inexplicable. Des Walker's combination of a cushioned defensive header and a clearance placed the ball neatly in the top corner to give Spurs the trophy they had handed to Coventry four years earlier. You'll never beat Des Walker? On this occasion he did it all by himself.

Spare a thought for Sunderland, whose wretched form and luck in 2003 were never better illustrated than in their home match against Charlton. Three down in half an hour was dire enough. The fact that two own goals from Michael Proctor and two wicked deflections were the cause summed up their season.

The best, however, are those moments that, had they occurred at the other end, would be lauded as pieces of sublime skill achieved only after months of work on the training ground.

- ☞ The start of the 1999–2000 season brought a rash of own goals in the Premier League. Frank Sinclair became Leicester's top scorer in reverse with two in successive games, both in the last minute.
- ☞ Occasionally, goalkeepers have obliged the opposition by throwing the ball into the net. Gary Sprake can take a bow for this: his video of gaffes would run to several hours.
- ☞ Pat Kruse got Cambridge United off to a flyer in 1977, scoring after only eight seconds. Unfortunately he was playing for Torquay, thus making history with the quickest-ever own goal.
- ☞ Chelsea's championship-winning season of 1954–55 was helped with a bizarre own goal at Leicester. It entered the records as 'Froggatt and Milburn, shared own goal', a unique achievement.

Gary Mabbutt's Knee.

**Title of a Coventry City fanzine,
named after the cause of their only
piece of silverware**

Life isn't always rosy for the Manc Machine.

Paisley, Bob

Liverpool

BOB PAISLEY MADE HIS DEBUT as a professional footballer for Liverpool in 1939, and retired as the most successful manager in the club's history in 1983 after 44 years of service. Although never a glittering international star, as a player Paisley was good enough to win a championship medal with Liverpool in 1947. When his playing career came to an end he joined the Anfield back-room staff, becoming a redoubtable deputy to the legendary Bill Shankly. When Shanks quit, Paisley took over as manager reluctantly, believing he was no more than a stop-gap for a bigger name. How wrong he was. Building on Shankly's legacy, Paisley remained at the helm for nine seasons, during which time Liverpool dominated both domestic and European soccer, winning six league titles, three European Cups and three league Cups – a haul of silverware that made this shy, quietly-spoken old man in a cardigan the most successful manager in the history of the English game.

☞ Paisley was the first Liverpool manager to lift the European Cup.

☞ He never won the FA Cup, either as a player or manager.

👆 Between January 1978–81, Liverpool were unbeaten at Anfield for a staggering 85 games (63 in the league).

👆 In 1978–79 Liverpool coasted to the title using only 15 players, two of whom played four games between them.

👆 He was voted Manager of the Year six times.

VITAL STATISTICS

Place of Birth:	Hetton-le-Hole, England	
Date of Birth:	23 January 1919 **Died:** 12 February 1996	
Caps:	0 (England) **Goals (International):** 0	
Clubs:	As Player: Bishop Auckland, Liverpool;	
	As Manager: Liverpool	
Trophies:	LT (1947), 1976, 1977, 1979, 1980, 1982,	
	1983; LC 1981, 1982, 1983; EC 1977, 1978,	
	1981; UEFAC 1976	

LEGEND RATING	
Achievement	10
Tactical Awareness	9
Motivation	9
Team Selection/Transfers	9
Personality	6
TOTAL	**43**

Pearce, Stuart
Nottingham Forest, England

THERE CAN BE FEW better examples of a player making the most of modest natural ability. Those tree-trunk thighs meant Pearce rarely lost a tackle, and he read the play astutely to make up for a lack of pace. His crossing and powerhouse shooting made him just as dangerous in attack and at set-pieces.

Pearce spent time in non-league soccer before signing for Coventry. Brian Clough recognised his leadership and commitment and snapped him up. Pearce served Forest well – 522 games are testimony to that. As it appeared his career was ending, Pearce had a flirtation with the manager's job at Forest, quickly realising a struggling Premiership club was no place for a beginner. He elected to continue playing at Newcastle and West Ham and, finally, Manchester City.

His passion and naked aggression made 'Psycho' first choice for England for a decade, and they struggled to find an adequate replacement until the blossoming of Ashley Cole.

Pearce has brought the same intensity and honesty to his manager's role at Manchester City, and earned the respect of neutrals as well as City fans. Football fans love a trier, and no one gave more for his country than Stuart Pearce.

👍 Pearce was distraught to have missed a crucial penalty in the shoot-out at the 1990 World Cup. His fierce exultation when he made amends at Euro 96 became an iconic image.

☞ The 'Psycho' nickname comes not just from his raw playing style, but also from the intensity of the stare in his clear eyes.

👍 Pearce was awarded an MBE in 1999, some reward for a player with scant few trophies to show for a dedicated career.

👎 In 1999 Pearce was involved in a horrific accident in which his car was crushed by a lorry: the lorry came off worst.

☞ Pearce's fondness for crunching punk rock has caused much mirth amongst press and team-mates. He claims that the more conventional music favoured by his colleagues gives him a headache.

VITAL STATISTICS

Place of Birth:	London, England		
Date of Birth:	24 April 1962	**Died:** n/a	
Caps:	78 (England)	**Goals (International):** 5	
Clubs:	Coventry, Nottingham Forest, Newcastle United,		
	West Ham, Manchester City		
Appearances:	Club (League): 570		
Goals:	Club (League): 72		
Trophies:	LC 1989, 1990		

LEGEND RATING	
Achievement	6.0
Skill	6.0
Teamwork	8.0
Passion	10.0
Personality	8.0
TOTAL	**38.0**

Pelé
Santos, Brazil

EDSON ARANTES DI NASCIMENTO is the greatest footballer of all time. No arguments.

Born in Tes Coracoes, a small provincial town in the Brazilian state of Minas Gerais, Pelé (as he is better known) began his career at Santos, forcing his way into the first team by the age of 16, and made his debut for Brazil a year later in 1958 when, at 17, he collected his first World Cup winner's medal in Sweden. Pelé went on to play in three more World Cup tournaments; he struggled with injuries in 1962, and again in 1966, but in 1970, playing in a deeper role, he was the architect of some of the finest football the game has ever known. Surrounded by players who were in tune with his alert mind and quick feet, Brazil produced unforgettable, almost perfect football.

Pelé played all his domestic football in his beloved white shirt for Santos, a career that spanned nearly 20 years. He retired in 1974, but was persuaded to return to the game a year later when, like Franz Beckenbauer, Bobby Moore and many other of his old adversaries, he signed a $4.5 m contract to play in the newly-formed NASL with New York Cosmos. Pelé has remained in football as an ambassador for the game, and has served a spell as Brazil's Minister for Sport.

☞ Only Ferenc Puskas of Hungary has bettered Pelé's tally of 77 international goals.

☞ When Pelé retired from Brazilian soccer, Santos also 'retired' his No. 10 shirt.

✍ Pelé scored a hat-trick in the 1958 World Cup semi-final, then two more in the final, including a mesmerising, acrobatic volley.

☞ Pelé's record as the only man to have played in three World Cup-winning squads is unlikely to be matched.

✍ Pelé scored in excess of 1,200 first-class goals in his career.

VITAL STATISTICS

Place of Birth:	Tres Coracoes, Brazil			
Date of Birth:	21 October 1940	**Died:** n/a	Achievement	10.0
Caps:	91 (Brazil)	**Goals (International):** 77	Skill	10.0
Clubs:	Santos, New York Cosmos		Teamwork	10.0
Appearances:	Club (All Senior Matches): 1363		Passion	10.0
Goals:	Club (All Senior Matches): 1283		Personality	9.0
Trophies:	WorC 1958, 1970; BLT 1956, 1958, 1960–62,			
	1964, 1966–68; WCC 1962, 1963		**TOTAL**	**49.0**

LEGEND RATING

Penalty Shoot-Outs
Despair And Derring-Do

THEY MAY BE A TERRIBLE WAY to lose a game, but they make for great theatre. Penalty shoot-outs made their debut in 1970, a device introduced to settle the mind-numbing tedium of something called the Watney Cup. Since then of course, they have gone on to settle some of the world's most important matches.

For England fans, memories of high-profile failures are fresh. At Italia 90, the team were just a few kicks away from the World Cup final, but with the scores locked at 3-3, Stuart Pearce and Chris Waddle missed to send Bobby Robson's team home. Lightning struck for a second time at Euro 96 with Germany again proving to be England's nemesis from 12 yards. Gareth Southgate was the culprit this time. Then in France 98 it was Argentina's turn to expose England's vulnerability from the spot, David Batty making it a hat-trick of shoot-out failures with a feeble effort in St Etienne. It was David Beckham – of all people – whose missed penalty sent hosts Portugal through to the semis in Euro 2004.

The prospect of penalties has even entered some teams' pre-match thinking. In the 1986 European Cup final, Steaua Bucharest, figuring they had little chance of beating Barcelona in open play, shamelessly played for 0-0 in the hope of pinching victory in the lottery of a penalty shoot-out. Incredibly it worked. Barcelona missed all their penalties and Steaua were crowned champions of Europe.

- Pearce, Waddle and Southgate turned their failure to financial advantage, starring in a TV advertising campaign for Pizza Hut.
- Controversially, penalties replaced second replays in the FA Cup in 1991. Exeter beat Colchester 4-2 in the first shoot-out.
- In 1994 Italy's Roberto Baggio blazed over the bar to hand Brazil victory in the 1994 World Cup final. The other errant Italian was the great Franco Baresi.
- David Batty volunteered to take a penalty against Argentina in France 98, even though he had never taken one in a game before.
- 1997. Marlow beat Littlehampton 11-10 on penalties in the FA Cup first qualifying round. The first 21 spot-kicks were scored.
- The 2005 FA Cup final becomes the first to be settled by penalties after Arsenal stifle Manchester United for 120 minutes. Paul Scholes misses the crucial kick and Patrick Vieira seals a scarcely merited win for Arsène Wenger's team.

'Maybe they were kicking the s**t out of O'Leary for missing it.'

Roddy Doyle misinterprets the reaction of David's team-mates after he scores the winning penalty against Romania during Italia 90, in *The Van*

Pearce misses for England at Italia 90 (left) and scores in Euro 96 (right).

Peters, Martin
West Ham United, England

THE THIRD OF THE 'HOLY TRINITY' of West Ham players in the 1966 World Cup-winning side, alongside Bobby Moore and Geoff Hurst, Peters had forced his way into the England reckoning the previous season, making his debut only weeks before the tournament began. An extremely versatile player – appearing in virtually every position for West Ham – he was a good tackler and passed the ball well with either foot, but his real gift was his ability to steal into the penalty area and score vital goals, a knack that earned him the nickname 'The Ghost'. His overall scoring record was better than nearly one in three games, an exceptional return for a midfield player. Unlike Moore and Hurst, Peters left West Ham while still in his prime, and won further trophies with Tottenham. Like many of his England contemporaries, he wasn't a success as a manager. It would have been interesting to see Peters in the modern game – his style would have suited the Premiership.

- Peters scored 'the other goal' in the 1966 World Cup final, and one of England's goals in the 3-2 defeat by Germany in the 1970 World Cup quarter-final.
- Peters teamed up with his England colleague Geoff Hurst after their playing careers were over – selling car insurance.
- The £200,000 Bill Nicholson paid West Ham for Peters was a British record.
- Peters even appeared in goal for West Ham, deputising as a substitute in only his third appearance for the club.
- As Spurs captain in 1975, Peters led a deputation to try and persuade Bill Nicholson to rescind his resignation.

VITAL STATISTICS

Place of Birth: London, England
Date of Birth: 8 November 1943   **Died:** n/a
Caps: 67 (England)   **Goals (International):** 20
Clubs: West Ham, Tottenham, Norwich City, Sheffield United
Appearances: Club (All Matches): 882
Goals: Club (All Matches): 220
Trophies: WorC 1966; CWC 1965; LC 1971, 1973; UEFAC 1972

LEGEND RATING	
Achievement	8.0
Skill	8.0
Teamwork	8.0
Passion	7.0
Personality	6.0
TOTAL	**37.0**

Platini, Michel
Juventus, France

THE FINEST EUROPEAN MIDFIELDER of the past 30 years, Michel Platini combined sublime skill with a goalscoring record that would put many international forwards to shame. Touch, vision and great accuracy with either foot made him a divine playmaker, but he added the virtue of a constant flow of goals, both from set-pieces and open play. After 10 years in the French league, he turned down a move to Arsenal in 1982 claiming, perhaps justifiably, that English clubs played too many games. The Gunners' loss was Juventus' gain, as trophies followed for the Italian giants. Platini's high point came in the 1984 European Championships when, teaming up with Jean Tigana and Alain Giresse in midfield, he skippered France to a famous victory on home soil. Platini's astonishing return of nine goals in five games, including two hat-tricks, made him the tournament's top scorer. His business interests brought about a shock retirement in 1987, but he was tempted by the French national manager's job three years later. An uneasy tenure, Platini resigned after France's premature exit from Euro 92 but became president of the France 98 World Cup committee and continues to enjoy a high profile as a special advisor to FIFA.

☞ Platini's penalty won the European Cup at Heysel in 1985, but the evening's earlier tragedy overshadowed everything.

🖐 Platini remains a strong critic of English club football, particularly its reliance on foreign players.

☞ His three World Cups included two as French captain, both of which brought semi-final defeats in 1982 and 1986.

👍 He scored the winner a minute before the end of a ding-dong-do against Portugal in the semi-final of Euro 84.

✍ Platini is the only player to have been voted European Player of the Year in three consecutive years – 1983, 1984 and 1985. Even the great Johan Cruyff had a year off!

VITAL STATISTICS

Place of Birth:	Joeuf, France
Date of Birth:	21 June 1955 **Died:** n/a
Caps:	72 (France) **Goals (International):** 41
Clubs:	AS Joeuf, Nancy, St Etienne, Juventus
Appearances:	Club (All Matches): 576
Goals:	Club (All Matches): 307
Trophies:	EuroC 1984; FLT 1981; SA 1984, 1986;
	CWC 1984; EC 1985

Achievement	9.0
Skill	10.0
Teamwork	9.0
Passion	9.0
Personality	8.0
TOTAL	**45.0**

LEGEND RATING

Mexico, 1986. Platini scores against Brazil in the World Cup quarter-final.

Play-Offs
All That Way For This

DERIDED BY MANY at their inception in 1987, the play-offs have become an integral part of the season, adding tension to matches that previously would have been meaningless. Initially the play-offs involved the top division side immediately above automatic relegation, and the three sides immediately beneath automatic promotion in the division below. This system was discarded after two years, and since 1989 the play-offs have involved only sides jostling for promotion, with relegation being automatic. The system still has its critics (Swindon Town's promotion in 1993, when they finished 12 points behind Portsmouth in Division One, is often cited as an example of the iniquities of the system). The first beneficiaries were Charlton, Swindon and Aldershot. Charlton edged out Leeds 2-1 in a replay after the two-legged final finished level, thus preserving their status in Division One. There have been one or two classic confrontations since. In 1995 Bolton reversed a two goal deficit to overcome Reading 4-3, while Sunderland and Charlton battled out a memorable 4-4 draw in 1998, the Addicks eventually winning 7-6 on penalties to retain their place in the Premiership.

- Sunderland had a ball in 1990. They scraped into the play-offs in sixth place in the Second Division, beat their great rivals Newcastle and lost 1-0 to Swindon at Wembley. The gods were shining on the Wearsiders though; Swindon were demoted for financial irregularities, and Sunderland got their promotion.
- In 1999, Manchester City were 2-0 down to Gillingham with a minute to go. They drew level and won on penalties. Not untypical of City's ups and downs in recent years.
- Ipswich lost to Sheffield United on away goals in 1997, Charlton in 1998 and Bolton after a 4-3 ding-dong-do at Portman Road in 1999. Revenge was sweet in 2000 as they battled past Bolton (5-3 this time) and beat Barnsley in the final.

'Not only have I had to give up chess because I don't have time anymore, but I'm also smoking myself to death. If we go through and win the play-offs at Wembley, I'll be smoking more than my old boss Menotti.'

Ossie Ardiles, then manager of Swindon, 1990

Bolton complete a remarkable turnaround against Reading in 1995.

Pride And Passion

Local Derbies

TALK ABOUT LOCAL DERBIES and people automatically think about Celtic v Rangers or the Merseyside rivalry between Everton and Liverpool. Go abroad and the talk is of the Milanese giants or the (almost literal) war between the Istanbul clubs.

Yes, these sporting duels are steeped in history and passion, but never believe that fans of smaller clubs don't harbour the same enmity and passion. Anyone who has witnessed the bitter contests between Stoke City and Burslem-based Port Vale, or the deep-rooted hatred at the heart of Cardiff City v Swansea fixtures, would never doubt it. Maybe lack of success adds piquancy to these rivalries; the derby match becomes the focal point of another year on the treadmill. It certainly lends intensity – albeit accompanied by some marvellous gallows humour.

These provincial rivalries extend abroad as well; supporters of Vitoria Guimaraes in Portugal are content to live in the shadow of the Lisboa and Oporto clubs, so long as they beat Sporting Braga! Fans of NEC Nijmegen in Holland have learned to live with the odd stuffing at the hands of PSV or Ajax because they can dine out on the joy of a victory over Vitesse Arnhem. Paroquial it may be, petty it may seem, but it is part of the pride and passion of football.

☞ West Bromwich Albion and Wolves have a bitter enmity. Both top sides in the 1950s, they have only flirted with the big time since, and it clearly rankles.

☞ Did you know that Celta Vigo v Deportivo La Coruna is a local derby? Coruna and Vigo are the two principal cities in Galicia, and the rivalry has intensified recently as both clubs have competed in the top half of La Liga.

☞ The celebrations at Portsmouth when a 4-1 victory over Southampton in 2005 effectively relegated the Saints after a long period of bossing the south coast were loud and long and unnervingly vitriolic.

☞ Suggestions that Hearts and Hibs merge to form one Edinburgh club saw the men behind the scheme bombarded with hate mail and death threats.

☞ Dublin hosts an often trouble-filled, socially divided derby; Shamrock Rovers, of the poorer side of Dublin, south of the Liffey, like nothing more than to hand out a chasing to the well-to-do Bohemians from the north side.

'I sometimes think you love Norwich more than you love me,' moans the wife.

'Aye,' husband replies, 'And I sometimes think I love Ipswich more than I love you.'

Wolves and West Brom get neighbourly.

Race, Roy
Melchester Rovers, England

WITH A CAREER spanning five decades, Roy Race's evergreen qualities put even Roger Milla and Peter Shilton to shame. Signing for his local club Melchester Rovers, he carried the dreams of every British schoolboy with a career that brought a string of league titles and European Cups. Unlike Bobby Moore, he never had the distinction of lifting the World Cup, but it was one of the few honours that eluded him. A blonde, dashing centre forward he wore the red and yellow of Melchester for nearly 40 years, first as player, then as player-manager. In 1993 Roy cheated death in a helicopter crash that forced the amputation of his left foot. He left Melchester for a short spell as boss of Italian legends AC Monza, but his heart was never in it. Surviving by the skin of his teeth, he suffered a crushing blow with the closure of *Roy Of The Rovers Monthly* in 1994, but rallied briefly with *Roy Race: The Playing Years* (1995). A comeback in *Match Of The Day* magazine ended when it ceased publication in 2001. Oh, and did we mention he was a cartoon character?

☞ 1954. He appeared on the front cover of boy's magazine *Tiger*, but it was a year before he made his debut, scoring twice in a 3-3 draw.

☞ 1959–60. Roy is endorsed by Bobby Charlton, who lent his name to the writing of the Race saga.

👍 1974–75. Appointed player-manager of Melchester Rovers. After a chequered career he resigned live on TV 18 years later, only to be reinstated the same season.

👎 1981–82. Survives a shooting. Five years later Race survives a terrorist bomb attack that kills eight team-mates.

👎 1994–95. In an increasingly desperate plot twist, Roy's wife Penny is killed in a car crash as the Races become the most tragic family since the Kennedys.

VITAL STATISTICS

Place of Birth: Melchester, England

Date of Birth: Unknown, Roy is timeless   **Died:** n/a

Caps & Goals (International): Unknown, but Roy has played for England for over 25 years

Clubs: Melchester Rovers (player-manager from 1974); As Player/Manager: Walford Rovers

Appearances & Goals: Club (League): Lost count over 35 years

Trophies: Too many to list – he is very successful

LEGEND RATING	
Achievement	9.0
Skill	10.0
Teamwork	10.0
Passion	10.0
Personality	10.0
TOTAL	**49.0**

THE PAPER FOR ALL FOOTBALL FANS!

ROY OF THE ROVERS

15th OCTOBER, 1977
EVERY MONDAY

8p

MEN OF MELCHESTER

ROY RACE

Roy Race

Racism

Don't Pretend It's Gone Away

ONE OF SOCIETY'S LARGEST BARNACLES has been attached to the game for decades. It was 1884 when Arthur Wharton turned out for Darlington to become Britain's first black footballer. One can only wonder what reception awaited him.

In the 1970s the rise of the National Front brought chanting inside grounds and the selling of racist literature at the gates. Clubs were not only ignorant of the problem but contributed to it, perpetuating the stereotype that black players lacked bottle or commitment. One popular theory also suggested they couldn't play in cold weather.

The situation today is much improved. Black players have successfully integrated all over Europe, although the problem has not disappeared. Attitudes have improved in Britain but worrying hotbeds remain in Italy, Iberia and the Balkans. Today's challenge for the British game lies in increasing the number of black people operating in football across the board. Black executives, referees, coaches, managers and board members are still an exception (the only current black member of England's set-up is Hope Powell, coach of the national women's team). Asian players and fans need to be similarly welcomed. Verdict? Much improved, but must try harder.

- April 2004. Ron Atkinson fires an on-air racist outburst against Marcel Desailly after Chelsea's Champions League defeat at Monaco. Rightly, it costs him all his media contracts.
- Prejudice extending into religious bigotry, Rangers' policy of signing only Protestants proved ignorance is not only skin deep.
- In 1995, followers of the racist group Combat 18 caused the abandonment of England's friendly in Dublin.
- October 2004. Spanish coach Luis Aragones racially abuses Thierry Henry in an attempt to 'motivate' Arsenal team-mate Jose Antonio Reyes. Are you Big Ron in disguise? The following month, Spanish fans racially abuse England's black players during a friendly in Madrid.
- October 2004. Courageous referee Rene Temmink abandons a league match between ADO Den Haag and PSV Eindhoven following fans' racist chanting.

'When I came into the assembly hall in South Africa it was full of blackies and it was getting f*****g dark when they were all sitting together.'

UEFA boss Lennart Johansson
(If you find this amusing, please take the book back to the shop, we don't want your money)

Ramsey, Alf
Ipswich Town, England

'ENGLAND WILL WIN the World Cup in 1966.' In 1963, this was a rare boast from a reserved and modest manager named Alf Ramsey. And yet, amazingly, it came true. The sight of Ramsey still seated impassively on the bench as the final whistle blew to signal England's victory over West Germany was in stark contrast to the outpourings of joy around him, but inside you can be sure his heart was stirring. Thirty minutes before he had roused an England team, shattered by Germany's injury-time equaliser to force the game into extra time, with the words: 'You've won it once, now you've got to win it again.'

Ramsey's motivational skills had been proven even before 1966. Four years earlier, in charge of what was a modest array of talent at Ipswich, he brought the First Division title to Portman Road for the first and only time in their history. His style was pragmatic rather than entertaining, and was a reflection of a playing style that brought him 32 England caps and a league title with Spurs. Knighted in 1967, he seemed untouchable, but England's capitulation to Germany and their failure to qualify for the 1974 Finals cost him his job. A brief managerial flurry at Birmingham notwithstanding, it was the end for Ramsey.

👍 Won the Second and First Division titles in successive seasons as player and manager.

☞ Furiously dubbed Argentina 'animals' following the 1966 World Cup quarter-final.

☞ Ramsey's innovative 4-4-2 formation led England to be dubbed the 'wingless wonders'.

☞ Ramsey was the FA's second choice for the England job; Burnley's Jimmy Adamson turned it down.

👎 Ramsey's first England game was a disaster. England lost 3-0 to France and were eliminated from the European Nations Cup.

VITAL STATISTICS

Place of Birth:	Dagenham, Essex, England	
Date of Birth:	22 January 1920	**Died:** 28 April 1999
Caps:	32 (England)	**Goals (International):** 3
Clubs:	As Player: Southampton, Tottenham;	
	As Manager: Ipswich Town, England national side,	
	Birmingham (caretaker)	
Trophies:	LT 1962; WorC 1966	

Achievement	9
Tactical Awareness	9
Motivation	9
Team Selection/Transfers	8
Personality	6
TOTAL	**41**

LEGEND RATING

Rangers
The Dream Team

LIKE THEIR OLD-FIRM NEIGHBOURS, Rangers have a large pool of successful candidates to pick from. Yet, while it's tempting to select a team based on medals won, the quality control needs to be more stringent.

For all the tabloid revelations and weight problems, in his prime Andy Goram was probably Scotland's finest goalkeeper. George Young represents the 'Iron Curtain' defence in the immediate post-war era, and the twin legends of Greig and Gough are impossible to ignore in central defence. Sandy Jardine is not on his natural flank, but is a far classier option than the left-back alternatives. The midfield is not short of trickery: Baxter and Gascoigne's on-field skills were every bit as extravagant as their bar bills. The other half of midfield is tinged with sadness. Who knows the heights Ian Durrant would have scaled had one rogue tackle not put paid to his career, while memories of Davie Cooper's wing play are always tempered with the tragedy of his sudden and shocking death at 39. In attack, Brian Laudrup, Rangers' most gifted forward of all time, is paired with their most prolific goalscorer.

- Rangers' 49 league titles are a Scottish record.
- Graeme Souness led Rangers out of their longest barren spell, laying the foundations in the late 1980s for a side that equalled Celtic's record of nine successive titles.
- On the bench, Derek Johnstone is preferred to one-time team-mate Colin Stein. Johnstone's two spells with the club over more than a decade earned him hero status.
- Terry Butcher was the pick of Rangers' English signings of the late 1980s. Other notables included Trevor Steven, Ray Wilkins and Chris Woods.
- John Greig was voted Rangers' greatest player of the twentieth century in an end-of-millennium poll.

Manager: Graeme Souness

4-4-2

Andy Goram (90s)

George Young (40s/50s) Richard Gough (80s/90s) John Greig (C) (60s/70s)
Sandy Jardine (60s/70s)

Paul Gascoigne (90s) Jim Baxter (60s) Ian Durrant (80s) Davie Cooper (70s/80s)

Brian Laudrup (90s) Ally McCoist (80s/90s)

Subs: Peter McCloy (G) (70s/80s) Terry Butcher (D) (80s) Ian Ferguson (M) (80s/90s)
Jorg Albertz (M) (90s) Derek Johnstone (F) (70s/80s)

Paul Gascoigne (left) and Ally McCoist celebrate another trophy.

Rant

Norway 2 England 1, 1981

'LORD NELSON! Lord Beaverbrook! Sir Winston Churchill! Sir Anthony Eden! Clement Attlee! Henry Cooper! Lady Diana! (lapses into frenzied Norwegian, roughly translated as 'we have beaten them all!') Maggie Thatcher, can you hear me? Maggie Thatcher! Your boys took a hell of a beating! Your boys took a hell of a beating!'

The scene: Oslo, 9 September 1981. A hapless England looked to have blown their World Cup qualifying hopes for the third successive tournament by losing 2-1 to a Norwegian team considered to be cannon fodder. News enough in itself, but the match passed into footballing folklore thanks to this joyful rant at the final whistle from the Norwegian radio commentator, Bjorge Lillelien, who, in a few breathless seconds, outdid even the most frenzied Brazilian broadcaster with his random grasp of British celebrity. England would love to consign this banana skin to a permanently sealed archive, but thanks to our hero it will be mentioned in perpetuity whenever the teams meet. Henry Cooper has never been in such exalted company.

- Lucky England still qualified for Spain 82 thanks largely to Romania's home defeat by Switzerland.
- England had been vilified months earlier by also losing to Switzerland.
- The team in Oslo contained four all-conquering Liverpool players, plus Kevin Keegan and Bryan Robson.
- The rant may have inflicted lasting damage, as the commentator died prematurely a few years later.
- Although Lord Nelson had only a single eye and one arm, he may have performed better than many of England's players that night.

SCORERS	**Norway:** Albertsen, Thoresen
	England: Robson
EVENT	World Cup qualifier, Oslo, 9 September 1981
NORWAY	(Man: Tor Roste Fossen)
	1. Antonsen 2. Bernsten 3. Aas 4. Hareide 5. Grondalen 6. Giske 7. Albertsen
	8. Thorensen 9. Okland (Pedersen) 10. Jacobsen 11. Lund (Dokken)
ENGLAND	(Man: Ron Greenwood)
	1. Clemence 2. Neal 3. Mills 4. Osman 5. Thompson 6. Robson 7. Keegan
	8. Francis 9. Mariner (Withe) 10. Hoddle (Barnes, P) 11. McDermott

Lord Nelson holds the telescope to his blind eye – could have been FA chairman.

Red Devils
The Manchester United Dream Team

LOVE 'EM OR LOATHE 'EM, you can't deny that Manchester United have enjoyed the services of some fabulous footballers. Many international teams would struggle to assemble a squad like this.

In goal, the choice of Schmeichel brooks no argument, he was a class ahead of Stepney. The defence is built around the post-war era, with Irish international Carey ably supported by fellow Busby Babe Edwards and Byrne, and Martin Buchan, United's one truly class player from the team that struggled through the 1970s.

The midfield is extraordinary. Bryan Robson can't get in the side. A player who was the mainstay of the England team for a decade or more can't make his club's Best Of! A reserve team would feature Robson alongside Paul Scholes, Paddy Crerand and Billy Meredith.

The forwards would be guaranteed to provide entertainment. Both volatile and intolerant of those less gifted, Best and Cantona would frustrate and fascinate in equal measure. And if it didn't work, Denis Law would enjoy playing alongside either of them.

☞ How do you choose between Matt Busby and Alex Ferguson, both knights of the realm? We couldn't.

👍 After the incomparable Charlton, Bill Foulkes' 682 appearances make him United's most loyal servant.

👍 Johnny Carey was an early example of the attacking fullback, a solid defender with good ball skills. He later became a successful manager of Blackburn Rovers.

☞ In the 1978 World Cup, Scotland manager Ally McLeod played Martin Buchan at fullback. Only when he returned him to the centre did their performances begin to pick up.

👍 Van Nistelrooy merits inclusion even after three seasons. Now we know why Fergie was prepared to wait to sign him.

Director of Football and Media Relations: Sir Matt Busby
Manager (and not allowed to talk to the press): Sir Alex Ferguson

4-4-2

Peter Schmeichel (90s)

Johnny Carey (40s/50s) Duncan Edwards (50s) Martin Buchan (C) (70s/80s)
Roger Byrne (50s)

David Beckham (90s) Bobby Charlton (60s) Roy Keane (90s) Ryan Giggs (90s)

Eric Cantona (90s) George Best (60s/70s)

Subs: Alex Stepney (G) (60s/70s) Bill Foulkes (D) (60s) Bryan Robson (M) (80s/90s)
Denis Law (F) (60s/70s) Ruud van Nistelrooy (F) (00s)

Players' cars were more modest affairs in the 1970s.

Red Letter Day For England

Germany 1 England 5, 2001

ALL THOSE YEARS of angst and frustration at England's inability to beat Germany were washed away in one glorious evening. Only a year before, England had given an abject performance at home to the same opponents, losing to a soft Dietmar Hamann free kick. There were five changes to the team from the previous October; Adams, Keown, Le Saux, Andy Cole, and Gareth Southgate all giving way to younger legs. England played with the exuberance of youth and, even after going a goal down in the early stages, remained determined to set the agenda. Gerrard crunched his Liverpool team-mate Hamann to remind him he wasn't going to dictate this game. The Germans were inept (they weren't very good in 2000, but Keegan was scared to have a go at them). Poor at the back, unimaginative in midfield and ponderous up front, they carried no threat. On this occasion England did what a good team should do and destroyed vastly inferior opponents. A team with four world-class players beat a team with (maybe) one.

OK, that's enough critical analysis. WASN'T IT GREAT!?

- German goalkeeper Oliver Kahn, one of the greats of the last decade, flapped about like a baboon in a straitjacket.
- The Germans were missing key players like Scholl and Jeremies. Tough.
- Canadian-born Owen Hargreaves, substitute for Gerrard, was playing on his home ground. He had impressed for Bayern in the European Cup final against Valencia.
- Eriksson exploited the space behind the German wing backs to great effect, Beckham and Gerrard dropping balls in for the excellent Gary Neville and Ashley Cole to pick up.
- Ferdinand was at fault for the German goal, but was near flawless after that.

SCORERS	**Germany:** Jancker
	England: Owen (3) Gerrard, Heskey
EVENT	World Cup qualifier, Munich, 1 September 2001
GERMANY	(Man: Rudi Voller)
	1. Kahn 2. Worns 3. Linke 4. Nowotny 5. Boehme 6. Hamann
	7. Rehmer 8. Ballack 9. Jancker 10. Neuville 11. Deisler
ENGLAND	(Man: Sven-Goran Eriksson)
	1. Seaman 2. Neville, G 3. Cole 4. Gerrard 5. Campbell 6. Ferdinand
	7. Beckham 8. Scholes 9. Heskey 10. Owen 11. Barmby

That scoreboard still brings tears to the eyes.

Referees

Who's The W****** In The Black?

REFEREES HAVE A TOUGH JOB, and media exposure has done them no favours. They make decisions without the benefit of seven cameras and slow-motion, and yet they still get far more right than wrong.

A good referee is like a well-behaved child or dog; all the more worthy of praise when their presence goes unnoticed. Unfortunately for the good referees, you tend to forget them; they have to be individuals who are happy with this subsidiary role.

Too many referees at the top level forget that people are there to watch the football, not them. Intoxicated by the fame offered by TV exposure, they go out of their way to make decisions based on fussy interpretations of rules that they would be better served ignoring altogether. Whilst the options for autobiography and media appearances remain, this is a trend that can only get worse. The celebrity referee is here to stay.

One welcome trend has been the increasing number of female officials. In 1991, Wendy Toms shattered the English glass ceiling by running the line during a Football League fixture. Her presence hastened the switch from 'linesmen' to 'referee's assistants'. Toms has since officiated in the Premiership and is a regular Nationwide League referee. Whatever the gender, consistency rather than the current level of mediocrity should remain the goal.

- Kim Milton Nielsen has become the *bête noire* of English hotheads. He dismissed David Beckham at the 1998 World Cup and has red-carded Wayne Rooney for sarcastic applause.
- Urs Meier was honoured by England fans following Sol Campbell's disallowed 'winner' against Portugal in 2004. Disgracefully, the *Sun* newspaper printed his email address – 16,000 messages followed, including death threats.
- In a 1978 World Cup match between Brazil and Sweden, Clive Thomas awarded a corner in the dying seconds. Brazil scored from a header straight from the corner, but Thomas claimed he had already blown for full-time and disallowed the goal.
- In March 2005, Anders Frisk threatened to quit refereeing in the wake of alleged harassment from Chelsea fans, who took issue with his handling of their Champions League tie in Barcelona.
- In 2005, Italian rules stating their referees must retire aged 45 nearly did for the career of Pierluigi Collina. Such nonsensical arbitration was overturned, allowing Europe's best referee to continue.

'I wasn't sure whether the linesman was indicating the ball had crossed the goal line or whether he had spotted the same offence as me. It wasn't offside. I saw an offence, although I can't remember what it was. In fact there were about eight or nine infringements I could have blown for before the player shot.'

Having denied Chesterfield a place in the FA Cup final, Elleray compounds an abysmal decision by justifying it with a nonsensical rant

Pierluigi Collina, the best referee in the world. Would you argue with him?

Renaissance For Rossi
Italy 3 Brazil 2, 1982

IF FIFA EVER DECIDE to award medals for the greatest matches in the World Cup, this one will be on the podium. The eventual winners knocked out the pre-tournament favourites in an absolute classic.

Brazil were defending a 24-game unbeaten record and needed only a draw to progress to the semi-finals while, by contrast, Italy had started the tournament in stuttering fashion, struggling in the first group stage with three draws.

The match twisted and turned throughout. Three times Italy led, only to be pegged back by Zico's brilliance in setting up Socrates and then Falcão who scored with a thunderbolt from the edge of the area. The difference between the teams proved to be the rejuvenated Paolo Rossi. None of his goals were exceptional, but a hat-trick against the world's best team was no mean feat. Admittedly, Brazil's back line was average at best, and their goalkeeper was just plain incompetent. Italy's back four, on the other hand, were immense. Marshalled by the evergreen Zoff in goal, they withstood everything Brazil could chuck at them in the last 15 minutes to win the day and break the hearts of neutral supporters around the globe.

☞ Bergomi showed impressive maturity after coming on as a first-half substitute. Most 18-year-olds would have shrunk from dealing with Zico and Eder.

☞ For Paolo Rossi, this was the day he came in from the cold. His ban following his part in a Serie A betting scandal was only lifted a few weeks before the tournament.

☞ 40-year-old Dino Zoff denied Brazil throughout. His save from Oscar with two minutes left won the game.

☞ It had been a torrid time for both of Italy's forwards. Antognoni had only recently recovered from a fractured skull.

☞ Rossi's goals against Brazil were his first of the tournament. He finished as its leading scorer with six.

SCORERS	**Italy:** Rossi (3)
	Brazil: Socrates, Falcão
EVENT	World Cup second round, Barcelona, 5 July 1982
ITALY	(Man: Enzo Bearzot)
	1. Zoff 2. Gentile 3. Cabrini 4. Tardelli 5. Collovati 6. Scirea 7. Oriali
	8. Conti 9. Rossi 10. Antognoni 11. Graziani
BRAZIL	(Man: Tele Santana)
	1. Waldir Peres 2. Leandro 3. Junior 4. Cerezo 5. Oscar 6. Luizinho
	7. Falcão 8. Socrates 9. Serginho 10. Zico 11. Eder

Rossi (centre, blue shirt) strikes another dagger into Brazilian hearts.

Revie, Don
Manchester City, Leeds United, England

WHETHER ONE REGARDS HIM as one of England's great club managers or the father of modern cynicism, Don Revie's influence on the domestic and national game is considerable. A competent, if unspectacular player, Revie was always a deep-thinking tactician, adapting his role as target man to a more deep-lying centre forward in a copy of the tactic deployed by the Hungarian striker, Hidegkuti. But it was as a manager that he excelled, notably with Leeds United. A struggling Second Division outfit in 1961 Revie had transformed Leeds into runaway league champions by 1969. His team, comprised of gifted and ruthlessly determined players like Jack Charlton, Billy Bremner and Johnny Giles, became feared as much for their ruthless professionalism as for their talent. The natural choice as England manager in 1974 following the sacking of Sir Alf Ramsey, Revie turned from saviour to sinner in three years. England's failure to qualify for a second successive World Cup Finals – and the discovery that he had been secretly negotiating a deal to manage the United Arab Emirates – saw him pilloried in the press. His boats burned, Revie disappeared completely from public life. Obituaries on his death in 1989 showed old wounds were not easily healed, although, to a man, his Leeds team spoke in his defence.

- PFA footballer of the year in 1955.
- Despite Leeds' success, Revie's team should have won much more, finishing league runners-up five times and losing three Cup finals.
- Leeds lost only two games in the 1969 season, the fewest ever in a 42-game campaign.
- 1969. Leeds establish a record of 34 consecutive league games unbeaten.
- Bob Stokoe claimed that Revie offered him a bribe to throw a vital league game. Stokoe gained his revenge years later in 1973, as manager of the Sunderland side that upset Leeds to win the FA Cup final.

VITAL STATISTICS

Place of Birth: Middlesbrough, England

Date of Birth: 10 July 1927   **Died:** 28 May 1989

Caps: 6 (England)   **Goals (International):** 4

Clubs: As Player: Leicester City, Hull City, Manchester City, Sunderland, Leeds United; As Manager: Leeds United, England national side, United Arab Emirates national side

Trophies: LT 1969, 1974; FAC 1972; LC 1968; UEFAC 1968, 1971

Achievement	8
Tactical Awareness	9
Motivation	8
Team Selection/Transfers	9
Personality	4
TOTAL	**38**

LEGEND RATING

Robson, Bobby
Ipswich Town, England, Newcastle United

EXCELLENT PLAYER. Great manager. Nice bloke. Few figures in football are treated with the universal respect accorded Bobby Robson. Robson's 35 years as a manager, eight of them with England, followed 17 years as a successful midfield player with West Brom and Fulham, where he played alongside the legendary Johnny Haynes. After retiring as a player Robson managed Ipswich for 13 years. During that time Robson bought and sold countless players but it was the signings of the Dutchmen Arnold Mühren and Frans Thijssen, two of the first overseas players to make a significant impact in English football, for which he is probably best remembered.

As England manager he survived an indifferent start, failing to qualify for the European Championships, but his record in two World Cups was impressive. In 1986 he took England to the quarter-finals and then, four years later, led them to the semis at Italia 90. On both occasions England lost out to the eventual tournament winners. After seven years abroad, he returned to his native North-East and revitalised a Newcastle United in sharp decline after ineffective management by Kenny Dalglish and Ruud Gullit. Chairman Freddie Sheppard's memory was short, though. His dismissal of Robson after an indifferent start to the 2004–05 campaign was shabby and ill-timed.

☞ He caused immediate controversy as England manager by omitting Kevin Keegan from his first squad in 1982.

✒ He enjoys good relations with the media these days, but was subjected to a vicious tabloid campaign to oust him as England manager in 1988 following a 1-1 draw with Saudi Arabia.

✍ He scored twice on his England debut in a 4-0 defeat of France, 1957.

☞ He has won only one English domestic trophy as a manager, the FA Cup with Ipswich in 1978.

☞ He left Ipswich for the England job after finishing second in the First Division in successive seasons.

VITAL STATISTICS

Place of Birth:	Sacriston, England		
Date of Birth:	18 February 1933	**Died:** n/a	
Caps:	20 (England)	**Goals (International):** 4	
Clubs:	As Player: Fulham, West Bromwich Albion;		
	As Manager: Vancouver Whitecaps, Fulham,		
	Ipswich, PSV Eindhoven, Sporting Lisbon,		
	FC Porto, Barcelona, Newcastle United		
Trophies:	FAC 1978; UEFAC 1981; CWC 1997; DLT 1991,		
	1992; PLT 1995, 1996		

	LEGEND RATING
Achievement	7
Tactical Awareness	8
Motivation	9
Team Selection/Transfers	8
Personality	9
TOTAL	**41**

Robson, Bryan

West Bromwich Albion, Manchester United, England

ENGLAND'S FINEST PLAYER of the 1980s was also one of their unluckiest. Although 'Captain Marvel' brought a huge midfield presence to bear for club and country, his catalogue of injuries threatened to make him more celebrated in the *Lancet* than the back pages. Robson's first World Cup Finals in 1982 saw him come of age, but the sight of him limping prematurely out of the following two tournaments left England fans mouthing the words 'if only'.

The heartbeat of West Bromwich Albion's finest post-war side, Robson later moved to Manchester United in search of the major prizes. It worked. He won FA Cup winner's medals in 1983, 1985 and 1990 and picked up a European Cup Winners' Cup gong in 1991. It looked like a league championship was going to elude him but, in the latter stages of his Old Trafford career, United finally came good, picking up their first title in 26 years in 1993. Robson played in only five matches that season, but no one in the country begrudged him his medal. His self-motivation and determination seemed ideal qualities for management, but despite leading Middlesbrough to two Wembley finals, his record in the league was poor, and his record in the transfer market was even worse. He was replaced as Middlesbrough boss by Steve McLaren in 2001. A disastrous spell at Bradford followed, but his stock rose when he saved West Brom from what seemed certain relegation in 2005.

- ✋ He captained England 65 times, second only to Bobby Moore.
- ✋ With 26 international goals he is the only non-striker in England's top 10.
- ✋ 1982. Scored after 27 seconds versus France, the quickest goal in World Cup Finals history.
- ✋ He lifted the FA Cup as captain three times (1983, 1985 and 1990).
- ☞ £1.5 m fee paid to West Brom by Man United in 1981 was a British record.

VITAL STATISTICS

Place of Birth:	Chester-le-Street, England	
Date of Birth:	11 January 1957	**Died:** n/a
Caps:	90 (England)	**Goals (International):** 26
Clubs:	West Bromwich Albion, Manchester United,	
	Middlesbrough	
Appearances:	Club (League): 568	
Goals:	Club (League): 114	
Trophies:	LT 1993, 1994; FAC 1983, 1985, 1990;	
	CWC 1991	

LEGEND RATING	
Achievement	7.0
Skill	7.0
Teamwork	10.0
Passion	9.0
Personality	7.0
TOTAL	**40.0**

Rooney, Wayne
Everton, Manchester United, England

YOU'RE 18, you've had a high-profile move to Britain's most famous club, but had to sit out the first few weeks with an injury. You get your chance; a big night, a Champions League game at Old Trafford. So what do you do? Play safe and pass sideways? Freeze and have a minger? No. You score a hat-trick. At least that's what you do if you're Wayne Rooney.

Rooney is without doubt the most exciting English player to have emerged in this writer's adult lifetime. Gascoigne had chutzpah; Le Tissier was a divine talent without desire; Owen a lethal bullet. Rooney has elements of them all, and if the combination comes to fruition he could finally turn England into a side capable of winning tournaments. His performances at Euro 2004 confirmed him as world class, and his appetite for the big games is healthy.

Rooney may be spared the burn out that threatens so many sporting prodigies; David Moyles handled him with kid gloves at Everton and Manchester United can afford to rest him occasionally. The regular suspensions his aggession and temper invite give him sporadic days off, too! The red mist should recede with age and maturity. Let's hope so, because at present Rooney's boorish and charmless demeanour detract from his status.

☞ Rooney made his Premiership debut against Spurs in August 2002, two months shy of his 17th birthday.

✎ He became Everton's youngest-ever scorer when he netted twice against Wrexham in a Worthington Cup match on 1 October 2004.

✎ Shortly afterwards a sensational last-minute winner against Arsenal made Rooney the Premiership's youngest-ever scorer, eclipsing Michael Owen.

✎ 12 February 2003, Rooney became England's youngest-ever player, again eclipsing Owen.

✎ A first England goal followed in the 2-1 win in Macedonia – surprise, surprise, eclipsing Owen's record as England's youngest scorer.

VITAL STATISTICS

Place of Birth:	Liverpool, England		
Date of Birth:	24 October 1985	**Died:** n/a	
Caps:	27 (England)	**Goals (International):** 10	
Clubs:	Everton, Manchester United		
Appearances:	Club (League): 105		
Goals:	Club (League): 30		
Trophies:	None		

Achievement	6.0
Skill	9.5
Teamwork	9.0
Passion	9.0
Personality	4.0
TOTAL	**37.5**

LEGEND RATING

Rough Justice

West Germany 3 (5) France 3 (4), 1982

THIS MATCH HAD EVERYTHING, including one of the great injustices a World Cup audience had ever witnessed. The game was delicately poised at 1-1 when France's Patrick Battiston burst clear onto the German goal, only to be cynically brought down on the edge of the area by a head-high challenge from German goalkeeper, Schumacher. Amazingly, Dutch referee Charles Corver failed to award even a foul – rough justice for the French fullback who was stretchered off with concussion and broken teeth.

With all neutrals baying for German blood, justice appeared to have been served as France swept into a 3-1 lead in extra-time with only 17 minutes left. But, settling for their two-goal advantage, the French sat back inviting German pressure. Germany seized the initiative and two goals in five minutes, the second a brilliant overhead kick from Fischer, saw them force a penalty shoot-out. Amazingly, France threw it away a second time. Schumacher saved Didier Six's kick to prevent a 4-2 lead, and repeated the trick to keep out Bossis's effort with the scores at 4-4. Then, as the shoot-out moved into sudden-death, Hrubesch applied the final, killer blow. The tears shed by French players were shared by football lovers everywhere.

☞ 'I'm convinced the world knows the best team lost. We only have ourselves to blame, though,' Michel Platini.

☞ Substitute Patrick Battiston had only been on the pitch for five minutes.

☞ 'He [Schumacher] is very sorry for what happened. It was an accident.' German coach Jupp Derwall, who even managed to keep a straight face.

☞ A French newspaper poll after the game revealed Schumacher to be the least popular man in French history, edging Adolf Hitler into second place.

☞ Justice finally prevailed as Italy beat Germany 3-1 in the final.

SCORERS   **W. Germany:** Littbarski, Rummenigge, Fischer
                   France: Platini (pen), Tresor, Giresse

EVENT   World Cup semi-final, 8 July 1982

W. GERMANY (Man: Jupp Derwall)
               1. Schumacher 2. Kaltz 3. Förster, K-H 4. Stielike 5. Briegel (Rummenigge) 6. Förster, B
               7. Dremmler 8. Breitner 9. Littbarski 10. Magath (Hrubesch) 11. Fischer

FRANCE   (Man: Michel Hidalgo)
               1. Ettori 2. Amoros 3. Janvion 4. Bossis 5. Tigana 6. Tresor 7. Genghini (Battiston)
               (Lopez) 8. Giresse 9. Platini 10. Rocheteau 11. Six

An anxious Platini escorts the stricken Battiston.

Rovers
The Blackburn Dream Team

BLACKBURN ROVERS' HEYDAY was in the nineteenth century. In an era when the FA Cup was the blue riband trophy, Rovers claimed it six times between 1884 and 1891, thanks largely to the goalscoring exploits of their centre forward, Jack Southworth. After a brief decline another great side emerged just before the onset of the First World War. With Bob Crompton at the team's heart, George Chapman at centre half, and Danny Shea banging in the goals, Rovers won the title in 1912 and 1914.

Under the management of Irishman, Johnny Carey, another Rovers revival took place in the 1950s. Although Carey's team contained no megastars, it was not short on fine players: Peter Dobing, Bryan Douglas and the prolific Bill Eckersley could hold their own in any company. They reached the FA Cup final in 1960.

The end of the maximum wage meant financial challenges for a small club like Blackburn, and an exodus of their best players led inevitably to another fallow period. Only when Jack Walker began to pour millions into the kitty did Rovers again become a force, the signings of Alan Shearer and Chris Sutton giving them a strike force good enough to bring the FA Premiership title to Ewood Park in 1995.

- Centre half George Chapman was pressed into service as a centre forward during the 1911–12 season. He responded with eight goals in as many games as Rovers surged to the title.
- ☞ The loyal and willing Fazackerley deserved to play in better Blackburn sides. He stayed at the club after retiring and contributed almost as much as a coach.
- ☞ Despite winning the championship the 1995 team was criticised for its direct tactics: two wingers, Ripley and Wilcox, providing the bullets for the SAS (Shearer and Sutton).
- ☞ Only the tricky winger Damien Duff makes it from the current team, but Graeme Souness has other exciting young talents in Matt Jansen and David Dunn in his improving side.

Manager: Johnny Carey

4-4-2

Tim Flowers (90s)

Colin Hendry (90s) George Chapman (1900s/10s)
Derek Fazackerley (70s/80s) Keith Newton (60s)

Damien Duff (90s/00s) Peter Dobing (50s/60s)
Bob Crompton (C) (10s) Ronnie Clayton (50s/60s)

Alan Shearer (90s) Bill Eckersley (50s)

Subs: Jimmy Ashcroft (G) (10s) Mike England (D) (60s) Tim Sherwood (M) (90s) Jack Southworth (F) (1890s) Danny Shea (F) (10s)

'Uncle' Jack Walker indulges in a little cabaret.

Rush, Ian

Liverpool, Wales

ONE OF THE GREAT instinctive finishers, Rush broke a stack of goalscoring records in his time with Liverpool. Discovered at Chester as a teenager, he was bought by the Anfield club in 1979 for £300,000.

As well as great poise in front of goal, Rush's best asset was his movement. Blessed with great stamina, he constantly dragged defenders out of position and deceived them with late feints and runs – the perfect foil for the spontaneous creativity of Kenny Dalglish. A defender once claimed that keeping tabs on him was 'like marking a ribbon'.

Rush never achieved the recognition he deserved abroad. This was due in part to being Welsh, which meant he never had the opportunity to shine in a good international team, and to his unhappy season with Juventus. Bought by the Italians for £3.2 m, Rush was sold back to Liverpool for £2.8 m the following year, observing, profoundly, that the experience had been 'like being in a foreign country'. Rush should have retired at Liverpool, as lacklustre spells at Leeds and Newcastle did nothing for his reputation. Better to remember him as the highest scorer in Liverpool's history.

- He scored a record 44 FA Cup goals, including five in finals (also a record).
- He scored 49 League Cup goals (this is a record held jointly with Geoff Hurst).
- Rush the record breaker: 'I am proud and privileged to have beaten the record of a great player like Roger Hunt.'
- Rush had played only 33 games in the Fourth Division for Chester when Liverpool stepped in.
- He was PFA and Football Writers' Player of the Year, 1984.

VITAL STATISTICS

Place of Birth:	Flint, Wales
Date of Birth:	20 October 1961 **Died:** n/a
Caps:	73 (Wales) **Goals (International):** 28
Clubs:	Chester, Liverpool, Juventus, Leeds United, Newcastle United
Appearances:	Club (All Matches): 584
Goals:	Club (All Matches): 253
Trophies:	LT 1982–84, 1986, 1988, 1990; FAC 1986, 1989, 1992; LC 1981–83, 1994, 1995; EC 1981, 1984

LEGEND RATING	
Achievement	8.0
Skill	9.0
Teamwork	9.0
Passion	8.0
Personality	6.0
TOTAL	**40.0**

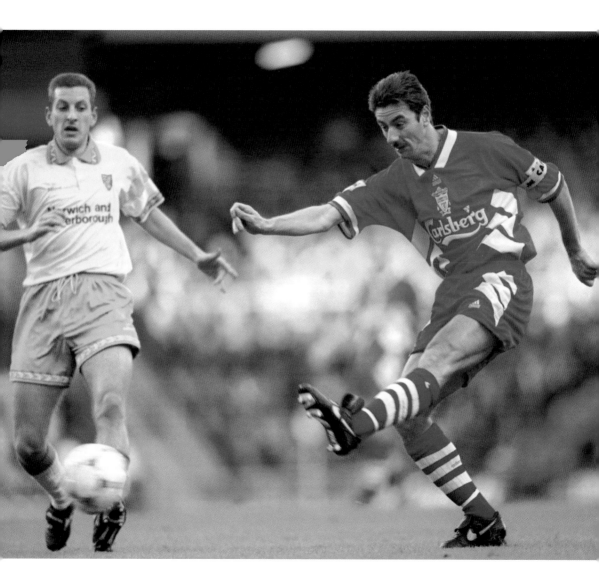

Saturday Night Fever
Match Of The Day

Until the BBC tried an experiment with its fledgling minority channel BBC2 in 1964, the only way to watch a league game was to turn up at the ground. That experiment was called *Match Of The Day*, and became a national institution and staple ingredient of Saturday-night viewing. Its first commentator, Kenneth Wolstenholme, was of the old school, a master of understatement and circumspect pronunciation. The programme was to eventually rely on Barry Davies and John Motson for its real colour, two men whose voices became synonymous with the show over a period of 30 years. In the early days only edited highlights from one or two games were transmitted but, following the arrival of Sky to the marketplace, the format was overhauled to include highlights of all matches from the top division. Presenters have come and gone down the years, the analytical approach of Jimmy Hill giving way to the smoothness of Des Lynam. More recently Gary Lineker was promoted to the anchor role, and it is he who currently introduces the show's coverage of FA Cup and international matches. Whatever the personnel, the signature tune has remained the same, acting as a musical comfort blanket to armchair fans for nearly four decades.

☞ The first broadcast on 22 August 1964 attracted only 20,000 viewers, less than half the crowd at Anfield as Liverpool beat Arsenal 2-0. First ever *MOTD* goal is scored by Roger Hunt.

✎ 1966. Promoted to regular Saturday-night slot following success of the BBC's World Cup coverage.

☞ 1980–82. *MOTD* yo-yoed between Saturday night and Sunday afternoon as ITV muscled in on the BBC monopoly.

☞ 1983. Live deal agreed with ITV, but a strike left screens football-free. Two years later *MOTD* lost league games for seven years to ITV.

✎ 1992. Deal with Sky returned league action to *MOTD*. A nine-year run ended on 19 May 2001.

✎ August 2004. *MOTD* returns to our screens after a three year absence.

'Those who participate provide the poetry. Those who commentate provide the prose – and not very good prose at that. That's why so many ex-players have taken up commentating. It's called missionary work.'

Gary Lineker addressing the Oxford Union in 1990 in a debate on the motion that 'this house believes it is better to commentate than participate'

Desmond Lynam, *Match Of The Day*'s smoothest anchorman.

Scholes, Paul

Manchester United, England

DESPITE UNITED'S big money signings of recent seasons, a key reason for their success has been the ability to spot and nurture young English talent. Whilst Beckham has grabbed the lion's share of off-the-field attention, none can doubt the huge contribution of a local Salford lad.

Scholes' great asset is his versatility. A ball-winning midfielder, his willingness to roll up his sleeves has been the chief reason why aesthetes like Cantona and Beckham found room to breathe. His ability to take up and prosecute goalscoring positions has also produced a goals-to-games ratio that many Premiership strikers struggle to emulate.

For England, he was one of the first names on the team-sheet for many years. His performance against Argentina at the 2002 World Cup Finals was one of the finest by any player in the tournament. His decision to retire from internationals in 2004 was sudden and odd. Ferguson would have hoped it would add zest to Scholes' performances for United, but instead they have declined in a puzzling manner.

Scholes will remian a United great, but maybe only a change of club will rekindle his lost spark.

- First season 1995–96 – makes immediate impact with 14 goals in 18 games.
- 1999 – scores in FA Cup final victory over Newcastle, thus winning a second double at 24.
- Biggest disappointment – suspended for 1999 Champions League final.
- 1999 – scores hat-trick for England in World Cup qualifier v Poland.
- Scholes' shyness is well-known. It is rare for him to give post-match interviews and he remains a grey, rather characterless figure off the pitch.

VITAL STATISTICS

Place of Birth:	Salford, Manchester, England				
Date of Birth:	16 November 1974	**Died:** n/a	Achievement	8.0	
Caps:	66 (England)	**Goals (International):** 14	Skill	7.0	
Clubs:	Manchester United		Teamwork	9.0	
Appearances:	Club (League): 329		Passion	8.0	
Goals:	Club (League): 87		Personality	4.0	
Trophies:	LT 1996, 1997, 1999, 2000, 2001, 2003;				
	FAC 1996, 1999, 2004; EC 1999		**TOTAL**	**36.0**	

LEGEND RATING

Seaman, David

Arsenal, England

DAVID SEAMAN cost Arsenal £1.3 m from QPR in 1990. Perhaps not a bargain on the same scale as Alex Ferguson's swoop for Peter Schmeichel, but not a bad bit of business. After joining the Gunners, Seaman helped the club to a succession of trophies, including the 1998 League and Cup double.

A usually reliable keeper, Seaman has been harshly pilloried for a couple of high-profile errors; in the 1995 European Cup Winners' Cup final he was lobbed by Real Zaragoza's Nayim from the half-way line and, against Germany in a World Cup qualifier in 2000, he was beaten from 35 yards by a Dietmar Hamann free kick. But those who criticise him for this conveniently forget the countless hours of impeccable service he gave both Arsenal and England. Seaman was England's number one for most of the last decade, a period in which only Tim Flowers and Nigel Martyn seriously threatened to displace him. He was outstanding at both Euro 96, France 98 and the 2002 World Cup Finals, despite his over-publicised mistake against Brazil. His fantastic, last-minute save in the 2003 FA Cup semi-final was the perfect riposte to critics who thought he was past his best.

☞ Seaman flirted with professional cricket as a youngster; he was a powerful fast bowler in Yorkshire league cricket.

✎ Not bad in the kitchen, either, Seaman was winner of a celebrity *Ready Steady Cook* programme in 1998.

☞ In a 1997 World Cup qualifier against Moldova Seaman captained England for the first time.

✎ Seaman redeemed himself for the Hamann goal, making a fabulous save moments before England took a 2-1 lead in the return game in Munich.

☝ January 2004: after half a season in poor form at Manchester City, injury forced his retirement, not the best swansong for one of England's finest.

VITAL STATISTICS

Place of Birth:	Rotherham, England
Date of Birth:	19 September 1963 **Died:** n/a
Caps:	75 (England) **Goals (International):** 0
Clubs:	Peterborough United, Birmingham, Queens Park Rangers, Arsenal, Manchester City
Appearances:	Club (League): 731
Goals:	Club (League): 0
Trophies:	LT 1991, 1998, 2002; FAC 1993, 1998, 2002, 2003; LC 1993; CWC 1994

LEGEND RATING	
Achievement	8.0
Skill	8.0
Teamwork	7.0
Passion	7.0
Personality	7.0
TOTAL	**37.0**

Shackleton, Len
Sunderland, England

ENGLAND MANAGERS have traditionally regarded talented individual players with suspicion, often ignoring them in favour of more workaday but malleable players. In recent times Glenn Hoddle and Matt Le Tissier were both victims of this peculiar mindset, while an earlier example is Len Shackleton. A plain-speaking Yorkshireman 'Shack's' blunt observations did not always go down well with managers and administrators, but plain was never an adjective to describe his play. He was the most skilful English player of the 1940s and 1950s. A small inside forward, he cut swathes through opposing defences with instant ball control and supreme dribbling ability. Moving to Newcastle in 1946 proved an important step in his career, as his performances at St James's Park made him a crowd favourite. But a clash with management saw him sold to neighbours Sunderland. It is at Roker Park where he will be most fondly remembered. If Shackleton was on form, so were Sunderland. His performances made a struggling First Division side a competent one, and it was probably no fluke that the fading of the great man's powers coincided with the club being relegated in 1957–58. That was to be Shackleton's final season. Sunderland have never found another like him.

☞ In 1935–36 Shackleton became the shortest-ever English schoolboy international, standing at a Lilliputian 4 ft 0 in.

☜ He scored six times on his debut for Newcastle in a 13-0 win over Newport.

☞ In his autobiography, Shackleton headed one chapter 'The Average Director's Knowledge of Football'. The rest of the page was left blank.

☞ The British transfer record was broken twice to buy Shackleton. Newcastle paid Bradford Park Avenue £13,000 in 1946, receiving over £20,000 from Sunderland 16 months later.

☞ His five England caps are a scandalous under-use of his talent. Paul Mariner won 35.

VITAL STATISTICS

Place of Birth:	Bradford, England	
Date of Birth:	3 May 1922	**Died:** 28 November 2000
Caps:	5 (England)	**Goals (International):** 0
Clubs:	Bradford Park Avenue, Newcastle, Sunderland	
Appearances:	Club (for Sunderland): 348	
Goals:	Club (for Sunderland): 101	
Trophies:	None	

LEGEND RATING	
Achievement	5.0
Skill	9.0
Teamwork	7.0
Passion	8.0
Personality	9.0
TOTAL	**38.0**

Shankly, Bill

Liverpool, Scotland

AFTER A PLAYING CAREER severely curtailed by the war, in which the highlight was an FA Cup winner's medal with Preston in 1938, Shankly entered football management with Carlisle, and started on his road to destiny. The apprenticeship was long and unglamorous; several years in the lower divisions with unfashionable clubs gave no indication of what was to come. Shankly seemed an odd choice for a struggling Liverpool in 1959, and their lean spell continued until 1964 when a league title finally came their way for the first time in 17 years. A further two championships, two FA Cups and a UEFA Cup followed before Shankly's retirement in 1974.

His contribution to Liverpool could never be measured in trophies alone, though. The wisecracking Scot laid the foundations of the 'boot-room' dynasty at Anfield, a think-tank of ideas and tactics that was to serve Liverpool well for 20 years. The continuity of playing style and management, and the philosophy of self-belief that characterised the club across that time were Shankly's legacy.

- Liverpool won the title in 1966 using only 14 players.
- Shankly never won the European Cup – the closest he came was a controversial defeat by Inter Milan in the 1965 semi-finals.
- An earthy humorist, Shankly's most famous observation was: 'Football is not a matter of life and death, I can assure you it is much more important than that.'
- 'The socialism I believe in is not really politics. It is a way of living. It is humanity. I believe the only way to live and be truly successful is by collective effort, with everyone working for each other, everyone helping each other, and everyone having a share of the rewards at the end of the day … it's the way I see football and the way I see life.' Bill Shankly

VITAL STATISTICS

Place of Birth:	Glenbuck, Ayrshire, Scotland
Date of Birth:	2 September 1913 **Died:** 28 September 1981
Caps:	5 (Scotland) **Goals (International):** 0
Clubs:	As Player: Carlisle United, Preston North End;
	As Manager: Carlisle United, Grimsby Town,
	Workington, Huddersfield Town, Liverpool
Trophies:	LT 1964, 1966, 1973; FAC 1965, 1974;
	UEFAC 1973

Achievement	9
Tactical Awareness	9
Motivation	10
Team Selection/Transfers	9
Personality	9
TOTAL	**46**

LEGEND RATING

Shearer, Alan

Blackburn Rovers, Newcastle United, England

NOT ESPECIALLY TALL, or particularly quick come to that, Alan Shearer is a striker who relies on strength and timing. He is also an exceptionally fine header of the ball – probably the best since Andy Gray – and possesses a thumping right foot.

Shearer emerged as a prodigy at Southampton, where he managed to shine in a mediocre side without making the breakthrough at international level. Then Jack Walker's cash, plus the promise of winning the sort of trophies that were always going to elude him at Southampton, lured him to Blackburn Rovers. At Ewood Park Shearer's scoring rate increased immediately, and his prolific partnership with Chris Sutton propelled Blackburn to the league title in 1995. He struck up a similarly fruitful partnership for England with Teddy Sheringham, a double-act that brought about the destruction of Holland (4-1) in the group stage of Euro 96.

That same year Shearer returned to Newcastle, his boyhood team. Since then he has been hampered by a series of injuries, but when fit has continued to score goals. Now retired from international football to protect his body from further punishment, Shearer is a lone figure of stability on the house of sand that is Newcastle Football Club.

A bland outward demeanour conceals a biting sense of humour and strong will. Shearer seems a certainty for Newcastle manager in the near future.

☞ Both Shearer's domestic transfers were record fees; his £15 m move to Newcastle was a then world record.

✍ He scored 37 goals in Blackburn's title-winning season. The following season he got 30 again, becoming the first player to reach the target in three consecutive seasons having scored 30 plus in the previous campaign.

✍ He was the youngest top-division player to score a hat-trick (17 years, 140 days, for Southampton in a 4-2 win over Arsenal).

✍ He scored in normal time and in the shoot-outs in two of England's recent high-profile matches (against Germany at Euro 96 and Argentina at France 98).

VITAL STATISTICS

Place of Birth:	Newcastle, England		Achievement	7.0
Date of Birth:	13 August 1970	**Died:** n/a	Skill	7.0
Caps:	63 (England)	**Goals (International):** 30	Teamwork	9.0
Clubs:	Southampton, Blackburn Rovers, Newcastle		Passion	9.0
Appearances:	Club (League): 537		Personality	8.0
Goals:	Club (League): 274			
Trophies:	LT 1995		**TOTAL 40.0**	

LEGEND RATING

Sheringham, Teddy
Tottenham Hotspur, Manchester United, England

'OH, TEDDY, TEDDY, went to Man United and he won f*** all!' they chanted gleefully as Manchester United did, indeed, finish his first season without a trophy. The next season was a different matter. Having been in and out of the team all year (Yorke and Cole were Fergie's preferred combination), Sheringham entered the big arena, coming on for the injured Roy Keane in the FA Cup final after only nine minutes. With a Premiership medal already safely stowed, another scoring appearance as a substitute saw Sheringham share in the third leg of United's treble triumph. From 'f*** all' to a unique hat-trick in 12 months.

Recognition for Sheringham came relatively late. Regarded as a journeyman at Millwall and Nottingham Forest, he blossomed at Spurs, forming a deadly combination with Jurgen Klinsmann. Accusing Spurs of lacking ambition he then left for United, but returned to his spiritual home for a swansong in 2001, immediately adding another dimension to an otherwise prosaic side. In subsequent spells at Portsmouth and West Ham Sherringham showed flickers of the old touch, but was too often off the pace in the Premiership.

Sheringham's partnership with Alan Shearer was instinctive and awesome, and they inspired England to the semi-finals of Euro 96.

- 1999. Scored as a substitute for United in both the FA Cup final (after 90 seconds) and European Cup final.
- Repeats the feat in England's vital World Cup qualifier against Greece in 2001, scoring with his first touch to level at 1-1.
- Sheringham's finest international performance came during Euro 96 as he and Shearer scored two apiece in the 4-1 destruction of Holland.
- ☞ Sheringham played in the 2002 World Cup Finals, becoming the oldest outfield England player to appear in the Finals.
- Sheringham was both PFA and Football Writers' Player of the Year in 2001.

VITAL STATISTICS

Place of Birth:	Highams Park, England	
Date of Birth:	2 April 1966	**Died:** n/a
Caps:	51 (England)	**Goals (International):** 11
Clubs:	Millwall, Aldershot, Nottingham Forest,	
	Tottenham, Manchester United, West Ham United	
Appearances:	Club (League): 693	
Goals:	Club (League): 277	
Trophies:	LT 1999, 2000, 2001; FAC 1999; EC 1999	

LEGEND RATING	
Achievement	9.0
Skill	8.0
Teamwork	8.0
Passion	7.0
Personality	7.0
TOTAL	**39.0**

1999. Sheringham tries the European Cup for size.

Shilton, Peter

Nottingham Forest, Southampton, England

PETER SHILTON CONTINUED PLAYING for so long that it seemed the only thing likely to persuade him to hang up his gloves was the arrival of his bus pass in the post. Having made his debut for Leicester in 1966, aged 17, he was still playing league football aged 47. His best spell as a club footballer was in Brian Clough's Nottingham Forest that won the European Cup twice, but he also played in the Southampton side that contained five England captains – himself, Keegan, Watson, Mills and Channon.

For a number of years Shilton played second fiddle or alternated with Ray Clemence in the England goal; at times it seemed that everyone bar the managers could see he was the better of the two men. He later made the number one jersey his own, and though he went on to record a record number of England caps (125), one wonders what tally he may have reached if his international managers had been more decisive. Shilton played in three World Cups, conceding only one goal in the 1982 tournament as England were eliminated without losing. Once he had ironed out early gremlins in his technique, Shilton became the complete goalkeeper. A great shot-stopper, although perhaps not in the same class as Gordon Banks, dominant in the area, and fast off his line.

- Shilton played his 1,000th league game for Leyton Orient against Brighton. Fittingly, he kept a clean sheet.
- Surprisingly, he only ever played in one FA Cup final, finishing on the losing side with Leicester in 1969.
- The £325,000 Stoke paid Leicester for Shilton was a world record for a goalkeeper.
- Shilton filed for bankruptcy in the 1990s, amid reports he had accrued heavy gambling debts.
- Shilton received an MBE in 1986, and an OBE in 1991.

VITAL STATISTICS

Place of Birth:	Leicester, England
Date of Birth:	18 September 1949 **Died:** n/a
Caps:	125 (England) **Goals (International):** 0
Clubs:	Leicester City, Stoke City, Nottingham Forest, Southampton, Derby County, Plymouth Argyle, Wimbledon, Bolton Wanderers, Coventry City, West Ham, Leyton Orient
Appearances:	Club (League): 1005
Goals:	Club (League): 0
Trophies:	EC 1979, 1980; LT 1978; LC 1979

Achievement	9.0	
Skill	9.0	
Teamwork	8.0	LEGEND RATING
Passion	9.0	
Personality	7.0	
TOTAL	**42.0**	

Simply The Best
Brazil 4 Italy 1, 1970

IT WAS THE GAME that settled the argument as to the greatest-ever team. Brazil had saved the best until last, perpetuating a philosophy that simply believed in scoring more goals than the opposition.

Their opponents were hardly makeweights. A team with Facchetti at its defensive heart and Luigi Riva a spearhead had seen off Germany in an epic semi-final – but they had the misfortune to run into a forward line with every great player at his peak.

The main surprise was that after 65 minutes, the score was still 1-1. Pelé's opener inside 20 minutes appeared to set up a procession, but the Achilles' heel that was Brazil's defence handed Boninsegna an equaliser before half-time. Once Gerson had restored the lead with a trademark long-range strike though, normal service was resumed. The fourth goal was pure Brazil, Carlos Alberto joyously lashing home after a gorgeous build-up saw the ball rolled languidly into his path by Pelé. It remains one of the World Cup's most repeated goals – a glorious souvenir of a peerless team.

- The match that won Brazil their third World Cup saw them awarded the Jules Rimet trophy outright.
- Jairzinho's goal meant he scored in all six games of the tournament.
- Mario Zagallo was the first man to win the World Cup as both a player and a coach.
- Zagallo coached Brazil again at France 98. They failed to repeat the performance, falling ingloriously to the hosts in the final.
- Pelé's opener was Brazil's 100th goal in the World Cup Finals.

SCORERS	**Brazil:** Pelé, Gerson, Jairzinho, Carlos Alberto
	Italy: Boninsegna
EVENT	World Cup Final, Estadio Azteca, Mexico City, 21 June 1970
BRAZIL	(Man: Mario Zagallo)
	1. Felix 2. Carlos Alberto 3. Brito 4. Piazza 5. Everaldo 6. Clodoaldo
	7. Gerson 8. Jairzinho 9. Tostao 10. Pelé 11. Rivelino
ITALY	(Man: Feruccio Valcareggi)
	1. Albertosi 2. Cera 3. Burgnich 4. Bertini (Juliano) 5. Rosato 6. Facchetti
	7. Domenghini 8. Mazzola 9. de Sisti 10. Boninsenga (Rivera) 11. Riva

Simulation
Or Cheating, As It's Commonly Known

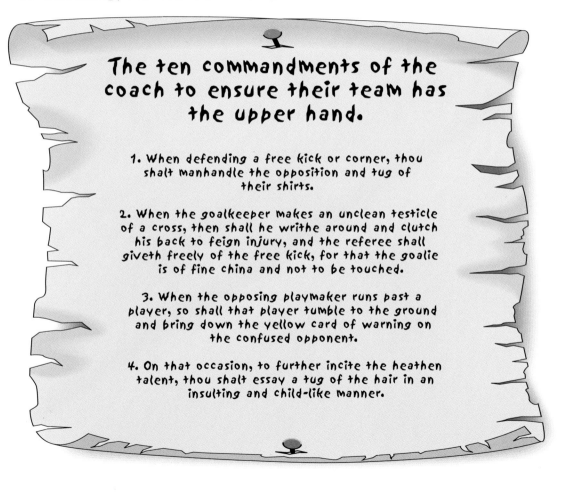

The ten commandments of the coach to ensure their team has the upper hand.

1. When defending a free kick or corner, thou shalt manhandle the opposition and tug of their shirts.

2. When the goalkeeper makes an unclean testicle of a cross, then shall he writhe around and clutch his back to feign injury, and the referee shall giveth freely of the free kick, for that the goalie is of fine china and not to be touched.

3. When the opposing playmaker runs past a player, so shall that player tumble to the ground and bring down the yellow card of warning on the confused opponent.

4. On that occasion, to further incite the heathen talent, thou shalt essay a tug of the hair in an insulting and child-like manner.

5. When the striker has pushed the ball too far past the defender, then shall he tumble to the ground in a melodramatic fashion, trusting in the inadequacy of the black-clad judiciary.

6. Whensoever a foul tackle is committed on a player, then shall that player wave his hand in supplication, demanding the yellow card of wrath for the pugilist.

7. Should, in the instance of commandment six, the tackled player be too busy rolling around in agony, then shall one of his nearby colleagues take upon themselves the onerous task of officious hand-waving.

8. Should a player be tackled in a robust and physical manner, so shall that player roll over to a count of five. The player shall then commence clutching a body part as if in agony, irrespective of whether any contact was made with that particular body part.

9. When a player's dramatic performance demands the attention of the physician, then shall that player be honour-bound to offend the opposition by skipping around like a lamb shortly after the departure of that physician.

10. Should a free kick or penalty be awarded to the opposition, then shall the defenders undergo a routine of gamesmanship and delay until the moment the kick is struck.

Somersaults and Salsa
The Fine Art Of Goal Celebration

OLD BLACK-AND-WHITE newsreel shots of footballers scoring goals and trotting, stony-faced back to the centre circle seem to come from a different game. No kissing, no cuddling, no diving, no fist-clenching, no ripping the shirt off, no gymnastics, no mime, no tableaux vivants. How dull it all must have been.

However, the amateur dramatics of the modern goalscorer have become tedious. The obligatory cupping of the ear to mock a silenced home crowd, the plunge to the knees by the corner flag – no wonder referees were instructed to curb the worst excesses. Whole teams were charging towards the scorer, engulfing them in scrums of adulation.

Who knows where it all started? Charlie George lying flat out on the Wembley turf after firing in the winner against Liverpool? Others have refined and re-defined the art: Hugo Sanchez, Real Madrid's great Mexican, with his trademark somersault; Klinsmann plunging to the ground in self-mockery of his reputation as a diver; Roger Milla and Lee Sharpe posing around the corner flag. Entire teams got involved in complicated routines, the most bizarre being Chelsea's reproduction of a classical painting following a strike by Roberto di Matteo. Oh dear.

👍 The most athletic? Peter Beagrie, the much-travelled winger, has treated many a ground to a somersault worthy of Sanchez.

👎 The worst? Has to be the awful baby-cradling pantomime introduced by Brazilian Bebeto at the 1994 World Cup.

👍 The silliest? Aylesbury Town, after a cup goal, waddling around on their knees doing the Aylesbury duck.

👎 The most irresponsible? Robbie Fowler pretending to snort cocaine off the dead-ball line.

👎 The most ill-judged? Not strictly after a goal, but at the end of the 1993 League Cup final, Tony Adams threw goalscorer Steve Morrow over his shoulder. Morrow broke his arm and missed the FA Cup final as a result.

'I made a two-fingered gesture towards the fans to show that I had scored twice. It must have been misinterpreted.'

Paul Peschisolido

Lee Sharpe: 'Tonight Matthew, I'm going to be Elvis.'

Souness, Graeme
Liverpool, Rangers, Scotland

SOUNESS AS A PLAYER was a manager's dream. He was possessed of great vision and passing ability, allied to a tremendous shot, but combined it with a steel and aggression that set him apart from other playmakers. His downside was a short fuse, and regular inability to curb the hard side of his nature.

His form in a moderate Middlesbrough side led Liverpool to lay out £325,000 for his signature – a British record that was to last only a month. A successful spell in Italy was followed by a return as player-manager of Rangers. Souness' first season at Rangers saw them win their first Scottish title for nine years. His sojourn as manager of Liverpool was more fraught. A degree of personal insensitivity, and some catastrophic signings led to his desmise – resignation after a 1994 FA Cup defeat by Bristol City. A spell at Blackburn Rovers saw a more mellow approach get Rovers promoted and then consolidate their place back in the Premiership.

A move to Newcastle saw a return to chaos as Souness struggled to tame a rebellious squad. A summer clear-out and the signing of Michael Owen restored some of the balance.

🖋 He signed Paul Stewart from Tottenham with a view to using him as Liverpool's main striker – possibly one of the worst signings ever by a major club.

🖋 Souness was pilloried in Liverpool for his dealings with the *Sun* newspaper, the paper that earned the eternal enmity of the city for their crass coverage of the Hillsborough disaster.

VITAL STATISTICS

Place of Birth:	Edinburgh, Scotland
Date of Birth:	6 May 1953 **Died:** n/a
Caps:	54 (Scotland) **Goals (International):** 4
Clubs:	As Player: Tottenham, Middlesbrough, Liverpool, Sampdoria, Rangers; As Manager: Rangers, Liverpool, Benfica, Blackburn Rovers, Newcastle United
Appearances:	Club (All Matches): 528
Goals:	Club (All Matches): 78
Trophies:	LT 1979–80, 1982–84; LC 1981–84, (2000); EC 1981, 1984; FAC (1992); SLT (1987, 1989–91)

MANAGER		PLAYER	
Achievement	7	Achievement	9
Tactical Awareness	7	Skill	8
Motivation	7	Teamwork	8
Team Selection/Transfers	7	Passion	7
Personality	6	Personality	6
TOTAL	**34**	**TOTAL**	**38**

LEGEND RATING

Southall, Neville

Everton, Wales

JUST WHEN YOU THOUGHT he had finally hung up his gloves, Neville Southall had a habit of popping up as stand-in keeper for yet another injury-hit club. What's more, each time he did so he seemed to have put on at least another stone, giving him the unfortunate appearance of a flying pudding. Yet, it is only recently that Southall has emerged as a figure of fun. In his heyday he was arguably the best goalkeeper in the world. His performances made Everton the only team in the 1980s to consistently challenge their rivals from across Stanley Park, and helped make the league title Merseyside's personal property. If Liverpool had enjoyed his services rather than the erratic Grobbelaar, Anfield's domination of club football would surely have been total. Oddly, despite such a lengthy playing career, Southall was a figure who shunned the camaraderie of his team-mates; after Everton matches he preferred a long, solitary drive home to his Welsh farm to a night on the town with his colleagues. Despite his heroics for Wales, they never qualified for a major tournament. So, like his countrymen Mark Hughes and Ian Rush, he was never afforded an opportunity to validate his reputation at the top level.

- 1990. Fined a week's wages after staging a one-man sit-down protest on the Goodison Park pitch at half-time.
- 1995. Already PFA Footballer of the Year, Southall won Everton the FA Cup with a great Wembley display against Man United.
- 1998. Southall won Torquay's Player of the Year award despite playing in only half their games.
- 2000. Southall played his last Premiership game at the age of 41, pressed into emergency service by Bradford.
- His 92 caps are a Welsh record.

VITAL STATISTICS

Place of Birth:	Llandudno, Wales	
Date of Birth:	16 September 1958	**Died:** n/a
Caps:	92 (Wales)	**Goals (International):** 0
Clubs:	Bury, Everton, Port Vale, Southend, Stoke City,	
	Torquay United, Bradford City	
Appearances:	Club (League): 701	
Goals:	Club (League): 0	
Trophies:	LT 1985, 1987; FAC 1984, 1995; CWC 1985	

LEGEND RATING	
Achievement	7.0
Skill	8.0
Teamwork	9.0
Passion	10.0
Personality	6.0
TOTAL	**40.0**

Spot-Luck

Brazil 1 France 1, 1986 (aet) (France Won 4-3 On Penalties)

WOULD PLATINI'S GENIUS carry the day against a talented, but curiously defensive Brazil? The match proved to be a tight affair – technically excellent but with few clear-cut chances. Careca opened the scoring with a fine strike, but Platini, celebrating his 31st birthday, pulled the French level. The game came alive in the last 20 minutes. Two minutes after Zico's entrance as a substitute, Brazil were awarded a dubious penalty. Four years before, Zico had tucked away a penalty in similar circumstances, but history was not to repeat itself – he missed, and the game headed into extra-time.

France were denied an obvious penalty when Bellone was upended by the goalkeeper, and Socrates, of all people, spurned an easy chance a minute later. And so to penalties. Socrates attempted a repeat of his nonchalant chip earlier in the tournament, but succeeded only in effecting a back-pass to Joel Bats. Platini, with a chance to all but seal the result, then blazed high over the bar, but following a miss by Julio Cesar, his midfield colleague Luis Fernandez struck the winning penalty for France.

☞ Penalty Shoot-out: Brazil: Socrates (missed), Alemao, Zico, Branco, Julio Cesar (missed)
France: Stopyra, Amoros, Bellone, Platini (missed), Fernandez.

☝ France lost to Germany in the semi-final (again), and their team broke up after the tournament. They would win the next Finals tournament in which they competed, in 1998.

☝ Socrates and Zico never played for Brazil again – the end of an era.

☞ Careca vied with Gary Lineker as the best striker in the tournament. Brazil might have achieved more if they had found him a decent partner.

SCORERS	**Brazil:** Careca
	France: Platini
EVENT	World Cup quarter-final, Guadalajara, 21 June 1986
BRAZIL	(Man: Tele Santana)
	1. Carlos 2. Josimar 3. Branco 4. Elzo 5. Julio Cesar 6. Edinho 7. Junior
	8. Alemao 9. Socrates 10. Careca 11. Müller
FRANCE	(Man: Henri Michel)
	1. Bats 2. Amoros 3. Tusseau 4. Fernandez 5. Bossis 6. Battiston
	7. Giresse 8. Tigana 9. Stopyra 10. Platini 11. Rocheteau

Zico (right) wriggles free from Fernandez.

Stein, Jock

Celtic, Scotland

JOCK STEIN'S EXPLOITS as a player merit more than a passing mention in the Celtic history books, having won the League and Cup in a five-year career at Parkhead. But it was his feats as manager that ensured his legendary status. Stein broke Rangers' domination of Scottish football in the 1960s, and presided over the most successful period in Celtic's history – a record run of nine consecutive league titles, including two domestic trebles.

Football and this son of a Lanarkshire miner nearly parted company in the early days, as he drifted from Albion Rovers to Llanelli before Celtic gave him his big break. Stein's most memorable accomplishment was bringing the European Cup to Glasgow in 1967 when, against an all-star Inter team, he masterminded a stunning 2-1 victory in Lisbon. In 1978, following a near-fatal car crash and a row over his appointment to the Celtic board, he left the club to take up the job of Scotland manager, where his eight-year tenure brought two successive qualifications for the World Cup. Tragically, Stein was not around to take his team to Mexico in 1986. During Scotland's final, victorious qualifying match against Wales in Cardiff he collapsed on the touchline and died of a heart-attack.

☞ Only one of his 26 managerial honours was not with Celtic (the 1961 Scottish Cup with Dunfermline).

☞ Stein managed Leeds United in 1978 for just 44 days, the same number as Brian Clough four years earlier.

☜ He reached the World Cup Finals as Scotland manager in 1982, but lost out to Brazil and the USSR in a strong group.

☞ Bill Shankly to Stein after Celtic's European Cup final win: 'John, you're immortal.'

☜ Alex Ferguson took temporary charge of Scotland after Stein's death, but failed to get them through the group stage at Mexico 86.

VITAL STATISTICS

Place of Birth:	Burnbank, Scotland
Date of Birth:	5 October 1923 **Died:** 11 September 1985
Caps:	0 **Goals (International):** 0
Clubs:	As Player: Albion Rovers, Llanelli, Celtic;
	As Manager: Dunfermline, Hibernian, Celtic,
	Leeds United
Trophies:	SLT 1966–74, 1977; SFAC 1961, 1965, 1967,
	1969, 1971, 1972, 1974, 1975, 1977; EC 1967

Achievement	10
Tactical Awareness	9
Motivation	9
Team Selection/Transfers	7
Personality	7
TOTAL	**42**

LEGEND RATING

Stiles, Nobby
Manchester United, England

OF THE MANY IMAGES from 1966, none captures the exultant English mood more than a gap-toothed Nobby Stiles jigging joyfully on the hallowed Wembley turf. Stiles had already created his national persona as a tough-tackling defensive midfielder, and developed seamlessly from an old-fashioned wing half into the artful dislodger of Sir Alf's famous 'wingless wonders' formation.

And yet it could have been so different. After the first round match against France, during which Stiles had perpetrated a nasty, high tackle in front of the royal box, Ramsey was instructed by the FA to drop him. He refused. The decision was not well received but, mindful of the player's value to the team, Ramsey stuck to his guns. Thus the stage was set for Stiles' greatest game, the semi-final versus Portugal and a memorable encounter with Eusebio. For all his trophies with Manchester United, including the European Cup also won at Wembley, Stiles' popularity was never higher than during that glorious, unforgettable fortnight in 1966.

- Dubbed 'The Assassin' by the Argentine press before Man United's World Club Championship match versus Estudiantes in 1968. A marked man, he was headbutted and unluckily sent off for dissent.
- He played for and managed Preston North End. Although promoted to Division Two in 1978, they were relegated three years later.
- He was awarded an MBE for services to football.
- Stiles' 420 United and England games yielded just 19 goals.
- He took over at the Canadian club Vancouver Whitecaps, but management was never his forte.

VITAL STATISTICS

Place of Birth: Manchester, England
Date of Birth: 18 May 1942 **Died:** n/a
Caps: 28 (England) **Goals (International):** 1
Clubs: Manchester United, Middlesbrough, Preston North End
Appearances: Club (League for Man Utd): 311
Goals: Club (League for Man Utd): 17
Trophies: WorC 1966; LT 1965, 1967; EC 1968

Achievement	9.0
Skill	6.0
Teamwork	7.0
Passion	8.0
Personality	7.0

TOTAL 37.0

LEGEND RATING

Strachan, Gordon

Aberdeen, Manchester United, Celtic, Scotland

WHEN MARTIN O'NEILL LEFT Celtic for personal reasons in 2005, the club replaced him with the only manager of comparable touch-line animation. Gordon Strachan had also left a club for personal reasons – Southampton the year before, after a respectable tenure that saw them reach the Cup final and mid-table safety. Elimination from the Champions League before the serious players had even entered was a terrible start, but the side have since recovered some equilibrium.

Strachan had a sound mentor. He was the creative spark in Alex Ferguson's Aberdeen side that challenged the Glasgow hegemony in the 1980s, and followed Ferguson to Old Trafford. Strachan left before the trophies began rolling in, but in doing so beat the master to the league title as Howard Wilkinson's workaday Leeds team sneaked the 1992 trophy.

Strachan was a feisty, passionate and skilful player. Never a conventional winger, he exerted great influence from wide positions, as his excellent distribution always offered the option of taking on the fullback. Unsurprisingly, he became a feisty and passionate manager too; his post-match interviews were often more entertaining than the preceding football match.

👍 He was voted Scottish Footballer of the Year in 1980 and English Footballer of the Year in 1992. The English award was greeted with an emotional: 'It's a tremendous honour. I'm going to have a banana to celebrate.'

👍 In common with other great players like Souness and Hansen, Strachan never made a powerful mark on the international scene. He played in the 1982 and 1986 World Cup Finals but was as uninspired as most of his compatriots.

👍 After a mobile phone rings at a post-match press conference: 'That'll be the Samaritans. They usually call me this time of day.'

VITAL STATISTICS

Place of Birth: Edinburgh, Scotland

Date of Birth: 9 February 1957 **Died:** n/a

Caps: 50 (Scotland)

Goals (International): 5

Clubs: As Player: Aberdeen, Manchester United, Leeds United, Coventry City; As Manager: Coventry City, Southampton, Celtic

Trophies: SLT 1980, 1984; SFAC 1982–84; CWC 1983; FAC 1985; LT 1992

	MANAGER		PLAYER	
Achievement	5	Achievement	7	
Tactical Awareness	6	Skill	7	
Motivation	8	Teamwork	9	
Team Selection/Transfers	7	Passion	8	
Personality	9	Personality	8	
TOTAL	**35**	**TOTAL**	**39**	

LEGEND RATING

Sunderland's Stunner
Arsenal 3 Manchester United 2, 1979

ACTUALLY, it wasn't a great match. But for exciting climaxes, no FA Cup final had witnessed drama like it since Stanley Matthews moved into overdrive in 1953. Arsenal had established a two-goal cushion by half-time and were content to run down the clock during the second half. United scarcely looked up to the task.

But with five minutes remaining, Gordon McQueen, still loitering in the penalty area after a badly-worked set-piece, turned in a speculative cross. Even now, Arsenal looked more than capable of holding their nerve. Enter Sammy McIlroy, who dribbled through a nervous and transfixed Gunners' defence two minutes later to toe-end the ball past the advancing Jennings. It squeezed tantalisingly inside his right-hand post, like a gently caressed snooker ball falling into a side pocket. In the stands the United fans lost it big time. Unfortunately for them, so did their team. From the restart, with just seconds to go, Arsenal moved the ball to Brady on the left wing, and the Irishman hit a wicked, curling cross over a flailing Gary Bailey on to the outstretched right boot of Alan Sunderland. The goal gaped, he scored, and the Cup was won at last.

☞ This was the second of Arsenal's hat-trick of successive Cup final appearances, and the only time they won. Ipswich and West Ham beat them in 1978 and 1980 respectively.

☞ This was Arsenal's 11th game of the competition, having taken five matches to overcome Sheffield Wednesday in the third round.

👇 This was Pat Rice's fourth final in an amazing run.

👇 For Dave Sexton, this was the nearest he came to a major trophy as United manager. He was sacked in 1981 after four barren seasons.

👇 Several hundred United fans left the stadium when their team were 2-0 down.

SCORERS **Arsenal:** Talbot, Stapleton, Sunderland
Manchester United: McQueen, McIlroy
EVENT FA Cup final, Wembley, 12 May 1979

ARSENAL (Man: Terry Neill)
1. Jennings 2. Rice 3. Nelson 4. Talbot 5. O' Leary 6. Young 7. Brady
8. Sunderland 9. Stapleton 10. Price 11. Rix
MAN UTD (Man: Dave Sexton)
1. Bailey 2. Nicholl 3. Albiston 4. McIlroy 5. McQueen 6. Buchan 7. Coppell
8. Greenhoff, J 9. Jordan 10. Macari 11. Thomas

Alan Sunderland (foreground) after scoring that late, dramatic winner.

Taylor, Graham
Watford, England

AFTER AN ORDINARY playing career with Grimsby Town and Lincoln, Graham Taylor moved into management at 28, his playing days ended by a serious hip injury. Moderate success led to his appointment as manager of Watford, and it was here that he made his reputation as he took the club from Division Four to the top flight in less than five years. Even more remarkably, his team even got amongst the big boys in 1983, finishing second in the First Division and losing in the FA Cup final to Everton. A strong defence and two fine wingers in Kevin Callaghan and John Barnes, later of Liverpool, enabled Watford to play a direct style with which many of their opponents simply couldn't cope. A move to more glamorous Aston Villa led to another second placed finish in 1990. An excellent club manager, particularly adept at getting the maximum return from modest players, it is unfortunate that Taylor will be eternally damned as the manager of one of England's poorest-ever national sides.

During his spell as boss in the early 1990s his selections were odd, and his long-ball tactics entirely unsuited to international football. Although his overall record is better than you might imagine, he will be remembered for his team's consistent failure to make any impact on major tournaments.

- 👍 After the debacle of the 1992 European Championships, Taylor's vilification in the press was unprecedented, and famously climaxed with one tabloid turning his head into a turnip on their back page.
- ☞ His return to management saw Watford achieve another promotion to the top flight in 2000, but this time immediate relegation followed.
- 👎 Taylor probably regrets allowing the shooting of a documentary that showed him issuing confusing, contradictory instructions to his players during England's 1994 World Cup qualifying campaign. The programme spawned a new national catchphrase: 'Do I not like that.'

VITAL STATISTICS

Place of Birth:	Worksop, England	
Date of Birth:	15 September 1944	**Died:** n/a
Caps:	0	**Goals (International):** 0
Clubs:	As Player: Grimsby Town, Lincoln City;	
	As Manager: Lincoln City, Watford,	
	England national side, Wolverhampton	
	Wanderers, Aston Villa	
Trophies:	None	

LEGEND RATING	
Achievement	6
Tactical Awareness	7
Motivation	9
Team Selection/Transfers	8
Personality	8
TOTAL	**38**

October 1993. An irate Taylor is restrained by the fourth official as England lose a crucial World Cup qualifier in Rotterdam.

Taylor Report
A Legacy Of Laziness

IN THE WAKE of the Hillsborough disaster, the government realised that further legislation was necessary. The aftermath of the 1971 Ibrox tragedy had brought the Safety of Sports Grounds Act, but this had failed to solve the problems of crumbling stadiums and terracing, and was anachronistic in its recommendations on crowd control. The responsibility for reform was placed in the hands of Lord Justice Taylor, a High Court judge. His first report, an interim version in August 1989, produced the Football Spectators Act and created the Football Licensing Authority (FLA), while his second in 1990 criticised many aspects of football administration and put forward 76 recommendations for improvement. The sobering conclusion of the Taylor Report was that British football could not be relied upon to put its own house in order, and that all parties – administrators, police and fans – had to share in the blame for the failings that had made British football grounds a serious threat to public safety.

A welcome side-effect of the Football Spectators Act was the scrapping of the Thatcher-inspired plans for compulsory identity cards. Perimeter fencing, a contributing factor in the Hillsborough disaster, has disappeared from British grounds but remains in Europe.

☞ March 1990. Chancellor John Major announced a 2.5 per cent reduction in the tax on football pools, releasing £100 m for ground redevelopment. The Football Trust added £40 m later in the year.

☞ Many wondered why clubs that lavished millions on transfers and wages should receive extra help from the taxpayer. Both Liverpool and Glasgow Rangers received £2 m, the maximum grant permitted to one club.

☞ Taylor's recommendations on all-seater stadiums have not been slavishly followed. All English league grounds should have converted by 1999–2000, yet Fulham were allowed to keep terraces open during their first season back in the Premiership.

The major issues addressed in the report:

- Terrace capacities. Taylor called for a 15 per cent reduction, with restrictions on self-contained pens and the opening of perimeter gates.
- A need to drastically modernise old grounds and increase safety facilities, including the replacing of terracing with seats.
- Ticket touting should be made illegal.
- A need for responsible behaviour by players and the media.
- An urgent need for consultation between clubs, officials and fans, in particular regarding hooliganism, segregation and racist chanting.

Plough Lane, Wimbledon. Condemned, and now dismantled.

Ten-Goal Payne
A Luton Legend

LUTON V BRISTOL ROVERS, Third Division South. True, 1936 was a time of simpler pleasures, but this wasn't a match that was likely to quicken the pulse. Except perhaps for Joe Payne who, with both of Luton's first-choice centre forwards out injured, was pressed into service as an emergency striker. Most of the home fans had never seen Payne before, so the opposition can hardly have quaked in their boots when the team-sheets were pinned up. But he soon changed that, helping himself to a first-half hat-trick. According to the cliché, you make your own luck in football. If this is true then Payne had his own factory and was mass-producing it. Incredibly, in the second-half he kept on scoring and Bristol Rovers were buried in the avalanche. With five minutes remaining, Payne's tenth goal of the game sealed a 12-0 win. No player had ever scored as many in a league game, and no one has come close to emulating his feat since. Joe Payne's piece of history is secure.

☞ Most irritated man? Tranmere's Robert 'Bunny' Bell, who had held the league record of nine goals in a game for less than four months.

☞ Despite this blip on the radar, 1935–36 was an uneventful season for both clubs. Bristol Rovers finished eighth, while Luton were 11 points off the pace in fourth.

☝ Unsurprisingly, Payne became first choice for the Hatters the following season. He carried on where had left off, and his 55 goals in the campaign remain a club record.

☞ Oddly, Payne did not score at all in the first 20 minutes. One hopes that any premature barrackers were suitably embarrassed at the final whistle.

'How long left, ref?'

Bristol Rovers' keeper in the 89th minute realises that the game might just be up. (Yes, you're right, we made it up.)

That Save, Pelé And Moore
Brazil 1 England 0, 1970

THE SCORELINE may not suggest a classic, but this was a match for the football purist. Pitting the defending champions against the team that would replace them at the tournament's end, this was a game notable as much for its defensive and goalkeeping qualities as it was for attacking flair. England appeared to have got out of jail in the first half as Gordon Banks made an incredible stop from Pelé's header, probably the best – and certainly the most replayed – save of all time. England could not repel the Brazilian attack for ever though, and on the hour they finally surrendered to the irrepressible Jairzinho, who fired home after good work from Tostão and Pelé.

The tone of the match was set by Bobby Moore's duel with Pelé, a real clash of the titans. This was Moore's finest game, his calm, interventionist style won the admiration of the Brazilian genius who made a point of exchanging shirts with the England captain after the two had embraced warmly at the final whistle. This mutual display of respect and affection, caught by camera lenses the world over, epitomised the dignity and style with which both players conducted themselves throughout their glittering careers.

- Both teams qualified for the quarter-finals, Brazil with a 100 per cent record, England with wins against Czechoslovakia and Romania.
- The match signalled the start of a great friendship between Moore and Pelé. The Brazilian paid a heartfelt tribute on Moore's death.
- Jairzinho's goal was one of seven in the tournament; he netted in all six games and finished as the top scorer.
- England nearly snatched a draw, only for Jeff Astle to miss a sitter after coming on as a substitute.
- This result was no disgrace for England; Brazil scored at least three goals in every other game at the Finals.

SCORERS	Jairzinho
EVENT	World Cup Finals group match, Estadio Jalisco, Guadalajara, Mexico, 7 June 1970
BRAZIL	(Man: Mario Zagalo) 1. Felix 2. Carlos Alberto 3. Piazza 4. Brito 5. Everaldo 6. Clodoaldo 7. Paulo Cesar Lima 8. Jairzinho 9. Tostão (Roberto) 10. Pelé 11. Rivelino
ENGLAND	(Man: Sir Alf Ramsey) 1. Banks 2. Wright 3. Cooper 4. Mullery 5. Labone 6. Moore 7. Lee (Astle) 8. Ball 9. Charlton, R (Bell) 10. Hurst 11. Peters

Banks makes THAT save.

They Think It's All Over
England 4 West Germany 2, 1966

'SOME PEOPLE ARE ON THE PITCH, they think it's all over … it is now. It's four'. Thus BBC commentator Kenneth Wolstenholme brought the curtain down on the 1966 World Cup. If he could claim royalties, he would now be wealthy enough to buy the FA itself. England's sixth game of the Finals brought a unique experience; for the first time in the tournament they went a goal behind, Haller taking advantage of a Ray Wilson error. But six minutes later, rising to meet a perfectly weighted free kick from Moore, Hurst leveled with a crisp header. In the second half England appeared to have won it through Peters with 12 minutes left, only for Weber to put celebrations on ice with a last-gasp equaliser. After 10 minutes of extra-time came the flashpoint. Hurst's shot rebounded off the underside of the bar and, controversially (and probably wrongly), Azerbaijani linesman Tofik Bakhramov awarded a goal to England. Hurst completed his hat-trick in the dying moments but by then the Germans were already a beaten side. The country that invented the game could finally call itself world champions.

- Geoff Hurst remains the only scorer of a hat-trick in a World Cup final. He found the net with his head, right and left foot.
- Germany added to an unenviable record. In five successive World Cup Finals, the team scoring first had lost.
- Ramsey rallied his troops before extra-time with his most famous words: 'You've won it once, now go and win it again'. He remained impassive on the bench at the final whistle.
- Hurst's selection was vindication for Ramsey. Greaves was the popular choice but Hurst replaced him for the quarter-finals and retained his place.
- Ramsey was knighted shortly after the victory. Both Bobby Charlton and Hurst have since received the same award.

SCORERS	**England:** Hurst (3), Peters
	West Germany: Haller, Weber
EVENT	World Cup final, Wembley, 30 July 1966
ENGLAND	(Man: Alf Ramsey)
	1. Banks 2. Cohen 3. Wilson 4. Stiles 5. Charlton, J 6. Moore 7. Ball
	8. Hurst 9. Charlton, R 10. Hunt 11. Peters
W. GERMANY	(Man: Helmut Schoen)
	1. Tilkowski 2. Hottges 3. Schnellinger 4. Beckenbauer 5. Schulz 6. Weber
	7. Held 8. Haller 9. Seeler 10. Overath 11. Emmerich

Hurst, far right, watches his second and England's third bounce on, sorry over, the line.

Thijssen, Frans & Muhren, Arnold
Ipswich Town

IN 1970S BRITAIN, foreign footballers were as rare as short back and sides, so when Spurs announced the signings of the Argentine stars Osvaldo Ardiles and Ricky Villa it caused a sensation. In comparison, Frans Thijssen and Arnold Muhren slipped into Portman Road almost unnoticed. But their deft skills and vision were soon the talk of the First Division.

Cultured midfielders both, they brought the passing principles of 'Total Football' to Ipswich and, in combination with the tigerish John Wark, formed the engine of Bobby Robson's 1981 UEFA Cup winners. Muhren later moved on to Manchester United in a lucrative deal. Although he won the FA Cup in 1983, his frequent injuries meant neither he nor United prospered (some would argue that his lengthy absence in the 1983–84 season cost United the title). His signing by Ajax in 1984 proved to be Muhren's Indian summer, and resulted in his recall for Holland. Aged 37, he was a member of the Dutch team that won the European Championships in 1988. Thijssen, meanwhile, struggled to maintain his form after leaving Ipswich, becoming an itinerant and peripheral figure.

- Thijssen was PFA Footballer of the Year in 1981, while Muhren won Ipswich's Player of the Year award in his first season (1978–79).
- Both were members of the Ipswich team that won the UEFA Cup in 1981, defeating their Dutch countrymen, AZ67 Alkmaar, 5-4 in the two-legged final.
- 'The man with velvet feet.' John Motson waxes lyrical over Arnold Muhren.
- In 1988 Muhren provided the cross for the best goal ever in the European Championships – Van Basten's stunning volley in the final against Russia.

VITAL STATISTICS
FRANS THIJSSEN

Place of Birth:	Heuman, Holland			
Date of Birth:	23 January 1952	**Died:** n/a	Achievement	6.0
Caps:	14 (Holland)	**Goals (International):** 3	Skill	8.0
Clubs:	NEC, FC Twente, Ipswich, Vancouver Whitecaps,		Teamwork	8.0
	Nottingham Forest, Fortuna Sittard, FC Groningen		Passion	7.0
Appearances:	Club (for Ipswich): 125		Personality	6.0
Goals:	Club (for Ipswich): 10			
Trophies:	UEFAC 1981		**TOTAL**	**35.0**

LEGEND RATING

1981. Muhren (left) and Thijssen hide their modesty with the UEFA Cup.

VITAL STATISTICS

ARNOLD MÜHREN

Place of Birth:	Volendam, Holland	
Date of Birth:	2 June 1951	**Died:** n/a
Caps:	23 (Holland)	**Goals (International):** 3
Clubs:	FC Twente, Ajax, Ipswich, Manchester United	
Appearances:	Club (for Ipswich and Man Utd): 226	
Goals:	Club (for Ipswich and Man Utd): 34	
Trophies:	CWC 1987; UEFAC 1981; FAC 1983; EuroC 1988	

Achievement	8.0
Skill	8.0
Teamwork	7.0
Passion	7.0
Personality	7.0
TOTAL	**37.0**

LEGEND RATING

Thirty-Six – Nil
Arbroath 36 Bon Accord 0, 1885

IMAGINE, IF YOU WILL, a possible post-match interview with the Bon Accord manager: 'Aye, the lads are naturally disappointed. We always knew it would be a tough game, it's difficult to come to one of the big clubs like Arbroath and get a result. Obviously, with some of our boys being a bit sketchy on the rules, like forgetting to change ends at half-time, it made it an uphill battle. But I do feel the game turned on a couple of major decisions. One was the kick-off. Had it not happened we might well have held out for a draw. Also, the referee missed a blatant handball leading up to their 29th goal, he must have been the only person in the ground who didn't see it. If television had been invented the replay would definitely have vindicated us. Still, at least we can concentrate on the league now.' One supposes the Bon Accord keeper didn't give up his day job as a piano tuner. Scotland's biggest slaughter since Culloden is a scoreline that will probably never be topped.

- On the same day and in the same competition, Dundee Harp beat Aberdeen Rovers 35-0.
- Arbroath met their match in the fourth round, losing 5-3 at Hibernian.
- Arbroath's only other Cup exploit is a run to the semi-final in 1947.
- The score would have been even higher but for the absence of goal nets, which were not yet in common use.
- This is still a world-record victory in an official match.

EVENT   Scottish FA Cup first round, 12 September 1885

ARBROATH   1. Milne, Jim snr 2. Collie 3. Salmond 4. Rennie 5. Milne, Jim jr 6. Bruce
7. Petrie 8. Tackett 9. Marshall 10. Crawford 11. Buick

BON ACCORD 1. Stevie Wonder 2. Long John Silver 3. Blind Pew 4. David Blunkett
5. Douglas Bader 6. Bonnie Langford 7. Basil Fotherington-Thomas
8. Thora Hird 9. Adeola Akinbiyi 10. Don Estelle 11. Toulouse Lautrec

INCREDIBLE VICTORY FOR ARBROATH

AFTER BEATING opponents Bon Accord by 36 goals to nil in the first round of the Scottish FA Cup yesterday, Arbroath's manager was said to be 'satisfied' with the way the match had gone for his team and that 'it was quite a convincing defeat'.

The Bon Accord side did not appear to find their form throughout the whole game, despite highly vocal support from their supporters, mainly family and friends of the players who all come from a small hamlet in the Grampian Mountains. Some questionable decisions were made by the referee, which worked in Arbroath's favour, giving them their 29th goal of the match.

Those Who Died Young
Footballers Cut Off In Their Prime

DYING AS A RESULT of a playing injury is mercifully rare. The most famous example was Celtic goalkeeper John Thomson, who in September 1931 was Scotland's hottest property. Diving at the feet of Rangers' Sam English, he sustained serious head injuries and died hours later in hospital aged just 22. The funeral briefly united the sectarian divide, but English was mercilessly barracked by some Celtic fans in the following fixture. Deeply upset, he was never the same player and left Rangers the following season.

Rangers can point to a more recent tragedy. In March 1995 their former winger and legend Davie Cooper collapsed and died from a brain haemorrhage while coaching youngsters for a television programme. The 39-year-old Cooper was as fit as he had ever been and had no history of previous illness. There are other examples. but the deaths of this Glasgow pair are particularly poignant, putting football, sectarianism, rivalry and trophies in their rightful perspective.

In June 2003, the shocking death of Marc Vivien Foe was a reminder that even the fit and active can be struck down. Playing in the Confederations Cup semi-final for Cameroon against Colombia, he suffered a heart attack on the pitch and died minutes later. He was 28 years old.

- In 1964 John White, a key member of Tottenham's double-winning side, was killed by lightning while sheltering under a tree during a round of golf.
- Laurie Cunningham and David Rocastle are the most recent English internationals to die prematurely. In 1989 Cunningham met his end behind the wheel of a car in Madrid, while Rocastle succumbed to cancer in 2001.
- Andres Escobar paid the ultimate penalty for scoring an own goal while playing for Colombia in the 1994 World Cup Finals. He upset a betting cartel and was murdered on his return.
- In 1897, Aston's Thomas Grice was fatally stabbed by his own belt buckle after what looked like an innocuous tumble.

'Bill Nicholson started to talk about identifying John White's body. He broke down ... he never broke down like that.'

Dave Mackay describes the effect of John White's death

Rangers' Davie Cooper, and Marc Vivien Foe. RIP.

Thrashings

Well, Des, It Was A Bit One-Sided Really

ARBROATH'S 36-0 DEFEAT of Bon Accord in 1885 is well documented as the world's biggest drubbing in a first-class game. Early fixtures were notorious for their mismatches; it would be churlish not to mention Preston's 26-0 caning of Hyde in 1887, the largest English score. In cup ties of yore, the pummelling of works' teams by well-drilled professionals was commonplace.

Despite tighter competition, mismatches still occur even at the top level (Revie's Leeds toying with Southampton in a 7-0 hammering in 1972 springs to mind). Even in the 1990s the cliché that there are 'no easy games nowadays' doesn't stand up to intense scrutiny. Manchester United versus Ipswich may have been a home banker in 1995, but 9-0 didn't result in too many claimed betting slips. But United's dominance of English football in the 1990s didn't stop them being humiliated 5-0 by Newcastle and Chelsea. Spare a thought, though, for Stanley Milton. On 6 January 1934 the Halifax goalkeeper trotted out for his debut against Stockport – and promptly let in 13 goals. Happily, he survived to be picked another day, which doesn't say much for their reserve keeper.

- American Samoa's 31-0 defeat set a new international record. FIFA weren't able to ratify the score immediately, as the scoreboard claimed 32-0.
- When Newcastle's keeper and outfield stand-in were both injured during a match at Upton Park in 1986, they turned to the vertically challenged Peter Beardsley to keep goal. West Ham won 8-0.
- Europe's record aggregate win is held by Chelsea, who once beat Jeunesse Hautcharage 21-0. The Luxembourg part-timers fielded a player with only one arm, and it wasn't the goalkeeper.
- 'We were lucky to get nil.' Oft-quoted preserve of the tight-lipped and ashen-faced manager.

'We are asking the Lord to keep the score down.'

American Samoa's coach, Tunoa Lui, prays for a miracle before a World Cup qualifier against Australia in April 2001; they lost 31-0

Ryan Giggs and Andy Cole celebrate United's latest mauling.

Too Much Bottle

Alcohol

DRINK HAS ALWAYS BEEN a strange contradiction in football. The misdemeanours of Premier League stars under the influence make for familiar tabloid revelations, yet at the same time Carling have poured millions into the FA's coffers with their sponsorship of the Premier League. At club level, the Blue Star brewery has added their familiar logo to Newcastle's black-and-white stripes in recent years. For British players, a lifestyle providing both plenty of spare time and plenty of cash has led to a thriving drinking culture. The skills of George Best and Jim Baxter can scarcely be mentioned without rueful references to the habit that so affected their lives. The great Brazilian Garrincha was to meet with an untimely end through his own alcohol addiction, while Billy Bremner's international career was curtailed following alcohol-induced incidents in a Danish nightclub. Modern casualties have included Paul Merson, and his former Arsenal team-mate Tony Adams who published an autobiography called *Addicted* in reference to his problems with the bottle. Today's use of dieticians and the cleaner habits of most continental imports have reduced the problem but, as the US government found, prohibition is completely unenforceable.

- A wilting Denis Compton was famously revived with a half-time tot of brandy during the 1950 FA Cup final. His second-half display helped Arsenal beat Liverpool 2-0.
- 1971. West Ham lost 4-0 at Blackpool in the FA Cup after several players break a club curfew and go drinking the night before. Among the players dropped for the next game is England captain Bobby Moore.
- England's footballers are snapped in the infamous 'dentist's chair' days before the start of Euro 96. The antics are repeated on the pitch, minus chair and alcohol, following Paul Gascoigne's goal in their group match against Scotland.

'I saw an advert saying "Drink Canada Dry" and thought it was an instruction.'

George Best explains his decision to cross the pond

Merse calls for a swift one from anyone with a hip-flask.

Top Toffees

Everton's Greatest

NINE ENGLISHMEN and two Welshmen make up this blend from Everton's four great eras. All positions are contentious save two; Southall is easily the best keeper and Dixie Dean is English football's most prolific goal machine. In defence, Newton and Wilson were two of England's classiest ever fullbacks, whilst the combination of Watson and Ratcliffe brought Everton a brace of titles in the 1980s. Two of the 1970 'holy trinity' are included, Ball and Kendall edging out Colin Harvey. Trevor Steven provides width, balance and sublime passing skills to right midfield, his left-footed contemporary Sheedy is usurped by the craftsman of the 1939 Champions, Joe Mercer.

In attack, Everton enjoy an embarrassment of riches in the classic centre-forward tradition. A forward line of Gray and Dean would make opposing defences quail. Lineker's prolific season reaped no reward and Rooney's premature departure precludes his presence.

☞ Everton's rich tradition of forwards is highlighted by the omissions from this squad – Bob Latchford, Roy Vernon and Graeme Sharp.

☞ Harry Catterick is preferred to Howard Kendall as manager. Although both won two titles, Kendall's second and third spells in charge presided over increasingly poor sides.

☞ Apart from Kendall, Colin Harvey also managed the side. His spell from 1987–90 was spent in Kendall's shadow, starting a decline from which they have never recovered.

☞ Seven of Everton's nine Championship sides are represented, the exceptions being 1891 and 1915, when competition was far weaker.

☞ Curiously, given these days of classy foreign imports, all of this squad are British except the tireless and inspirational Gravesen.

Manager: Harry Catterick

4-4-2

Neville Southall (80s/90s)

Keith Newton (60s/70s) Dave Watson (80s/90s)
Kevin Ratcliffe (C) (80s/90s) Ray Wilson (60s)

Trevor Steven (80s) Alan Ball (60s/70s) Howard Kendall (60s/70s)
Joe Mercer (30s)

Dixie Dean (30s) Andy Gray (80s)

Subs: Gordon West (G) (60s/70s) Brian Labone (D) (60s)
Thomas Gravesen (M) (2000s) Tommy Lawton (F) (30s) Joe Royle (F) (70s)

Manager Howard Kendall beams with another League title.

Total Football

Holland, 1970s

BUILDING ON THE SUCCESS of the great Ajax club team, Michels took a squad assembled around that side to the 1974 World Cup Finals. They had scraped through qualification, a late goal against Norway eliminating Belgium, but in Germany they were a revelation, comfortably the best team of the tournament despite their loss to the hosts in the final. All the players were comfortable on the ball, while their movement and passing were exquisite. 'Total Football' at its poetic best. Van Hanegem, stately and cultured, and the vigorous Neeskens were the team's engine room in midfield. What is often forgotten is how tough the Dutch were. If the attack wasn't firing, they were able to dig in; Krol, Rijsbergen, Haan and Neeskens were superb footballers, but they were not afraid to leave a foot in when necessary. And above all there was Cruyff. With all that talent behind him and the wiry strength of Rensenbrink next door, he was the icing on the cake, full of tricks and pace. Four years later in Argentina, without Cruyff and Van Hanegem, they were less persuasive, but still formidable opponents, and some awesome long-range shooting at altitude saw them through to a second final. Sadly, they lost again, securing their status as the greatest team never to win anything.

☞ The managers who built the two great club sides were the managers for the two World Cup campaigns (Michels from Ajax, and the Austrian, Ernst Happel, from Feyenoord).

☝ Cruyff missed the 1978 World Cup after a dispute with Happel, followed by Van Hanegem.

☞ The 1978 campaign saw twins play in a World Cup final for the only time. Winger Rene van der Kerkhof had featured in the 1974 final as a sub, and he was joined by brother Willy in 1978.

☝ Arie Haan's winning goal against Italy in 1978, effectively propelling Holland into the final, was from a preposterous distance, easily 40 yards.

Manager: Rinus Michels

Key Players
Wim Suurbier (D) Ruud Krol (D) Wim Rijsbergen (D)
Arie Haan (M) Wim Jansen (M) Wim van Hanegem (M)
Johan Neeskens (M) Johnny Rep (M/F) Johan Cruyff (F)
Rob Rensenbrink (F)

Trophies
None (beaten in 1974 and 1978 World Cup Finals)

Johan Cruyff, the best of an extremely talented bunch.

Trautmann's Final
Manchester City 3 Birmingham City 1, 1956

ON THE FACE OF IT, this was a routine FA Cup final. The underdogs did not defy the odds, there were no comebacks, last-minute winners or 40-yard scorchers. One goalkeeper's performance, though, was unique. Bert Trautmann was already giving a fine display for Manchester City when he dived at the feet of Birmingham forward Peter Murphy and was knocked unconscious. Only partially revived, he was involved in another jarring collision five minutes later. The newsreel footage of Trautmann massaging his neck did not reveal the whole story. It wasn't until days later, after he had completed the match and picked up a winner's medal in City's 3-1 victory, that the full extent of his injury was diagnosed. Incredibly, x-rays revealed that he had suffered a broken neck and should not even have been standing up, let alone playing football. Had the modern system of three substitutes and a keeper on the bench been applied, Trautmann would almost certainly have been replaced immediately and his heroism thus diluted. In the event, his performance produced one of the FA Cup's most famous episodes in an otherwise unremarkable match.

- Trautmann was Footballer of the Year in the same season.
- Having been a German soldier and POW in the Second World War, his arrival at Maine Road brought protests and boycotts by City fans.
- Trautmann made a full recovery and was back in the team six months later.
- This match saw Trautmann overshadow Manchester City's star player, future England boss Don Revie.
- Trautmann was a converted keeper, having preferred to play centre half in his native Bremen.

SCORERS	**Manchester City:** Hayes, Dyson, Johnstone
	Birmingham City: Kinsey
EVENT	FA Cup final, Wembley, 5 May 1956
MAN CITY	(Man: Leslie McDowall)
	1. Trautmann 2. Leivers 3. Little 4. Barnes 5. Ewing 6. Paul 7. Johnstone
	8. Hayes 9. Revie 10. Dyson 11. Clarke
B'HAM CITY	(Man: Arthur Turner)
	1. Merrick 2. Hall 3. Green 4. Newman 5. Smith 6. Boyd 7. Astall
	8. Kinsey 9. Brown 10. Murphy 11. Govan

Trautmann dives in the challenge that was to break his neck.

TV & Film

Screen Soccer

FOOTBALL HAS PROVIDED a source of inspiration for dozens of filmmakers over the decades, yet for the most part they have been of a distinct 'B' movie standard. Perhaps the most famous football film is the improbable *Escape to Victory*, which tells the unlikely story of a group of prisoners of war – Bobby Moore, Pelé and Ossie Ardiles included – who plot their escape during a match against a German army team. *There's only one Jimmy Grimble*, is the latest attempt to depict the dreams and despairs of any football-mad youngster while *Gregory's Girl* cleverly used football to give an insight into the angst of adolescence. Television drama-makers have also turned to football on a regular basis, and seem particularly fascinated by the increasing presence of women in the game. In 1989 Cheri Lungi topped the ratings as *The Manageress* in charge of a struggling club, while the long-running BBC drama *Playing the Field*, based on the Doncaster Belles, charted the trials and tribulations of a women's team.

Later film offerings have included a decent stab at dramatising Nick Hornby's groundbreaking book *Fever Pitch*. In 2002, *Bend it Like Beckham* provided a novel take on an Asian girl trying to break into UK women's football. The greatest success story has to be Vinnie Jones, who has reinvented himself as a hard-man movie actor.

☞ Pelé flirted with the big screen twice in the 1980s. He first appeared in the POW drama *Escape to Victory* and again two years later in the little known *Young Giants*.

☞ *Beyond The Promised Land*, a Man Utd authorised fly-on-the-wall glimpse of Becks and the rest during the 1999–00 season, was only shown in Manchester cinemas.

☞ The boot was on the other foot when *Footballers' Wives* hit the small screen in 2002. 'They're young, they're rich, they're sexy, and they've got everything money and fame can buy,' screamed the publicity puff.

☞ *The Arsenal Stadium Mystery* is the earliest example – a 1939 black and white murder mystery set against a Highbury backdrop.

'The fans' favourite, a movie which understands like no other what makes football great.'

A *Guardian* film critic referring to the star-studded 1981 movie, *Escape to Victory*

A scene from the risible *Escape to Victory*. Look, no dirt.

United Bury Their Ghosts
Manchester United 4 Benfica 1, 1968

TEN YEARS ON, this was the night that laid the ghosts of Munich to rest. At the final whistle Bobby Charlton's face, distorted with emotion, told its own story. This was a victory for the dead as well as for the living, a fitting tribute to the Busby Babes who had perished on the tarmac on that fateful night of 6 February 1958.

The pre-determined venue for the European Cup final was a huge advantage for Matt Busby's team, as half of Manchester decamped to Wembley to cheer on their heroes. They saw a cagey, goalless first half, but a rare header from Charlton appeared to have won it for United just before the hour. But Benfica pulled level through Jaime Graca after 75 minutes, and the goal galvanised the Portuguese champions. Pressing hard, Eusebio eluded Stiles in the dying minutes, only to be denied by Stepney's parry when a winner seemed certain. This incident proved to be the turning point. In extra-time United, lifted by their supporters, were irresistible. A goal of characteristic genius from George Best set them on their way, his dribble through the entire defence unleashing raptures of relief around Wembley. Kidd and Charlton twisted the knife, and Benfica were finished.

👌 Apart from Busby and Bobby Charlton, centre half Bill Foulkes was the only other Munich survivor involved in the match.

👆 For Denis Law, it was a bittersweet night. He watched the match from a hospital bed recovering from a knee operation.

☞ Foulkes' words after the game were moving: '…for those of us who lost our friends … our victory seemed the right tribute to their memory'.

👌 The aftermath brought several more honours. Busby was knighted, while George Best was named English and European Footballer of the Year.

☞ The 1968 team, like the Busby Babes, was largely home-grown. Only Alex Stepney and Paddy Crerand had cost a fee.

SCORERS	**United:** Charlton (2), Best, Kidd
	Benfica: Graca
EVENT	European Cup final, Wembley, 29 May 1968
MAN UTD	(Man: Matt Busby)
	1. Stepney 2. Brennan 3. Dunne 4. Crerand 5. Foulkes 6. Stiles 7. Best
	8. Kidd 9. Charlton 10. Sadler 11. Aston
BENFICA	(Man: Otto Gloria)
	1. Enrique 2. Adolfo 3. Humberto 4. Jacinto 5. Cruz 6. Jaime Graca
	7. Coluna 8. Jose Augusto 9. Eusebio 10. Torres 11. Simoes

Best (no. 7) turns away after scoring United's crucial second.

Unsung Heroes
Never Mind The Badge Kissers

LOYALTY IS OFTEN cited as the quality most lacking in the modern game. Ronaldo's search for a bigger pot of gold at Real Madrid, thus ignoring Internazionale's patience with his rehabilitation, is the most glaring example.

For the less gifted, the options are more prosaic. Some players, whether out of devotion or expediency, have demonstrated season after season of unyielding service. Goalkeepers often figure in clubs' appearance records due to their ability to eke out a longer career. Pride of place must go to Steve Ogrizovic. He remained as understudy for years at Anfield watching Ray Clemence positively ooze rude health. He not only lasted another 16 years as Coventry's No. 1 but showed enough consistency to set a club record for number of appearances.

As far as clubs go, West Ham has enjoyed a greater percentage of long-servers than almost any other. Some, like Bobby Moore, enjoyed almost every decoration possible. Spare a thought for fellow defender Billy Bonds, who chalked up a Hammers' record of 663 appearances. Despite proving himself a model of consistency, his sole reward was a single England call-up. He never even got on the pitch.

☞ March 1978. Chelsea's twin stalwarts Ron Harris and Peter Bonetti each make their 700th appearance for the club on the same day.

☞ Ian Callaghan, despite 18 years of success at Anfield, waited 12 years between England caps before being recalled by Ron Greenwood in 1978.

✍ John Trollope played 770 games for Swindon over 20 years, finally hanging up his boots in 1980 – an amazing record for an outfield player.

✍ The award for Best Uncapped Player. Step forward Tony Brown of West Brom. He holds two club records, 574 appearances and 218 goals, but never got an international sniff in 17 years.

'He is part of the furniture, like a granddad. He's a miserable old git but he has such presence'

Veteran Portsmouth keeper Alan Knight receives a dubious tribute from team-mate Paul Hall

Venables, Terry

Tottenham Hotspur, England

UNTIL RESCUING MIDDLESBROUGH from the clutches of Division One in 2001, Terry Venables had never taken a footballing job north of Tottenham. In a managerial career that has spanned three decades his English employers have been almost exclusively in London, serving to reinforce his reputation as the cockney geezer with more than a hint of the Essex wide-boy about him – a reputation, it has to be said, he added to by resigning as England coach to defend himself in court against accusations of financial misdoings. Fans were sorry to see him leave the England post. As 'the people's choice' to succeed Graham Taylor he was a huge success, only narrowly failing to take England to the final of Euro 96. Venables has always had a reputation as a manager with imagination and foresight; from his time at Crystal Palace to his resurrection of Barcelona, his teams have played with flair and innovative tactical formations. At the Nou Camp he led Barca to their first league title for 11 years in 1985, and was unlucky not to add the European Cup to his sideboard the following year when, famously, all five of his allotted penalty-takers missed their kicks in the shoot-out against Steaua Bucharest in the final. He was a better coach than he was a player; despite being tipped for greatness at schoolboy level his career drifted after his second and final England appearance.

- 1991. In partnership with Alan Sugar, Venables bought Spurs. Two years later, a bitter High Court battle ended with Sugar gaining sole control.
- 1995. A judge described Venables' court evidence as 'wanton' and 'not entirely credible'.
- 1997. Venables enjoyed a brief spell as Australian national coach, then bought Portsmouth for £1.
- 2002–03 proved a tough one for Venables. He started as Leeds' potential saviour but left before its end with Leeds in trouble.

VITAL STATISTICS

Place of Birth:	London, England	
Date of Birth:	6 January 1943	**Died:** n/a
Caps:	2 (England)	**Goals (International):** 0
Clubs:	As Player: Chelsea, Tottenham, Queens Park Rangers, Crystal Palace; As Manager: Crystal Palace, Queens Park Rangers, Barcelona, Tottenham, English national side, Portsmouth, Australian national side, Middlesbrough, Leeds United	
Trophies:	PLA 1986; FAC 1991	

Achievement	6	
Tactical Awareness	9	
Motivation	8	**LEGEND RATING**
Team Selection/Transfers	9	
Personality	7	
TOTAL	**39**	

Venables was one of the few to bring out the best in Paul Gascoigne (right).

Vieira, Patrick

Arsenal, France

PATRICK VIEIRA and Emmanuel Petit were the twin midfield turbines of the Arsenal side that won the League in 1998, a season the pair rounded off by collecting World Cup Winner's medals with France. Add a European Championship Winner's medal in 2000, and another double in 2002, and it adds up to a tidy few years for the Senegalese-born Vieira.

Vieira first emerged at Cannes where he captained the side in the French First Division at the ripe old age of 18. From there he wasted little time securing a move to AC Milan but, after failing to break into the side, he was soon whisked away for £3.5 m by his compatriot and admirer, Arsène Wenger. That fee now looks like a steal. Wenger bought a player with skill and good distribution, but also immense strength. Since arriving in England Vieira has improved with every season, and there are signs that the fuse on his temper, so often the source of his disciplinary problems, is growing longer with age. Failure in the 2002 World Cup Finals seems to have simply driven Vieira on even harder, but injury saw him miss France's Euro 2004 quarter-final defeat by Greece. His intense rivalry with Roy Keane, another uncompromising figure with an equally quick temper, has been one of the Premiership's great sub-plots in recent years.

Vieira's transfer to Juventus in summer 2005, left Arsenal with a yawning gap which is proving costly at the start of the 2005–06 season.

- After being dismissed in his first two games of the 2000–01 season, he had to be persuaded not to quit English football by Arsène Wenger.
- He played only two games in Milan's first team – their loss.
- Vieira's last contribution as a Gunner was to tuck away the penalty that saw Arsenal pinch the FA Cup in a shoot-out after having been outplayed by Manchester United.

VITAL STATISTICS

Place of Birth:	Dakar, Senegal	
Date of Birth:	23 June 1976	**Died:** n/a
Caps:	83 (France)	**Goals (International):** 4
Clubs:	Cannes, AC Milan, Arsenal	
Appearances:	Club (League): 336	
Goals:	Club (League): 34	
Trophies:	SA 1996; WorC 1998; EuroC 2000; LT 1998, 2002, 2004; FAC 1998, 2002, 2005	

Achievement	9.0
Skill	8.0
Teamwork	8.5
Passion	9.0
Personality	5.5
TOTAL	**40.0**

LEGEND RATING

Villa, Veni, Vici
The Aston Villa Dream Team

ASTON VILLA'S LONG HISTORY dictates that their Dream Team draws its personnel from a group of players spanning several generations. One of the dominant sides in the early years of the Football League, Villa won the championship six times before 1910, and remained in the top division for most of the next five decades, before the rot set in the 1960s. The next Villa side to make an impact won the league in 1981, and were a team largely without international stars – which might explain why only Cowans, Gray and Gidman make this all time 16 (Dennis Mortimer and Peter Withe also came close).

Goalkeeper Sam Hardy was the first great England goalkeeper, and John Devey was Villa's most glamorous player in those early years. Massie, Walker and Dixon, though unfamiliar names to modern fans, were all excellent midfielders and David Platt would have enjoyed feeding off the nod downs of aerial superpowers, Hitchens and Gray. There are no representatives from the current, rather colourless team, although Ian Taylor deserves a mention for service and consistency, and Gareth Barry is Villa through and through.

- Charlie Aitken made a club record 656 appearances, many of them during Villa's days in the lower divisions.
- Nigel Spink's second game for Villa was the 1982 European Cup final. He was drafted into the team just 10 minutes after kick-off, after Jimmy Rimmer ricked his neck in the warm-up.
- Gerry Hitchens ('The Blond Bomber') shocked Villa fans by leaving for Internazionale in 1961, the same summer Jimmy Greaves also departed for Milan.
- Dixon and McParland played in the 1957 FA Cup final against Man United, with McParland scoring both goals in a 2-1 win.
- Gordon Cowans, though never given a lengthy run in the England team, was the lynchpin of Villa's European Cup success.

Manager: Ron Saunders

4-4-2

Samuel Hardy (10s)

Stan Lynn (50s) Paul McGrath (90s)
Gareth Southgate (C) (90s) Charlie Aitken (70s)

John Devey (1890s) Gordon Cowans (80s)
David Platt (80s/90s) John Dixon (40s/50s)

Gerald Hitchens (50s) Andy Gray (80s)

Subs: Nigel Spink (G) (80s/90s) John Gidman (D) (80s)
Alex Massie (M) (30s) Billy Walker (M/F) (20s) Peter McParland (50s)

1982. Villa's European Cup triumph.

Waddle, Chris
Newcastle United, Olympique Marseille, England

A WINGER RELYING ON SKILL and quick feet rather than exceptional pace, Chris Waddle's roots may have lain in the traditional North-East heartland of England, but it is on the south coast of France that he acquired legendary status. Waddle prospered in his native Newcastle, attracting a substantial offer from Spurs in 1985. Although regular England caps followed, his fitful, fragile skills never sat well with a domestic audience. It took a move to Marseille in 1989 for Waddle to blossom; he won three league titles, became the creative heartbeat of the side and was idolised by the locals.

At international level, Waddle's greatest success was at Italia 90, but his tournament ended in ignominy. In the semi-final shoot-out with Germany, Waddle shaped to take England's fifth penalty with a country's fate in his hands. His spot kick sailed hopelessly high and wide, and England crashed out.

In 1992 Waddle returned to England with Sheffield Wednesday, but after four years in which the Yorkshire side promised much without actually lifting silverware, he ended his career as a novelty attraction in the lower divisions. His current national profile is maintained by regular radio summaries.

🖋 Waddle was one of many 1980s fashion victims to sport a mullet. He dispensed with it once, only to let it re-grow for Italia 90. Maybe the drag coefficient contributed to his feeble penalty.

☞ The £4.5 m paid by Olympique Marseille was the third-highest transfer fee at the time.

✍ In 1993 Waddle scored for Sheffield Wednesday in the FA Cup final against Arsenal, but finishes on the losing side in the replay. His consolation is the PFA Player of the Year award.

☞ In 1987 Waddle released an execrable pop single with Spurs team-mate Glenn Hoddle. 'Diamond Lights' by Glenn and Chris reached number 12 and gained the pair an appearance on *Top Of The Pops*.

VITAL STATISTICS

Place of Birth:	Hedworth, England		
Date of Birth:	14 December 1960	**Died:** n/a	Achievement 5.0
Caps:	62 (England)	**Goals (International):** 6	Skill 8.5
Clubs:	Newcastle United, Tottenham Hotspur, Olympique		Teamwork 7.0
	Marseille, Sheffield Wednesday, Falkirk, Bradford		Passion 6.5
	City, Sunderland, Burnley, Torquay United		Personality 7.5
Appearances:	Club (League): 598		
Goals:	Club (League): 120		
Trophies:	OLT 1990, 1991, 1992		**TOTAL 34.5**

LEGEND RATING

Wandering Stars
The Bolton Dream Team

BOLTON, ONE OF THE Football League's founder members, have had two outstanding sides, and both are well represented here. Dick Pym and Jimmy Seddon played in all three of their FA Cup wins in the 1920s, while David Jack, Ted Vizard and Joe Smith played in the first two. In the 1950s another well-drilled outfit reached two more FA Cup finals, winning in 1958. The three representatives from that team, left back Tommy Banks, goalkeeper Eddie Hopkinson and striker Nat Lofthouse, were all England internationals.

Since then the club has been up and down; a spell in the 1970s trying to cement a place in the top flight preceding the club's only year in Division Four. In the 1970s Bolton were inspired by the flamboyant genius of Frank Worthington and the graft of Peter Reid, both of whom make the squad. So too does Paul Jones, who formed a formidable central defensive pairing with current manager Sam Allardyce, during the same era.

A revival started by Bruce Rioch and continued with great skill by Allardyce, has seen the club's stock rise enormously in the last decade. A team largely made up of mercenaries has been well-served by the likes of McGinlay, Bergsson, Frandsen and N'Gotty and the new captain for 2005–06, Kevin Nolan.

☞ Long-serving Welsh winger Ted Vizard won 22 caps while with the Trotters. Though not a prolific goalscorer, he was the main supply line for striker Joe Smith.

♗ Gudni Bergsson joined with a reputation as a jobbing right back, but was transformed into an excellent centre half and crowd favourite, playing better at 36 than he had at 26.

♗ Bolton are enjoying their longest run in the top flight for over 40 years, and in the 2005–06 season found themselves playing in Europe for the first time in their history.

☞ Unluckiest omission: Jussi Jaaskelainen. A few more years and he may become as much of a Wanderers legend as Hopkinson.

Manager: Bill Ridding

4-4-2

Eddie Hopkinson (50s/60s)

Jimmy Seddon (20s) Gudni Bergsson (90s)
Paul Jones (70s) Tommy Banks (50s/60s)

Per Frandsen (90s) David Jack (20s)
Peter Reid (70s) Ted Vizard (20s)

Frank Worthington (70s) Nat Lofthouse (50s)

Subs: Dick Pym (G) (20s) Bruno N'Gotty (D) (00s) Kevin Nolan (M) (00s)
Joe Smith (F) (10s/20s) John McGinlay (F) (90s)

Wembley, 1958. Nat Lofthouse is chaired with the FA Cup.

Wembley

England

ORIGINALLY NAMED The Empire Stadium, Wembley has several nicknames including 'The Old Lady' and 'The Venue of Legends'. Built in the space of 300 days at a cost of under £750,000, it was the brainchild of architects John Simpson and Maxwell Ayrton, who worked together with the engineer Sir Owen Williams.

It opened for the 1923 Cup final between Bolton and West Ham. The first myth was duly created, as over 200,000 fans stormed the gates and were cleared with the aid of PC George Storey on his famous white horse Billy. Since then, the famous twin towers have played host to 72 FA Cup and 24 League Cup finals, as well as several European club finals. It was England's venue for Euro 96, but its greatest moments were reserved for the 1966 World Cup.

In staging the Finals, England had the advantage of playing all six games at Wembley. Charlton's goal against Mexico and Rattin's dismissal for Argentina provided the prologue and first act. The dramatic finale was reserved for the final; Hurst's hat-trick, Stiles' jig and Moore receiving the trophy are national mementos destined to be handed down through the generations.

- ☞ Wembley was the main venue for the 1948 Olympic Games.
- ⚒ Amazingly for a stadium then holding 100,000, it was built in less than a year by construction experts McAlpine. Its first intended use was for the British Exhibition.
- ☝ Despite its pageantry, Wembley was overdue a refit and closed in 2000. Its last game was very disappointing, as England squelched to a 1-0 defeat against Germany in a World Cup qualifier. It was also the last England game with Kevin Keegan as coach.
- ☞ A new chapter will begin with the reopening of Wembley for the 2006 FA Cup final. Despite fears to the contrary, the FA have guaranteed that the stadium will be ready in time. Precedent suggests we should not be too surprised if some sort of fiasco ensues.

VITAL STATISTICS

Location:	London, England
Local Club:	None
Date Built:	1923
Current Capacity	
(before closure):	80,000
Max. Capacity:	126,947

Wembley Wizards
Scotland, 1928

THIS WAS A TEAM celebrated not for its domination of an era, but for one game. And if, as the chant goes, you know your history, it was the sweetest game ever for all Scotland fans. The England versus Scotland clash at Wembley in 1928 ought not to have held any terrors for the home side; in the corresponding fixture the previous season, England had triumphed 2-1 at Hampden Park. Nothing could have prepared them for what was to come. Some of Scotland's best players, like so many after them, were plying their trade in England so, in theory at least, the two teams should have known each other's games well. Indeed, many of them were club team-mates. Scotland's half back and captain Jimmy McMullan was the passing playmaker of Manchester City, and was to emerge as the man of the match. With targets as mobile as Alex James (Preston, later Arsenal), Alex Jackson (Huddersfield) and Hughie Gallacher (Newcastle) he was not short of players to hit. With England frozen like startled rabbits in the headlights of a juggernaut, Jackson helped himself to a hat-trick, leaving James and Gibson to notch the other two in a thumping 5-1 victory. For Scottish fans, that 1928 win was a symbolic act of defiance, a footballing equivalent of Bannockburn – which is why they still sing about it today.

☞ In the context of the Home Internationals, Scotland's victory was meaningless. Both teams were playing merely to avoid the ignominious wooden spoon.

☞ England blamed the heavy pitch for the result, claiming it gave the smaller, nippier Scots an advantage.

☞ Not only was it a thrashing, it was England's first defeat at Wembley.

☞ Gallacher and James commanded huge transfer fees. Gallacher was sold to Chelsea in 1930 for £10,000, while James cost over £8,500, when Herbert Chapman took him to Arsenal in 1929.

☞ England's team contained no lack of firepower; Dixie Dean scored a record 60 goals in the same season. He scarcely got a kick.

Manager: None
(team was picked by committee)

Key Players
McMullan (M) Alex James (M) Gallacher (F) Jackson (F)

Trophies
None (but this Scottish side became famous for inflicting such a heavy defeat on the Auld Enemy on their own turf)

Man-of-the-match Jimmy McMullan is mobbed after Scotland's 5-1 demolition of England.

Wenger, Arsène

Monaco, Arsenal

WHEN BRUCE RIOCH FAILED to work out at Arsenal, everyone was looking around for the big-name British manager who would take his place. It came as something of a shock when they appointed Arsène Wenger, who was then working as a coach in the J-League in Japan.

His first season in full charge as a manager, at Nancy, was inauspicious – they were relegated. A move to Monaco in 1987 allowed Wenger to show his worth. A team containing Glenn Hoddle, who was to recommend him to Arsenal, won the French league a year later.

In his time at Arsenal he has introduced a new methodology and turned them from 'boring, boring Arsenal' into an exciting, creative attacking team. On the downside, the team have been beset by disciplinary problems; a disgraceful exhibition in a match against Manchester United saw them lucky to avoid even more serious censure from the authorities.

Wenger's team seem to have learned from that, and their performance in going through the 2003–04 season unbeaten was an immense achievement. Since then lack of ambition in the transfer market has seen them overtaken by Chelsea, and success in Europe continues to prove elusive.

☞ Strasbourg won the league title when Wenger was a player there, but he only appeared three times in that season.

👍 Wenger took Nagoya Grampus Eight from third-bottom to runners-up in the J-League in his first season.

👎 He was charged with serious disrepute after an altercation with the fourth official in the opening game of the 2000–01 season. A 12-match touchline ban was later overturned.

👍 A few flaky imports in the early years have given way to some inspired scouting. Unknowns (to British audiences) like Fabregas, Clichy, Reyes and Van Persie come straight into the side and perform at a high level.

👎 Wenger, surprisingly for such a smart man, has allowed his disputatious relationship with Alex Ferguson to get under his skin. In 2004 he was fined £15,000 for accusing Ruud van Nistelrooy of cheating.

VITAL STATISTICS

Place of Birth: Strasbourg, France

Date of Birth: 1 January 1950   **Died:** n/a

Caps: 0 (France)   **Goals (International):** 0

Clubs: As Player: Strasbourg; As Manager: Nancy, Monaco, Nagoya Grampus Eight, Arsenal

Trophies: FLT 1998; LT 1998, 2002, 2004; FAC 1998, 2002, 2003, 2005

Achievement	9.0
Tactical Awareness	8.5
Motivation	8.0
Team Selection/Transfers	8.0
Personality	7.0
TOTAL	**40.5**

LEGEND RATING

White Horse Wembley
Bolton Wanderers 2 West Ham United 0, 1923

THE NEWLY COMPLETED Empire Stadium at Wembley had been chosen as the venue for the Cup final. Amazingly, it was not an all-ticket event, a fact which resulted in mayhem.

A realistic estimate is that 250,000 people turned up to a stadium built to hold 100,000. Most of them were allowed in, with a result that at the scheduled kick-off time of 3 p.m., thousands of fans covered the pitch.

The day was saved by one PC Storey. Mounted on his horse Billy, he helped push back the throng to just beyond the touchlines with such success that the game started only 44 minutes late. Legend has it (falsely) that he managed this feat single-handed when in fact, Billy's distinctive white appearance was the only one visible from a distance.

After such a delay, and with the crowd encroaching to within inches of the pitch, the game was not a classic. David Jack gave Bolton an advantage after two minutes that they seldom looked like losing. J.R. Smith's goal after 53 minutes would have grabbed the headlines in any other year. They had already been written by a single white horse.

☞ The FA was worried about the appeal of the new stadium and had advertised widely for fans to attend. They had to refund 10 per cent of the gate to spectators with pre-paid tickets who were unable to get to their seats.

☞ PC Storey was not scheduled to be at Wembley that afternoon. He answered an emergency call in Central London to report to the ground once the crowds got out of hand.

☞ The FA could not abandon the game: King George V was there.

☞ Bolton's first goal was aided by West Ham defender Jack Tressdern, who was caught up in the crowd after taking a throw-in, allowing David Jack a free passage. Jack's shot knocked out a spectator pressed against the net.

SCORERS	Jack, JR Smith
EVENT	FA Cup final, Wembley, 28 April 1923
BOLTON	(Man: Charles Foweraker)
	1. Pym 2. Haworth 3. Finney 4. Nuttall 5. Seddon 6. Jennings 7. Butler
	8. Jack 9. Smith, JR 10. Joe Smith 11. Vizard
WEST HAM	(Man: Syd King)
	1. Hufton 2. Henderson 3. Young 4. Bishop 5. Kay 6. Tressdern
	7. Richards 8. Brown 9. Watson 10. Moore 11. Ruffell

Wingless Wonders
England 1966

IT IS A LINE-UP that England fans can recite like a mantra. And yet it is a team almost as notable for the players it does not include as those that it does. The fullbacks were good, honest professionals – but functional. Jimmy Armfield was a classier right back than George Cohen, whilst Ray Wilson can count himself lucky that Terry Cooper did not arrive on the other flank until three years later. Bobby Moore and Gordon Banks provided the defensive class, natural choices in any England team. And though the midfield was solid, the emergence of Alan Mullery and Colin Bell for the next World Cup certainly hadn't weakened it (indeed, some would argue it was improved by their inclusion). The forwards present a knotty problem. Geoff Hurst vindicated his late selection, his four goals in the last three games saw off Argentina in the quarter-finals and West Germany in the final, but the player he replaced, Jimmy Greaves, was an even more prolific scorer (his 44 goals in 57 games is England's most impressive modern ratio by a distance). Roger Hunt may be the lucky man here. Whatever the argument, and many feel the 1970 side was even better, no one can deny this XI their place in England's hall of fame as the nation's only World Cup winners.

☞ This side was dubbed the 'wingless wonders' due to Alf Ramsey's reluctance to use wide players.

✍ From 1958 to 1970, only England broke Brazil's dominance of the World Cup.

☞ Cohen and Wilson were capped for a further two years. The young Alan Ball was a regular until 1975.

✍ After winning the Jules Rimet trophy, England remained undefeated for nearly a year, until Scotland beat them 3-2 at Wembley.

Manager: Alf Ramsey

Key Players
Gordon Banks(G) George Cohen (D) Ray Wilson (D)
Nobby Stiles (M) Jack Charlton (D) Bobby Moore (D)
Alan Ball (M) Geoff Hurst (F) Roger Hunt (F)
Bobby Charlton (M) Martin Peters (M)

Trophies
WorC 1966

Alf Ramsey and Bobby Moore flank the Jules Rimet trophy.

Wright, Billy

Wolverhampton Wanderers, England

WHEN BILLY WRIGHT passed Bob Crompton's record number of England caps in May 1952 it was his 42nd appearance. That he went on to more than double that record is a testimony to his talent, consistency and downright resilience. Wright was unlucky to play in an era when insularity reigned in British football, so was never able to develop his game properly against the more creative European sides. In 1953 he bore the brunt of criticism after England had been led a merry dance by the Hungarians at Wembley, having taken flak after the humiliating defeat to the USA in the 1950 World Cup. Abysmal tactics and selection meant Wright never made an impact on a major tournament – that was left to his natural successor, Bobby Moore.

His experiences at club level were not dissimilar. Despite Wolves' dominance of the domestic game in the 1950s, their performances in the European Cup were disappointing – a narrow defeat to Schalke, and a hammering by Barcelona. Old-fashioned he might have been, but Wright was a player of enormous integrity, an honest pro who never gave less than his lung-busting best whether playing at half back or, as he did later in his career, in the centre of defence. Disciplined, determined and fearless he was also the perfect captain.

- In 1959 Wright made his 100th appearance for England, fittingly against Scotland. England won 1-0.
- Wright missed only three games in reaching his century. Eighty-five of his 100 appearances were as captain.
- Wright's last match for England was against the USA; an 8-1 win was partial revenge for the embarrassment in 1950.
- Wright had four years as Arsenal manager in the early 1960s, but achieved nothing and was lost to the game soon after.
- Wright was PFA Player of the Year in 1952, and was awarded a CBE on his retirement. A monument was constructed two years after his death, and now stands outside Molineux.

VITAL STATISTICS

Place of Birth:	Ironbridge, England	
Date of Birth:	6 February 1924	**Died:** 3 September 1994
Caps:	105 (England)	**Goals (International):** 3
Clubs:	Wolverhampton Wanderers	
Appearances:	Club (League): 490	
Goals:	Club (League): 13	
Trophies:	FAC 1951; LT 1954, 1958, 1959	

LEGEND RATING	
Achievement	8.0
Skill	8.0
Teamwork	9.0
Passion	10.0
Personality	6.0
TOTAL	**41.0**

Zidane, Zinedine

Juventus, Real Madrid, France

MARSEILLES' MOST FAMOUS footballing son has seen his career soar to unimaginable heights from inauspicious beginnings at Cannes. A three-season period from 1998 brought him winner's medals in World and European finals for France, and a world-record £45 m move from Juventus to Real Madrid, after his goals helped the Turin club to two Serie A titles. Madrid assembled their team around the Frenchman, playing some breathtaking football; a Zidane special to win the 2002 Champions League was just one highlight.

His crowning moment must remain his two goals in Paris against Brazil to bring France their first World Cup. Zidane's two-footed skills and movement bemused Brazil throughout the game, as they had bemused defenders all through the tournament. The dose was repeated two years later at Euro 2000, and Zidane was a superstar.

A slightly stooping, balding figure, he lacks the charismatic looks of Batistuta or the natural athleticism of Figo, but remains an inspiration for late developers everywhere. His professional debut was in 1986 and he remained in relative obscurity with Cannes and Bordeaux before Juventus signed him 10 years later; unthinkable humility for the most influential player in the game around the turn of the century.

His performances have been inconsistent, even lacklustre in recent times; perhaps the spur of a last hurrah in Germany will re-ignite him.

☞ Amazingly, Zidane's first goal did not arrive until five years after his debut for Cannes.

✍ Not always the hero, his five years at Juventus brought six red cards.

✂ He was voted World Footballer of the Year in 1998 and 2000 and European Footballer of the Year in 1998.

✎ He received the *Legion d'Honneur* from the French President Jacques Chirac in 1998.

☞ Zidane's international career was resurrected when Raymond Domenech persuaded him to rethink his retirement in an effort to secure qualification for the 2006 World Cup.

VITAL STATISTICS

Place of Birth:	Marseille, France		
Date of Birth:	23 June 1972	**Died:** n/a	
Caps:	98 (France)	**Goals (International):** 29	
Clubs:	Cannes, Bordeaux, Juventus, Real Madrid		
Appearances:	Club (League): 482		
Goals:	Club (League): 86		
Trophies:	SA 1997, 1998; WorC 1998; EuroC 2000; EC 2002		

Achievement	10.0
Skill	9.0
Teamwork	7.0
Passion	9.0
Personality	7.5
TOTAL	**42.5**

LEGEND RATING

Zola, Gianfranco
Chelsea, Italy

HE MAY BE SARDINIA'S most celebrated footballer since Luigi Riva but, after thrilling crowds at Stamford Bridge during the closing seasons of his career, Gianfranco Zola is now regarded as an adopted Londoner. Too small to be a target man and never a prolific goalscorer, Zola's mercurial ball skills have created countless goals for grateful team-mates and made many accomplished defenders look like hapless novices. His trademark free kicks rely on guile and spin rather than outright power, but he still boasts a strike rate better than some penalty-takers. None was more memorable than his opener for Chelsea on their most famous European night, a 3-1 victory over Barcelona in a Champions League quarter-final in 2001. Zola repeatedly cut an international defence to ribbons that night.

A genial and honest man, Zola made true on a promise to return to Sardinia in 2003, helping Cagliari win promotion back to Serie A the following season.

Ironically, given his dead-ball prowess, it is a missed penalty for which Italian audiences will best remember him; his uncharacteristic failure against Germany in Euro 96 resulted in the *Azzuri's* elimination from the tournament. Never a Championship winner in Italy or England, and never a huge international success, Zola will nonetheless be remembered as one of the most abundantly gifted players of his generation.

- 1996. Zola became a *bête noire* for England fans after scoring the only goal in a World Cup qualifier at Wembley.
- 1997. Named Footballer of the Year, despite joining Chelsea in mid-season.
- 2001. 'There's only one Mrs Zola.' Song sung by Chelsea fans after Zola's wife was reported to have persuaded him to remain at the club for another season.
- 2002. Scored an audacious mid-air back-heeled volley versus Norwich in an FA Cup replay, probably his best-ever strike for Chelsea.

VITAL STATISTICS

Place of Birth: Sardinia, Italy
Date of Birth: 5 July 1966   **Died:** n/a
Caps: 35 (Italy)   **Goals (International):** 7
Clubs: Nuorese, Torres, Napoli, Parma, Chelsea
Appearances: Club (League): 468
Goals: Club (League): 150
Trophies: SA 1990; UEFAC 1995; FAC 1997; CWC 1998; LC 2000

LEGEND RATING	
Achievement	6.0
Skill	9.0
Teamwork	9.0
Passion	8.0
Personality	7.0
TOTAL	**39.0**

Index